*A Study of
U. S. Racial
Attitudes Today*

Black
and
White

William Brink

Louis Harris

A CLARION BOOK
PUBLISHED BY SIMON AND SCHUSTER

A Clarion Book
Published by Simon and Schuster
Rockefeller Center, 630 Fifth Avenue
New York, New York 10020
All rights reserved
including the right of reproduction
in whole or in part in any form
Copyright © 1966, 1967 by Newsweek, Inc.

FIFTH PAPERBACK PRINTING

SBN 671-20240-5
Library of Congress Catalog Card Number: 67-19815
Manufactured in the United States of America
by Murray Printing Co., Forge Village, Mass.

Contents

Preface

IT WAS IN THE SULTRY summer of 1963 that *Newsweek* magazine made its first massive, in-depth study of the Negro revolution in America. The course of this remarkable, contemporary social upheaval had been developing week by week since the day in 1954 when the U.S. Supreme Court returned its historic verdict outlawing segregation in the nation's public schools. But by 1963 there seemed to be a deep and dangerous void of understanding between the races—a great lack of meaningful dialogue over what the revolution was all about. In the intervening years the Negroes had been marching and demonstrating, sitting-in and lying-in, and chanting an unfamiliar refrain called "We Shall Overcome!" As the years wore on, there seemed to be no end to the demands of the Negros, or to the parade of limp bodies carried from the streets into waiting police patrol wagons in the cities of the North and the South. For whites accustomed to seeing the Negro largely as a performer on TV or at the baseball park, 1963 was a puzzling time. What exactly did the Negroes want? Who were their leaders? And how far were they prepared to go? The very future of America's social structure, it seemed, depended upon reliable answers to these questions.

Normally, journalists sample public opinion by going into the streets, collaring a handful of relevant people, and recording their opinions (a hoary journalistic joke is that the first taxicab driver encountered by the reporter is an unfailing source of popular sentiment). Clearly, this method was inadequate to the task of delineating the greatest mass protest since the American Revolution itself. Thus the editors of *Newsweek* decided on a unique marriage of the relatively new art of professional opinion sampling with the age-old art of journalism. Louis Harris and Associates, a man and an organization that had won nationwide recognition for polling in the political field, was chosen to apply the same clinical, dispassionate statistical yardstick to the Negro revolt. In July of 1963 more than 1,000 Negroes were polled by the Harris organization with an exhaustive questionnaire, and later the same technique was applied to some 1,200 white Americans in a separate survey. These surveys yielded an unprecedented portrait of a revolution taken at its flood tide. They were printed in *Newsweek* cover stories (July 29, 1963, for the Negro survey; October 21, 1963, for the white study) and later expanded by the present authors into a book that has become a reference work for American high schools and colleges.*

In retrospect, those early surveys were nothing if not prophetic. They confirmed that the Negro's struggle was an "authentic, deep-seated, broadly based revolution"—and one destined to go on and on. The revolt was aimed not at overthrow of the established order—as many of the world's revolutions have been—but simply at recognition for the Negroes and a full share in affluent American white society. Its dominant tactic was nonviolence, its prevailing spirit high hope. But the surveys also revealed a dangerous undercurrent of unrest.

* *The Negro Revolution in America*, Simon and Schuster, New York, 1964.

"Violence will remain a constant risk of the revolution. . . . The flashpoint is likeliest in the Northern slums. . . ." they reported.

All of us, of course, are only too aware of the course of American social history since 1963. The Negro's struggle for equality brought him significant gains, but it also led to ugly riots in the Negro ghetto of Watts in Los Angeles in 1965, and later to similar outbreaks in the ghettos of other great cities across America. At the same time the bitter new cry of "black power" arose to challenge the old nonviolent, integrationist main line of the revolution. By 1966 the Negro's protest had clearly reached a new and critical phase—one that dismayed and even frightened many white Americans. And so it was that *Newsweek*'s editors turned once again to the Harris organization. This time, in the summer of 1966, the Harris survey was conducted among blacks and whites at the same time, with the same kind of detailed questionnaires used in 1963, but updated to reflect changing conditions (see Appendix A, Appendix B). In all, 1,059 Negroes and 1,088 whites were sampled in every part of the United States. As in 1963, the Harris organization also polled a select group of 100 Negro leaders to provide a contrast of their more sophisticated views with those of rank-and-file Negroes. The selection of these Negro leaders was, admittedly, no easy task. Since 1963, any number of Negro activists had emerged in the nation's headlines, but not all of them represented any really significant body of Negro opinion. At the same time, some Negro leaders in the arts, the professions and business were, in their own quiet way, as influential as any of the activists. In consultation with Negroes themselves, *Newsweek* finally chose a list of leaders representing every facet of the Negro community from Martin Luther King to Sammy Davis, Jr. (see Appendix C).

The results of this massive effort were published in a 30-page *Newsweek* cover story of August 22, 1966. But as before, there was so much rich material unused, and so much more to say about this most extraordinary chapter in American history, that the authors decided to set forth the full story in this book. In the main, it is based on the 1966 *Newsweek*-Harris surveys, but the reader will find much that is new and provocative in the complete recital of events since 1963. Scattered through the texts are abbreviated statistical tables from the Harris surveys; in Appendix D, these and other tables are treated in full.

Throughout the Negro revolution, the modern American press has played a large role in the very development of that revolution. One is tempted to believe that if the revolt had occurred in an earlier day, one of less widespread mass communications, it might never have gotten off the ground at all. In the beginning of the present struggle, the detailed reporting of newspapers and news magazines, as well as the ever-present eye of the television camera, helped greatly to arouse the nation's sympathy for the black men marching and singing in the streets. But by the same token, this searching coverage also helped to impede the Negro's cause when he began rioting in the streets, and to turn sympathy into backlash. The day may come—if, in fact, it has not already arrived—when responsible news media may have to weigh very carefully the kind of treatment they give to the onrushing events of the Negro's protest. It remains the conviction of the authors, however, that the cause of racial harmony will best be served if whites and blacks at least *understand* each other. This book therefore is dedicated to informing the reader not only of what has happened since 1963, but how and why.

As with any other undertaking of such magnitude, the authors are indebted to a host of helpers, principally the loyal interviewers and New York staff of the Harris organization who provided the basic raw material, and the staffers of *Newsweek* Magazine, who literally roamed the nation and the world to add flesh and blood to the bare statistics. In Vietnam, *Newsweek*'s Saigon bureau chief Everett Martin and his staff took weeks out from the frantic pace of an escalated war to provide material for a chapter on the Negro G.I. To reach all those included in the Negro leadership survey, a *Newsweek* correspondent interrupted Thurgood Marshall in the midst of a meeting in Montreal, and another talked with Negro author James Baldwin in a Beirut bar. Covering the Negro revolution is not without its hazards. In the summer of 1966, Karl Fleming, for many years a respected reporter of the civil-rights story in the South and now *Newsweek*'s Los Angeles bureau chief, was clubbed to the ground by a band of young Negroes and seriously injured while attempting to cover a new outbreak in Watts.

The authors additionally owe a large debt of gratitude to Lucy Kramer and Anne Hetfield of *Newsweek*'s research staff, who spent long hours checking the accuracy of the statements herein, and to Mrs. Laura G. Efrein, who tracked down and assembled much of the source material used. Finally, they are especially indebted to Osborn Elliott, editor of *Newsweek*, who originated the race studies in the first place, and who cast his practiced eye over the finished manuscript.

WILLIAM BRINK
LOUIS HARRIS

Black
and
White

CHAPTER 1

At the Crossroads

AMERICANS ARE, ON THE WHOLE, a tolerant people and a generous people. They have fought lofty wars of liberation, sacrificing their sons with not much more assurance than that a principle was at stake. Since World War II they have bank-rolled their shattered allies and the underprivileged nations of the world, with only an occasional wince at the pinch on their pocketbooks. They have opened their hearts to the oppressed and their shores to the homeless. They have done all that—but they have not seen fit to grant to America's 21 million Negroes the freedom that was guaranteed them by the Constitution of the United States and reinforced by Abraham Lincoln's Emancipation Proclamation.

Why? The answer, of course, is rooted in three centuries of American history. No nation can, overnight, shed a prejudice ingrained for three hundred years—years in which the Negro always has been an alien creature with an alien skin in an alien world. James Baldwin, the sensitive Negro author, has written of his people: "You were born where you were born and faced the future that you faced because you were black and *for no other reason* [italics his]. You were born into a society which spelled out with brutal clarity, and in as many ways as possible, that you were a worthless human being."*

Yet it is instructive now to recall the events of 1963, when the Negro American's modern twentieth-century revolution reached flood tide. At the time, the spectacle of a race writhing in the chains of its bondage and struggling to get free moved many Americans profoundly, or at the very least pricked their conscience. Suddenly they realized—as never before—that they were being called to account for those three hundred years of prejudice. At that point, no one had any clear idea where the Negro was going, but he seemed to be on his way, and in and out of government the white world embarked on truly extraordinary efforts to help him. Such was the climate of good will, in fact, that many tolerant Americans were ready to believe that the Negro's revolt would simply roll on to a successful conclusion (that was the period of wry jokes like "I can't get a job, I'm a white man"). Sympathy for the black cause ran strong when the police dogs bared their fangs and Bull Connor bellowed his defiance at Birmingham, Alabama, in 1963. It probably reached a high point, in the opinion of most civil rights observers, at that heart-stopping moment when the Negro columns went down before the police billies in the Selma march of 1965. But not too long after Selma came Watts—that awful four days when the Los Angeles ghetto went up in flames and 36 people died. After that, the Negro's revolution was never quite the same again. After all the years of nonviolent supplication since the U.S. Supreme Court school desegregation of 1954, the Negro revolt gave way to outright riot, to bitter internal dissension in the Movement itself, and to a rising white backlash. The year 1966 became not the year of deliverance for the Negro, but the year when it dawned on all Americans—black and white—that equality for the Negro was

* *The Fire Next Time*, Dial Press, New York, 1963.

a far greater problem than anyone had imagined, and its solution was probably more remote than ever.

IN ACTUALITY, THE NEGRO'S search for equality has followed closely the classic pattern of most revolutions. Crane Brinton, Harvard's distinguished professor of history, notes in his study of the subject that there are at least three principal requisites for the birth of a revolution.* First, revolution most often takes place in a society that is economically progressive, but in which the fruits of progress are not distributed evenly throughout the population. This is certainly true of U.S. society, and of the Negro's place in it. Secondly, the government should either be corrupt or else ineffective in trying to institute reforms. The Federal government today is hardly corrupt, nor is it ineffective. But it certainly did very little to help the Negro during the ninety years between emancipation and the beginning of his American revolution. A third condition is that the upper classes, and especially the upper-class intellectuals, have enough leisure to develop social consciousness and take up causes. Leisure born of rising affluence, of course, is a mark of American society today, and the Negro has in fact drawn much support from upper-class sympathizers and intellectuals (he has, however, perhaps drawn more from young college students). Brinton also found that a revolution flourishes best when the country is not involved in any international conflict, which tends to distract attention from the cause. This is one condition lacking in the Negro revolution, since the United States has become deeply involved in war in Vietnam. In fact, the Vietnam war is cited by civil-rights leaders as one very specific reason why the Negro's revolt has slowed: many of those who once worried about the Negro's plight now worry about the war.

Some sort of erosion is almost always present in a revolution. After the initial burst of agitation (Brinton speaks of the ef-

* *The Anatomy of Revolution*, Vintage, New York, 1957.

ficacy of a "few good dramatic riots" to help things along),
what often follows is a period of moderation—a difficult and
prolonged time of trying to implement and consolidate the
gains made. In Cuba, Fidel Castro accomplished a rather rapid
takeover in the few short years from 1956 to 1959, only to come
face to face with the difficult task of rebuilding the economy
of his isolated country. The danger is that moderation very
often leads to impatience, the rise of extremism and even a
reign of terror. As the academicians have plotted the course, it
is precisely here that revolutions can come unstuck and the
hard-won gains can be lost. Only when this critical period is
weathered does moderation return and a constructive evolu-
tion begin.

If the parallel with the Negro's revolution in America is not
perfectly exact, it is nevertheless striking. For after the long
hot summer of 1966, impatience with "gradualism" began rising, moderates were under attack, and a new generation of
militants was clamoring for stronger measures. This was the
year when the cry of black power—that vaguely menacing appeal to the Negro's racial pride—first sprang from the lips of
Stokely Carmichael, the new young head of the Student Nonviolent Coordinating Committee, and Floyd McKissick, the
new head of the Congress of Racial Equality. This was the
year when the more extreme black nationalist groups began
boasting of their stockpiles of guns and calling for open war-
fare. This was the year when swarms of ghetto Negroes, frustrated at their miserable plight, rose up in bloody Watts-style
riots in the Hough slum of Cleveland (where Negroes roamed
the streets with guns and firebombs and four people were
killed), on the West Side of Chicago (the scene of summer-
long violence in 1966), and a score of other places.

In truth, it was hardly surprising that the Negro's Movement had taken such a turn. The black man's revolt has been
so amorphous, so formless, that there never has been a master
plan for its completion. All along it was recognized that as
Freedom Road moved from the lunch counter to the private
domain of the white man, as it moved from the rural South to

the festering slums of the North, the going would get rougher. And as the going got rougher, the Negro leaders themselves began to squabble over how to proceed. Angry, intolerant men, the black power advocates were questioning the most basic precepts of the revolution—nonviolence as the method and integration as the goal. Their cries for black political and economic power, for going it alone, for violence in return for violence, put moderates like Whitney Young, Jr., of the National Urban League and Roy Wilkins of the National Association for the Advancement of Colored People sorely on the defensive. Even more on the defensive was the Reverend Dr. Martin Luther King, Jr., winner of the Nobel Prize for Peace and the very symbol of nonviolent protest.

If these were troubling times for the Negroes, they were equally so for the whites. Plagued as always by the certain knowledge that the Negro is entitled to his rights, the whites felt themselves being pressed too hard. Two Presidents (Kennedy and Johnson) had reminded them that the Negro's cause is just, and Congress had been busily enacting laws to implement the Negro's rights. Now the Negro himself seemed ready to fight at the slightest provocation. Many white liberals, feeling themselves betrayed and no longer wanted by the most militant of the Negro leaders, turned to debating the Vietnam war. White moderates grew apathetic (very possibly the worst blow the Negro cause could suffer would be white boredom) or openly hostile. Above all, many whites began to feel genuine fear—fear for their very safety on the streets. No matter how hard SNCC's Stokely Carmichael tried to explain black power in reasonable terms, every time he appeared on television he sounded more to whites like the voice of terror.

Perhaps inevitably, public support for the Negro began to wane and opposition began to rise into what has been loosely called the white backlash. The term is something of a catchall —a convenient way to cover every possible white reaction from pure apathy to unadulterated bigotry. Backlash also implies a sudden switch in sentiment, which may not be the case. Some observers (New York's liberal Senator Jacob Javits is one) feel that the backlash *is* a sudden thing, a new sense of revulsion brought on by the terror talk and the call to reverse racism of a few Negro leaders. But more think that the white backlash in reality is the age-old prejudice of whites rising to the surface, an "out from under the rocks phenomenon," as one social psychologist has called it. However it is defined, white backlash was a stark reality in waning 1966, causing Congress to emasculate and finally scuttle the civil-rights bill that would have given the Negro one of his most cherished goals—open housing—and contributing to the defeat of some liberal candidates at the polls in November.

AT THIS CRITICAL JUNCTURE of the Negro's revolution, the *Newsweek* survey has a special value, for it shows very clearly how the attitudes of whites and blacks have changed since 1963, and precisely where they stand now.

In the case of whites, there is no question that their attitudes toward the Negro have softened measurably since 1963, even in the South. Fewer whites would object today to sitting next to a Negro in a movie or on a bus. Even white objections to integrated housing and intermarriage have dipped a few percentage points, though they remain strongly opposed.

But whites also are deeply upset by the disturbing course the Negro's struggle has taken. Very nearly half of them admit to feeling uneasy on the streets now (the percentage is higher in the cities), and such is the spectre of violence that nearly two-thirds are opposed to even peaceful demonstrations. Moreover, there has been a distinct and foreboding split in the ranks of the whites themselves. Tolerance for the Negro is highest among middle and upper-class whites who are the farthest removed from the struggle. The tolerance is a good deal less among poorer-class whites who must confront the Negro on the inflammatory edges of the big-city ghettos. These are people whose homes are their castles, and they can get fighting mad over the incursions of the Negro, as they showed in Cleveland's Hough and Chicago's West Side in 1966. Perhaps even as much as the Negroes, these people feel far removed from the centers of power where the decisions are made that affect their lives; in their view they are taking the heaviest pressure, unfairly left to carry the white man's burden. Yet they are not the only ones feeling the pressure. Some 70 per cent of all whites think the Negro is trying to move too fast. And their plain message to the black man is: Cool it.

What about the Negroes? They, too, have changed a bit since 1963. Recognizing the rising white resistance, they are somewhat less optimistic now than they were three years ago about their chances for further progress. But, just as the white man's attitude toward the Negro has softened, so have the Negro's doubts about the white man. Blacks remain thoroughly convinced that they will overcome some day, and their aim has never changed. They still want their share of the American good life: decent jobs, decent schools, decent homes, nothing less than integration across the board. The majority of Negroes also remain committed to nonviolence, and put their trust in the leadership of Martin Luther King and the counsel of the moderates. Yet just as there is a minority of belligerent whites, there is a minority of Negroes who profess themselves lured by the siren call of black power. There is a minority of Negroes who think riots like the one in Watts have helped the black cause more than they have hurt. And there is a small but potentially dangerous minority that is ready to join the riots.

The staccato outbreaks of strife in the streets during the hot summer of 1966 were such that many thoughtful people on both sides of the color line honestly feared that there might well be a racial explosion. Some feared that Communists and their ilk were moving in to exploit the race issue; in Cleveland, a grand jury charged that Reds and trained agitators fomented the riot in Hough, although the U.S. Attorney General's office found no such evidence. At one point, Vice-President Hubert H. Humphrey stepped forward to propose a moratorium on Negro demonstrations in the nation's major cities, lest they provoke more riots. His proposal went unheeded, but it was symptomatic of the rising concern. Indeed, there is ample evidence in the *Newsweek* survey that the disenchanted minorities—white and black alike—represent a dangerous potential for violence. Northern ghettos particularly are a tinderbox waiting to be ignited. At the same time, the minority represented by the new black power militants is another threat. Neither Stokely Carmichael nor Floyd McKissick may command the legions of Martin Luther King, but they conceivably could rally several million Negroes to their banner. And the course of history has often been shaped by that same kind of minority.

Plainly, America has reached a crisis of color, and both sides are at the crossroads. Probably the devoutest wish of the whites is that the Negro's revolt will simply sputter and die, leaving them peacefully alone with their prevailing—if ambivalent—view that "I don't have anything against the Negro, but after all, he does drive down property values." But in their hearts they know that the task of emancipating the Negro, promised a hundred years ago by Abraham Lincoln, is far from complete.

For the Negroes, the excruciating dilemma is how to move ahead without further alienating the white community, for no one except the most intolerant militant among the Negroes supposes that the cause can be won without white support. Primarily the crisis for the Negro is a crisis of the moderates. If the classic course of revolutions is not to be followed, the moderates must find a way to prevent the zealots from taking over. Theirs is the task of pursuing further progress without losing headway, or, what could be worse, seeing their hard-fought gains taken away.

At what may well be called the mid-passage of the Negro American's revolution, there can be no doubt that the revolt is slowly but certainly changing shape. From what was in the beginning a simple monolith of protest, it is becoming a vastly complex machinery of clashing ideologies and conflicting tactics, of new faces and new ideas. How America's greatest social challenge will ultimately turn out, no one can claim to know. But one thing certain is that the Negro's search for his birthright will go on. He has come too far now to stop. He has tasted equality under the law and found it sweet. And he will not cease walking and talking, pushing and prodding, until the final prize of equality in fact has been won.

CHAPTER 2

Progress—and Unfinished Business

THE NEGRO'S QUEST FOR EQUALITY in contemporary America has been a slow, agonizing attrition—a piecemeal dismantling of the status quo that has taken him many years, and may well take many more before he is finished. In the beginning, after the U.S. Supreme Court's school desegregation order in 1954, the Negro's gains were measured in terms of an Autherine Lucy installed in the University of Alabama, or a handful of children entered in Little Rock's Central High School. Later a rash of Freedom Rides and sit-ins began to win for the Negro a seat in the front of the bus or at a lunch counter in the Deep South. Very often there was bloodshed and sometimes death, as in the case of the awful riot (2 dead, 375 injured) that attended the enrollment of James Meredith in the University of Mississippi at Oxford in 1962. In those troublesome times, first President Eisenhower and then President Kennedy were obliged on occasion to call out Federal troops and marshals to quell or forestall violence. And as the

Negro's Freedom Road slanted northward into the big-city slums, it ran into a great deal more trouble. Whereas before it had been the white man who had fomented the strife in the streets, now it was the Negro who rioted—in Watts and Hough and San Francisco. Massed police and mobilized National Guards became commonplace. White resistance began mounting, and the Negro's triumphant surge forward ground almost to a halt.

Yet bleak as the outlook may now seem, the Negro's modest gains since he first challenged white authority in the 1950s add up to an impressive amount of progress. For there is no question but that the black man's demand for his birthright has sunk deeply into the conscience of many whites. Since the revolution reached full stride in 1963, there have been earnest efforts to provide the Negro better jobs and to improve his housing—even to present him to public view. Where once the Negro was truly the Invisible Man of Ralph Ellison's novel —"I am invisible . . . simply because people refuse to see me," Ellison wrote—he now confronts America daily from advertisements and television commercials. Most important of all, his cause has moved the highest authority in the land: his own government. The Civil Rights Act of 1964 stripped away the galling "white only" signs from public accommodations, and greatly strengthened the attack on segregation in the schools and discrimination on the job. The Voting Rights Act of 1965 enfranchised masses of Southern blacks for the first time since Reconstruction. The United States also declared war on the poverty that afflicts so many Negroes, and Lyndon Johnson— the first Southern president in a century—took up the Negro's own freedom cry when he went on national television to promise: "We shall overcome!"

Indeed, Negroes themselves are almost awed at what they have wrought in a comparatively few years and with a relatively small number of their 21 million people actively involved in the struggle. The *Newsweek* survey clearly established that the biggest single mark of progress to the Negro is the simple fact that after three centuries of being ignored, he has finally made the white man recognize his plight. If this is not so tangible as a fatter pay envelope or more food on the table, it is nevertheless of incalculable benefit to the Negro; it not only sustains his hope for the future but lifts up his spirit and fills him with a swelling sense of pride. As a Negro factory hand in Buffalo, New York, put it: "We are prouder of ourselves, and more aware of ourselves as a people."

But there have been tangible gains as well. Responding to a direct question in the survey, very nearly 70 per cent of all Negroes say they are better off now than they were three years ago, and the figure rises above 70 per cent for Negros living in the South. "I remember when a Negro wasn't allowed in the ball park grandstand or in the eating places downtown," said Howard R. Davis, 57, of St. Louis, Missouri. "Things have come a long ways." In Indianapolis, Indiana, Juanita Corbitt observed: "We feel more free entering restaurants, motels and hotels. The churches are becoming integrated. White ministers are pastoring Negro churches and the congregations are mixing." A Negro housewife in Cassville, Georgia, added: "The kids are getting along fine in the white schools. I am making more money than I ever have, and when I ride the bus, I sit where I want."

As these comments suggest, one of the most striking results of the survey was the degree to which laws and court edicts have been effective in tearing down racial barriers. Purists have long contended that full equality in fact for the Negro cannot be legislated—that no law can open the hearts and minds of white Americans. That may still be so. But largely unrealized by many whites is the considerable amount of progress of the Negro in areas of official sanction—jobs, voting rights, public accommodations and education. In 1963, Negroes were asked in the *Newsweek* survey to compare their status with their lot five years before. In the 1966 survey, they were asked to compare their status with 1963. The following table graphically illustrates the results:

WHERE NEGROES HAVE MADE THE MOST PROGRESS

	Better off		Worse off		The same	
	1966	1963	1966	1963	1966	1963
	%	%	%	%	%	%
Education	58	39	3	5	23	35
Restaurants	55	36	2	4	27	44
Jobs	54	45	9	15	32	33
Voting	53	31	1	2	38	58

NOTE: "Not Sure" answers excluded.

THE NEGROES HAVE TAKEN a hard look at these gains and portioned out the credit for them. Not surprisingly, they give the Federal executive branch, under President Johnson, and Congress, the highest marks for helping the Negro. But very surprisingly, they have done a complete flip-flop in the case of other institutions that were roundly condemned as obstructionist in 1963. For example, white motels and hotels were resented by nearly 3 to 1 in 1963; now they are praised by more than 2 to 1. Movie theaters were criticized by 2 to 1 three years ago; now they get a 4 to 1 endorsement. White business was frowned on by 2 to 1 in 1963; now it is considered helpful to the Negro cause by better than 3 to 2. White bus lines were condemned by nearly 4 to 3 in 1963; now they are favored by 5 to 1. One clear implication of these figures is that the Negro is remarkably flexible in his attitudes toward whites.

The unhappy truth, however, is that not all Negroes have shared in the fruits of civil-rights victories. "I ain't improved none," was the flat comment of a Negro waiter in Columbia, South Carolina. John Burgess, 37, of Long Island City, New York, said this: "Things are the same. I'm still forced to raise my family in inadequate surroundings and there is still discrimination in the white man's attitude." And a 37-year-old farmhand in Franklin, Louisiana, told the survey: "Just look at this house. One side of it is falling down. Every time I ask

'The Man' to do something about it, he say that maybe he will if I do better in the fields."

The 1966 *Newsweek* study shows that the best gains have been made by Negroes of the South, where, of course, they have been the most disadvantaged. And among the Southern Negroes, the ones who have fared the best are middle- and upper-income Negroes, who in general are better educated and more apt to know—and ask for—their rights. Thus, while 53 per cent of all Negroes say their voting rights have improved, the figure for the South is 67 per cent, and it is 69 per cent for Southern Negroes in the middle- and upper-income brackets. In the case of their acceptance in restaurants and other public accommodations, improved now for 55 per cent of all Negroes, the figure for the South is 61 per cent, and 74 per cent for better off Southern Negroes.

But the survey demonstrates all too clearly that the Negroes who have shared the least in the rewards of progress are those living in the big-city slums and ghettos, mainly in the North. On the general question of progress since 1963, answered favorably by nearly 70 per cent of all Negroes, only 29 per cent of low-income slum Negroes can see any progress. Similarly, in the specific areas of jobs, or eating in restaurants, or education and voting rights, the ghetto Negro trails far behind. In the case of jobs, for example, only 24 per cent of them feel they are better off now, compared with 54 per cent of Negroes overall. For education, the figures are 39 per cent to 58 per cent. Thus, as substantial and heartening as the Negro's progress has been, there remains a great deal of unfinished business. For the slum Negro, certainly, but for others as well, there is still a long way to go in the three areas that concern the black man most: jobs, education and housing.

JOBS

The year 1966 was one of unparalleled prosperity for America. Production, profits and payrolls were at all-time peaks. Literally millions of new jobs were opening up and employers were crying for workers. The unemployment rate for the United States was down below 4 per cent, very close to what some economists consider the irreducible minimum. Yet the Negro Americans were not keeping pace with whites in sharing the great good life. True, their total employment level had been rising since 1957, and individually—as shown in the *Newsweek* survey—many could point to improvement in their work situation. But in the fall of 1966 the unemployment rate for Negroes was 7.8 per cent—twice the national average and no better than it was ten years ago. And in the midst of the greatest affluence the United States had ever seen, 40 per cent of Negro families were earning less than $3,000 a year, which, by the government's own yardstick, officially classifies them as poor.

The irony for the Negro is that probably in no other area has there been such a concerted effort—both government and private—to help him as there has been in the case of jobs. In July of 1965, Title VII of the Civil Rights Act of 1964 took effect, making it illegal for employers to discriminate in any phase of employment—from hiring to firing—on the grounds of race, color, religion, sex or national origin. Administered by the Equal Employment Opportunity Commission, the law first applied to employers (and union hiring halls and employment agencies as well) with 100 or more people, but by 1968 will embrace those with as few as 25 workers. The EEOC has been as much concerned with how Negroes are treated on the job as it has with opening more jobs for them, but its enforcement machinery is time-consuming and cumbersome. In its first year of operation, EEOC was swamped with more than 3,000 complaints from Negroes. Another arm of the government is the Labor Department's Office of Contract Compliance, which watchdogs defense contractors. Both are pushing vigorous programs to reduce job discrimination, and the OCC has begun to file suits against lagging firms in defense industry.

Spurred on by the government and by the tight labor pinch, but in many cases by a genuine desire to help, large areas of U.S. business have been opening the doors to Negroes. The evidence of real effort is everywhere. No official count is available, but literally hundreds and hundreds of companies with former "all-white" hiring practices have admitted Negroes. Some unions have begun to lower their traditional bars to Negroes. Corporation recruiters more and more scour the college campuses for promising Negro graduates. Many companies that already have Negro employees have made a conscious effort to move them up to jobs formerly closed to them. One 1966 study showed that U.S. Steel at its Birmingham, Alabama, plant alone had 800 Negroes working in jobs formerly held by whites. There are now more Negro airline stewardesses, more Negro radio announcers, even more Negro advertising men. Since 1961, some 350 U.S. corporations, including many blue-chip firms like General Electric and Xerox, have been enrolled in the White House's Plans for Progress, a voluntary program in which they pledge to make active efforts to provide equal job opportunities. Many of these firms have increased their Negro employment by 50 per cent and more. Some have even instituted such peripheral programs as giving Negro school teachers summer work, to augment their meager incomes.

Why, with all this effort, are so many Negroes out of work, or poorly paid? The answer, quite simply, is that too many Negroes lack the education or skills necessary to compete in today's highly mechanized and computerized society. Over and over, during the great job shortage of 1966, employers wailed that they would be only too glad to take on more Negroes if they could find any with the proper skills. The same lack, employers said, prevented them from moving Negroes already on the payroll into higher jobs. Because of deprived backgrounds, poorer educational opportunities and high drop-out rates, young Negroes are at a disadvantage even as they enter the labor market. In the summer of 1966, the U.S. Department of Labor reported that whereas the jobless rate for white youths aged 14–19 was 10.9 per cent, it was a whopping 26.9 per cent for young Negroes. But basically, the Negroes suffer from the age-old ravages of discrimination. In all the years when they could never aspire to anything more than the most menial jobs, not many Negroes bothered to aim higher. Thus when their golden opportunity arrived, many were ill-prepared for it.

The Negroes, of course, understand their handicap very well, but so also do the government and many businesses. A great many of America's largest corporations have massive training programs benefitting the Negro (and whites who want to raise their skills as well). Some are on-the-job training programs, some are after-hours classes where employees can complete their high school education. Some companies, such as Pacific Telephone & Telegraph, even go out into the ghettos to assure young Negroes that there are jobs open for them, to advise them what the qualifications will be, and urge them to finish their studies. Negroes also benefit from the government's multi-billion-dollar war on poverty, which lays heavy emphasis on job training. Both the Job Corps and the Neighborhood Youth Corps, financed by the Office of Economic Opportunity under the anti-poverty program, provide work experience, education and counseling for young people. The Department of Health, Education and Welfare runs two programs of vocational training, aimed largely at family heads. The biggest single program of all is the Labor Department's Manpower Development and Training project, devoted to on-the-job training. Again, these programs help disadvantaged whites, too, but since the Negro is the most poverty-stricken and jobless of all U.S. citizens, they help him more. During 1966, in fact, the Labor Department began signing job-training contracts with industry specifically designed to aid "disadvantaged minorities."

Negroes are properly appreciative of all the efforts on behalf of the black man: two-thirds of them, for example, approve of the Federal anti-poverty programs. But their leaders are far from satisfied. They feel, for one thing, that progress has not been fast enough—that a Negro accountant here or an airline stewardess there do not add up to enough numbers. "We're still talking in hundreds, not thousands," an Urban League official in the South observed. The Urban League runs a massive employment service of its own, called the National Skills Bank. Some Negro leaders feel that too much of business's seeming concern is sheer "tokenism"—a rush to hire a few "house Negroes" for appearance's sake. They also feel that the Negroes have made very little gain in the matter of their pay, a factor that may depend more on the largesse or good offices of the white employer than the force of law or public opinion. In the *Newsweek* survey of 1963, 54 per cent of all Negroes said their wages had improved in the previous five years. In the 1966 study, 55 per cent of them noted improvement in pay —hardly any change at all.

There is evidence to suggest that for all its participation in the struggle to help the Negroes find jobs, U.S. business is not doing all it could. In 1966, the National Industrial Conference Board, a non-profit research organization, completed a study (financed by a $195,000 grant from the Ford Foundation) of the Negro employment experience of 47 major American companies. The survey confirmed that the companies are trying hard to accommodate the Negro. But it also found that many of the firms—like the Negroes themselves—were caught unprepared by the sudden pressure on them to hire more blacks, and are still groping for new employment policies. Moreover, the NICB found that there is often a gap between company policy and practice—that equal opportunity doesn't work very well if it is not enunciated from the top with enough force to impress the lower echelons of business. Concluded the NICB: "Few of the companies studied are doing as well as they say they want to or as well as their top officers think they are doing."

EDUCATION

In the little more than a decade that has passed since the U.S. Supreme Court ordered desegregation of the public schools with "all deliberate speed," its wishes have been carried out with a good deal more deliberateness than speed. This is not to say that there has been no progress. As the Negroes themselves can attest, there has been, though hardly at a rate that would cause Martin Luther King or the NAACP's Roy Wilkins to turn handsprings. Not too long ago, the number of Negroes admitted to white schools in the hard-core South was measured in fractions of percentage points. That has changed somewhat. In the 1963–64 school year, for example, figures of the Southern Education Reporting Service showed that the number of Negro children attending integrated schools in the South was a miniscule 0.8 per cent. By the 1964–65 school year, that figure was up to 2.25 per cent, and by the beginning of the 1965–66 school year it had taken a triple jump to 6.01 per cent. The estimate for the 1966–67 school year was 12 per cent. Considering the immensity of the problem, this was progress, though no great numbers of children were involved (12 per cent means 360,000 out of a total of 3 million Negro children in southern schools) and integration in many cases amounted to no more than a few Negro children installed in a white school, or a few whites in a Negro school. The situation in higher education may not be much better. In the *Newsweek* survey, Negroes split almost even, 44 to 41 per cent, on whether a qualified member of their race can really get into a top college on an equal basis with whites.

In 1965, however, what amounted to a brand new ball game began under Title VI of the Civil Rights Act of 1964, which banned discrimination in any program assisted by Federal funds. The clear intention of the Executive Branch of the government was to use the potent weapon of Federal millions to achieve integration where court edict had largely failed. The blunt message to schools: no desegregation, no money. For the time being, at least, the U.S. Office of Education did not concern itself with schools in the North, except to consult with school officials there who had desegregation problems, to accept pledges of compliance, and to process complaints. While there are no reliable statistics on how much de facto segregation remains in the North, the Negroes have made gains there, largely through their own efforts of protest and demonstration. But in the 17 Southern and border states where segregation has been a long-standing policy, the United States asked for detailed desegregation plans, with the hope that the primary schools could integrate four grades over each of the next two years, reaching full integration in the 1967–68 school year.

In the first year there was considerable confusion over the law, and consequently an uneven pattern of compliance ranging from token to total. Many school districts submitted so-called "freedom of choice" plans in the belief that these would soften desegregation. Under freedom of choice, pupils name their school preference, but since they often tend to stick with their own kind, the result can be less integration than under an arbitrary plan. Some districts failed to respond to the government's directive at all.

In the spring of 1966, therefore, Commissioner of Education Harold Howe II promulgated a set of new—and in the South's view—stringent guidelines to take effect that fall. Among other things, the new rules ordered the closing of small inadequate schools maintained solely for Negroes, and said the freedom-of-choice plans would be acceptable only if they actually produced a significant amount of desegregation. And the guidelines went one long step further: they directed that the teaching staffs must be desegregated, too.

That tore it. All summer the South seethed in rebellion, charging in particular that desegregation of teachers went directly against the law, which specified that the government should not become involved in employment practices. Howe's office conceded this point, but argued that it was not trying to dictate the employment policies of Southern schools, only asking that teachers be *assigned* in such a way as to help end racial identity of the schools.

The debate erupted on Capitol Hill, where Southern congressmen, and some Northerners as well, took up the school cause. Howe was denounced as an "education commissar." The upshot was that when Congress passed the $6 billion school-aid bill of 1966, both House and Senate struck out a provision that would have given special consideration to schools trying to achieve racial integration. The angry House also struck at Howe by forbidding him to bus children (or teachers, for that matter) to other schools to speed desegregation. Cried Rep. Paul A. Fino, a Bronx, New York, Republican who was one of the Northern sympathizers: "I don't want to spend money so a socialized quack like Howe can bus pupils. The child you save may be your own." Actually, Howe's office had not ordered any busing until Title VI, though some Southern school districts had adopted busing as one method of complying with Howe's orders. But no matter. It seemed certain that Howe's policies alone were not the only spark that set the school issue aflame. By the time the debate reached Congress, the white backlash was cracking ominously, and Howe was a convenient target. Even so, there was genuine turmoil in the schools of the South, and the ultimate outcome of the government's ambitious program remained to be seen.

On a nationwide basis, the dimension of the school problem was graphically illustrated when the long-awaited Coleman Report appeared. Probably not too many Americans realize it, but the Civil Rights Act of 1964 contained a little-noticed section directing the U.S. Commissioner of Education to conduct a survey into "the lack of equal educational opportunities" by reason of race, religion or national origin. Over the next two years, a blue-ribbon team headed by James S. Coleman, professor of social relations at Johns Hopkins University, carried out the most massive inquiry in the history of U.S. education. In the major portion of the survey, nearly 600,000 children in 4,000 schools in all 50 states were tested and questioned. In addition, 60,000 teachers in these schools were questioned and self-tested, and the principals of the schools were also questioned. Under the title *Equality of Educational Opportunity,*[*] the findings of the Coleman group appeared as a comprehensive, 737-page document in the summer of 1966. Coleman himself made it plain that the survey was not primarily concerned

[*] U.S. Government Printing Office, Washington, D.C. Price: $4.25.

with finding out how much segregation there is in the nation's public schools; rather, the study focused on student achievement, with the ultimate goal of finding out how equal white and Negro children are in ability when they leave school. Even so, the Coleman investigators did make a value judgment on the extent of school segregation, and arrived at this conclusion:

"The great majority of American children attend schools that are largely segregated—that is, where almost all of their fellow students are of the same racial background as they are."

Almost 80 per cent of all white children in the first grade, the Coleman study found, attend schools that are from 90 to 100 per cent white. More than 65 per cent of all Negro pupils in the first grade attend schools that are between 90 and 100 per cent Negro. For both black and white children, segregation is more nearly complete in the South, where most of them attend schools that are 100 per cent white or Negro. The study also found that the same pattern of segregation holds—though not quite so strongly—for teachers. In the nation as a whole, the average Negro elementary pupil attends a school in which 65 per cent of the teachers are Negro; the average white elementary pupil attends a school in which 97 per cent of the teachers are white.

The obvious conclusion of the Coleman Report is that white children are the most segregated, which is another way of saying that the Negroes have not been very successful in crashing the gates of white schools. Nor are they even close to matching whites in achievement, once they are in school. In its qualitative findings, the Coleman group reported that at every grade level tested in the elementary and high schools, including the 12th and final grade, Negro pupils scored well below whites in all standard skills.* Moreover, the report found, the Negro's deficiency does not decrease with more schooling, but actually worsens, and the gap between Negro and white widens. In

* The reasons have much to do with the Negro's blighted environment, but this question is so critical and controversial that it will be discussed in a later chapter on the Negro family.

verbal skills, for example, the median score for Negroes in the first grade was 45.4. For whites it was 53.2—a difference of 7.8 points. In the 12th grade, the median Negro score was only 40.9, the white score 52.1—a difference of 11.2 points.

The Coleman findings are enough to give Negro civil rights leaders great pause. Negroes have pressed not only for more integration of the schools, but for a better education for their children. The latter is especially true in the great cities of the North (New York City is an example), where Negro leaders, recognizing the difficulty of integrating schools buried deep in all-Negro neighborhoods, have tended to ask instead for better facilities and better teachers. The Coleman study suggests that they are making, at best, slow progress both quantitatively and qualitatively. It also suggests that gradualism as a concept for school integration is not working well enough.

After the first great school integration battles of the late 1950s, public attention was drawn away from education while the Negroes themselves directed their protest to other areas of discrimination. Very possibly many white Americans simply thought that somebody, somewhere, was doing something about school integration, as the Supreme Court had wanted. But Harold Howe, the plain-speaking, Yale-trained Commissioner of Education, put the matter bluntly when he delivered a speech in New York in June 1966. "We seem," said Howe, "to have been lulled into a blind faith in gradualism, a mindless confidence that some morning, some year, a suddenly transformed electorate will spontaneously and joyously decide that this is the day to integrate America. Well, it's not going to happen."

HOUSING

In the early part of 1966, Dr. Martin Luther King, having deserted for the moment the home base of his Southern Christian Leadership Conference in Atlanta, Georgia, moved into a $90-a-month, four-room flat in the heart of Chicago's West

Side slum, to call attention to the miserable housing conditions of his race. The dramatic effect of this was diminished a bit when the startled landlord, learning that Nobel Peace winner King was among his tenants, hastily dispatched eight workmen to steam off the old wallpaper and paint the walls, repair the broken windows and plumbing, and clean the place up. But King was deadly serious, and throughout the summer he led marches through the city's residential areas (once he was hit in the head with a rock) in a concerted "end the slums" drive. For King it was his first real beachhead outside the South—a fact that was enough in itself to dramatize the concern of Negro leaders with their race's housing plight. In no other area of the civil rights struggle has the black man made so little progress.

In the *Newsweek* survey, 43 per cent of all rank-and-file Negroes in 1963 felt that their housing conditions were better; in 1966 the result was the same, 43 per cent. In other words, no progress at all. Some economic groups, such as middle- and upper-income Negroes of the North and South, actually feel they have lost ground. And only 29 per cent of *Newsweek*'s Negro leadership sample, the special group of 100 Negroes prominent in their race, can point to any progress in their housing. Moreover, the Negroes think they know where to put the blame: of all essentially white institutions, they distrust real estate companies almost as much as they do the police.

When it comes to his housing, of course, the Negro has substantially less going for him than in any other area of discrimination. Seventeen states* and 33 cities now have laws banning discrimination in private housing but, over and over, officials concede that any reasonably clever real estate man can find ways to worm around them. Since 1949, the U.S. government has poured more than $5 billion into urban renewal, but by the end of 1965 all that this had resulted in was

* Alaska, California, Colorado, Connecticut, Indiana, Maine, Massachusetts, Michigan, Minnesota, New Hampshire, New Jersey, New York, Ohio, Oregon, Pennsylvania, Rhode Island, Wisconsin.

new dwellings for only 25,000 Negroes, compared with 48,000 poor whites. Naturally, the picture is not uniformly bleak. All over the country, more than 1,000 civic organizations, neighborhood associations, in some cases even realty boards, are working to promote open housing in their communities. Two examples are the posh, wealthy suburbs of Winnetka, Illinois (Chicago), and Shaker Heights, Ohio (Cleveland), though it is another question how many Negroes can afford to live there. Some U.S. business firms have made efforts to improve housing in the vicinity of their plants, recognizing that their workers—both black and white—will be better workers if they have better housing conditions. One rather remarkable experiment is that of the U.S. Gypsum Co. in New York's Harlem, where it has set about renovating slum apartment buildings on its own hook. Gypsum, a Chicago-based maker of building materials, makes no attempt to disguise the fact that it hopes to encourage a rebuilding boom in the slums, and thus profit from the increased sale of its products. But it takes the further view that if it can help the slum dwellers in the process, so much the better. Its buildings have been a signal success with Negroes, and civic planners are impressed by the fact that Gypsum has spent an average of only $9,100 to renovate each apartment, compared with the $22,500 per unit it costs for new urban renewal construction. Now other U.S. manufacturers have undertaken similar programs.

Above all, Congress in 1966 passed the much-debated Demonstration Cities bill (after first stripping it of any racial overtones), which authorizes $1.3 billion for the rebuilding of some of the worst slums in selected cities throughout the country—selected, that is, to demonstrate what can be done with urban blight. Unlike urban renewal, the measure is concerned not only with the physical rebuilding of slums, but with tying together all of the Great Society's welfare programs to improve the cultural and educational life of the oppressed—black or white—as well. As an imaginative approach to the manifold evils of the slums, Demonstration Cities is perhaps the most important single piece of legislation enacted thus far under President Johnson's welfare programs, and it certainly is a bright hope for the future.

In the matter of housing, however, the basic problem for the Negro is that he has run smack into the white man's deepest prejudice, save for social mixing and intermarriage. Particularly to lower- and middle-class whites, their homes are their biggest single possession and they remain gripped by the prejudice that Negroes are too slovenly to live with, and by the old fear that property values will fall if Negroes move in. Even where the Negroes have made inroads into white neighborhoods—as they have—they often simply chase the whites to the suburbs and end up living in an all-Negro neighborhood again. In the great urban ghettos, of course, their plight remains almost unrelieved.

In the summer of 1966, white prejudice began boiling over on the edges of the Negro neighborhoods where the Negroes were pushing hardest, and there were border clashes in Cleveland, Brooklyn, Baltimore and Chicago. Nowhere was the basic confrontation of the races over housing better illustrated than when Martin Luther King proposed to march into Cicero, Illinois, an all-white suburb of Chicago (the former headquarters of Al Capone) inhabited largely by blue-collar workers of Eastern European extraction. No black man had set foot in Cicero since 1951, when a Negro was driven away by mobs, and the mutterings now from whites raised the specter of a terrible riot. Indeed, so great was the explosive potential that Chicago officials could not tolerate the march; instead they sat down with King and agreed to a covenant pledging the city to work actively for open housing. King called off his march. The gauntlet later was snatched up by CORE, but by that time the heat was off and only sporadic violence marked CORE's march.

Cicero was a significant victory for the Negro, but it was short-lived. A summer of riots and the angry cries from the black power advocates were taking their toll of white tolerance. On Capitol Hill, Congress was considering its third major civil rights bill, this one to remove discrimination from the selection of juries, and the sale or rental of housing. Even before the measure neared a vote, the housing section had been all but emasculated with amendments. But whereas Congress once had the will to help the Negro, now it did not. In the Senate, fully one-third of the Democrats voted against the cloture needed to shut off a Southern filibuster. Two-thirds of the Republicans did likewise, and even President Johnson failed to twist arms with his customary vigor. The bill died ingloriously, without even coming to a floor vote, and while blame could be laid at both Democratic and Republican doorsteps, Majority Leader Mike Mansfield came closest to the truth when he said the bill was scuttled by the "rioting, marches, shootings and inflammatory statements which have characterized this simmering summer." By all odds, it was the greatest single defeat suffered by the Negroes in all the long, hard climb upward since 1954. Open housing now seemed more remote than ever, and in the gloom that settled over the Negro community, Martin Luther King spoke for many when he said: "It surely heralds darker days for this era of social discontent."

IT CAN NOW BE SAID that in 1966 America simply was not ready for open housing. Under the pressure of the law, the Negro protest, and his own conscience, the American white has begun to yield—however grudgingly—in the areas that touch his private life the least—voting rights, or public accommodations, or jobs. Even education is in a sense peripheral, for the white child need spend only a few hours with Negroes in an integrated school; after that the Negroes vanish somewhere into a private world of their own. But the white man is not quite ready to see the Negro move in next door, and the battle there has scarcely been joined. Putting everything together, and sensing the danger of rising white resentment, the Negroes are able to see very well that the road ahead will be harder, at least for the short term. In the *Newsweek* survey, their expectations of future gains fall a few percentage points lower than in 1963. One basic trouble is that most of the white man's efforts to help the Negroes have benefitted those best able to take advantage of the help—the middle- and upper-class Negroes. Negro employment in the professional and technical fields has climbed more than 100 per cent in the last ten years; vast opportunities have been opened for those who happen to be lawyers or physicists. But automation has eliminated many of the menial jobs formerly open to the poorer classes of Negroes, and despite the lowering of some union bars, they still find it hard to crash the ranks of plumbers, or painters, or construction workers. In education, opportunities on the college level have improved greatly; some schools even exhibit a preference for Negro applicants over whites with equivalent credentials. But, as we have seen, the Negro in the elementary and high schools too often falls below the achievement of the white student, even when there is a conscious effort to improve his books and physical equipment. In housing, the shining high-rise towers of urban renewal provide homes largely for better-off Negroes and result in "urban removal" to even more squalid quarters for the poor blacks. The result is a widening rift in the Negro class structure, the upper classes becoming ever more complacent and satisfied with their progress, the poorer classes ever more frustrated at their lack of progress. Yet it would be a vast mistake to underestimate the upward surge that virtually all Negroes have experienced. There is almost no way to measure the exhilarating sense of freedom that has come to many Negroes over the past few years. Most notably in the field of public accommodations, but elsewhere too, they have—after three long centuries of denial—tasted the sweet fruit of release. And they have been given a tantalizing glimpse of what total acceptance into the mainstream of American society could mean. Perhaps because of this, the Negroes retain an abiding—and possibly unrealistic—faith in ultimate victory. Nearly 70 per cent of them are utterly convinced that over the next five years the white man's attitude will improve, his resistance soften. Despite the agonies of summer 1966, the Negro's final goal has changed not at all; over and above the piecemeal gains he has made, he still wants total integration. By 80 per cent Negroes want to work on the job with whites, by 70 per cent they want to send their children to school with whites, and by 68 per cent they want to live in mixed neighborhoods. At mid-passage in the revolution, how to accomplish that is now the most urgent task of their leaders.

"I Became a Savage"

ALMOST EVERYTHING BAD *that can happen to a young Negro in the ghetto has happened to Reginald Eccleston, a lithe, bearded 21-year-old who lives in the sprawling, squalid Bedford-Stuyvesant slum of Brooklyn, New York. As a teen-ager, he was a street-gang fighter, he was a high school drop-out, he used dope. "I became a delinquent, I became a savage," he said. At sixteen he was arrested for statutory rape. "Did I do it . . . yes, I did," he told the* Newsweek *reporter who interviewed him in mid-1966. "But make sure you put in statutory there, so some people don't get the wrong idea."*

Eccleston has spent his whole life in Bedford-Stuyvesant, sharing a corner of an old seven-room apartment with fourteen brothers and sisters, his taxi-driver father and overworked mother. "We used to be on welfare," he said. "We didn't get the money, just the food. But they said my father made too much money to get it. With all those children, how can a man make too much money?"

Reginald (his pals call him Butch) dropped out of high school in his senior year—"they were going to keep me back anyway"—but he had already learned all the ways to skip school and had missed whole semesters. "You sign in in the morning," he said, "then you cut out. If the police run up on me I say I got the day off. The police never know what's going on in school. I'd cut out, then maybe I'd go to the movies, or I would stay in the lunchroom and encourage others to go with me; we'd get a party going."

He found school just another extension of the Negro's second-rate existence. "The teachers, they come from other parts of town. They don't know the kids, they never asked how you felt about certain things. Christopher Columbus and all those cats, maybe there was a black guy next to him; maybe he was a black guy. They don't emphasize the part the black men are playing. You get a brainwash instead of an education. Black kids are beginning to get rebellion of the system." He paused a moment, then asked: "What color do you think Christ was? The Bible says he had hair like a lamb. There's only one kind of man has hair like a lamb."

Reginald Eccleston's own rebellion might have led him into even worse troubles had he not met the men who run the government's Youth in Action agency in Bedford-Stuyvesant. To Reginald these were people "who care about people," and he signed on for $45 a week to act as a liaison man, urging the Negroes to join up in Head Start and other youth activity and training programs.

He was a good choice for the job. Padding through his town in monk sandals, past the kids playing ball in the street and past the morose men and women perched on the stoops, he speaks the language of the slums—that strange cryptic dialect that is not really intended for white ears. One day on a street corner he met three of his old cronies, tough, gangling youths as tense as the mood of a ghetto night.

"Hey, Butch, what you doin', man?" one called, and answered himself, "The poverty program, yeah, everybody's got a program, but nothin' ever happens."

"Wait a minute, baby," said Reginald. "We're just telling you what's coming, we're telling you what's happening, man."

"What is happening, baby?" asked another. "The big cats living on Sugar Hill, the minute anybody makes it out of here they go uptown and they forget about us, they never put money back in. What have we got? We better get something or we is going to explode."

"There is power," answered Reginald. "First we have to get this person out of our minds, brothers. There's only two kinds of power, economic and political, that's power."

"Are you going to hang out with us then?" one pal asked.

"Yes, brothers," Reginald assured them, and they went their way.

Eccleston sits up late at night, reading the Economic Opportunity Act over and over, trying to find new ways to apply it in his work. "I don't like to read books, about some guy who goes to the jungle or somewhere and tells you about it, or about somebody's life. I never had the opportunity to read, I was too busy trying to survive. The Economic Opportunity Act, you know, political things . . . any type of knowledge I get I spread throughout my people. I try to motivate my people on how they can strengthen their economic life."

And Reginald Eccleston dreams for himself the kind of impossible dreams that used to be the private preserve of white 21-year-olds. "I hope someday to be President of the United States. I don't think I'll really make President, but if I reach for the top, maybe I can make Senator." He drew deeply on a cigarette and added: "I hope someday I will meet a beautiful woman. When I'm President, she must be the fuel for my fire."

But along with these soaring hopes, Eccleston also understands only too well the almost incurable despair of the slums.

"The trouble here is people have nothing to do," he said. "That's why there is such a large sex problem, they haven't got anything else to do. The parents, they're concentrating on how to feed you. We need a recreation center and more activity, especially for the girls. The boys dominate the playgrounds. I don't think we need civil rights, we need human rights."

Reginald Eccleston recalls often now his own narrow brush with disaster when he ran with the street gang and was lucky to escape with three years' probation for rape. "Yes, I tried drugs," he admitted. "I stopped. Some people are just stronger than others, I guess. I just couldn't see myself being any kind of addict."

But he approves of smoking marijuana. "It goes into the back of your head and pulls out the beautiful things," he said. "You need something to stand on. We can't say 'We're Americans' and stand on that. We need something to relax and get a little joy."

CHAPTER 3

Crisis of Leadership

WHEN JAMES AUBREY NORVELL, a 40-year-old unemployed clerk from Memphis, leveled a 16-gauge automatic shotgun at James Meredith one sultry June day in 1966, the three shots he pumped off in rapid succession were perhaps as fateful as any fired anywhere in the turbulent civil-rights revolution. Meredith fell wounded, knocked out of his brave little march into Mississippi before he had covered scarcely thirty miles. A mystic, scarred more deeply than anyone will ever know by his year of hate and torment at the University of Mississippi, Meredith had set out with only the most loosely defined goal: a hope that if he could walk through his native state unharmed in primary election week, it would encourage his people to swallow their fears and register to vote. Norvell's blasts made him a martyr, even if he didn't die. But very soon, history made him almost irrelevant.

Throughout the years of the Negro revolt, its leaders have had to stage their own demonstrations, arrange their own confrontations with the white man in order to make him pay attention to their demands. The attempted assassination of Meredith, with its hovering headlines and tight-in television cameras, was an opportunity not to be missed. A loner who believes he has a divine mission to salvage civilization, Meredith had neither asked for nor received organizational support for his march. But now all the leaders of the major civil-rights groups came racing to his hospital bedside in Memphis: Martin Luther King of the Southern Christian Leadership Conference, Stokely Carmichael of the Student Nonviolent Coordinating Committee, Floyd McKissick of the Congress of Racial Equality. Even the leaders of the old-line Establishment, Whitney Young, Jr., of the Urban League and Roy Wilkins of the NAACP, flew down from New York to take a hand.

The first task was to convince Meredith that his march must go on, but now as a massive national effort. Once he agreed, the coast-to-coast wires crackled with calls for volunteers. Logistics, the sheer complexity of organizing a march of thousands, were forgotten momentarily in the scramble to get the show back on the road.

But that night, in a tense meeting that went on until morning, the Big Five leaders began to fall out over what the purpose of the renewed march should be. Ever the moderates, Wilkins and Young wanted a single—and hopefully attainable —goal: a stronger civil-rights bill than the measure then up before Congress. Firebrands Carmichael and McKissick wanted a strong attack on President Johnson. What came out was a compromise stridently titled a "Manifesto" that did not call the President names, but demanded the saturation of the South with Federal voting examiners and a multibillion dollar "Freedom Budget" to help the Negro poor. Martin Luther King found he could live with the compromise and signed it along with Carmichael and McKissick. Wilkins and Young, liking not even the title, packed up and went home.

If this was a revealing split in the leadership ranks, there was more to come. As the enlarged new march surged forward through Mississippi, into taunts and jeers from whites and occasional tear gas and gun butts from the police, the harassed leaders of SCLC, SNCC and CORE maintained an outward show of unity. But when they stopped to address the eager Negro townsfolk who gathered along the way, they seemed to be speaking different languages.

At Greenwood, Mississippi, Stokely Carmichael rose before the black throng to cry:

"The only way we gonna stop them white men from whuppin' us is to take over. We been saying freedom for six years and we ain't got nothin'. What we gonna start saying now is black power."

"Black power!" the crowd roared.

"Ain't nothin' wrong with anything all black," shouted Carmichael, "'cause I'm all black and I'm all good. Now don't you be afraid. And from now on when they ask you what you want, you know what to tell them."

"Black power!" cried the crowd in rising crescendo. "Black power! Black power! Black power!"

This was a strange new war cry, one that carried ominous overtones of black racism, go-it-aloneness, and even violence. To the blacks who heard it, it seemed to have a compelling, magical attraction. Almost in desperation, Martin Luther King, the architect of nonviolence, fought back.

"We must never stoop to the white man's level of violence," he thundered to the crowds. "Don't forget yourselves, we're in a majority nowhere."

In the end, King gained control of the crowds; after all, he was the celebrity who had drawn them in the first place. The march wound to an orderly halt at the steps of the state capitol building in Jackson, Mississippi. But King thereafter trudged home to Atlanta forced to concede that Carmichael—more than he—had shaped the real message of the march. James Meredith himself would always be remembered as the man who bore the buckshot of race hatred. But in the history of the Negro's revolution, the march would mark the point where the widening rift in its leadership became glaringly public, and where the most basic underpinnings of the revolt—its tactics and its goal—came under direct challenge.

Since the early beginnings the method of the revolution had been nonviolence, the ultimate goal integration. But the new militants, with their chants of black power, had altogether different ideas. Nonviolence, they suggested, may well have outlived its usefulness, for the Negroes will never convince the white man of their determination unless they return violence waged against them with violent self-defense. As for integration, the black power advocates maintained that it is really irrelevant, that it will be self-defeating until the Negroes learn to take pride in their race. Otherwise they will simply carry with them into white society the servility that has marked their lives until now. What the black power champions want is to change the whole thrust of the revolution. They want to stop chipping away at the barriers of white prejudice to gain an immediate entry here and an immediate entry there. Instead, they would shore up the political, economic and cultural strength of Negro society until it can bargain on more nearly even terms with whites. Even the successes of the revolution thus far grate on them, for they seem like concessions granted grudgingly from above, not rights negotiated between equals.

Obviously, this is a very fundamental cleavage, and in retrospect it may have been inevitable. The Negro's revolt began with the courtroom skirmishes of the NAACP over school integration in the 1950s. But successful as many of these were, they were infinitely time-consuming, and many Negroes—especially younger ones—grew impatient. Boycotts and demonstrations became the order of the day, spreading like wildfire through the South and the North. Many were spontaneous, but the man who shaped their character was Martin Luther King. Indisputably the spiritual leader of his people, able to move them profoundly with his platform eloquence, King drew the concept of nonviolence principally from his study of Gandhi. He was convinced that this was the surest road to the white conscience; if the Negroes had nothing else, they (and their white sympathizers) would use their bodies in passive protest.

And so they did, during the long hard years of the early 1960s. Yet even then the Negro's revolution was essentially

formless. There was no central headquarters, recognized as
such by Negroes and whites. No one leader, not even Martin
Luther King, could presume to say that he led *all* the Negroes.
When SNCC and CORE joined the fray at the turn of the present decade, they were more aggressive, more militant. Occasionally there were intramural debates among the civil-rights
groups over tactics, and competition for headlines and funds.
Still, a loose alliance dictated by what were then common
aims, as well as the sheer immensity of their task, held them
together.

But as the Negro's revolt moved into the Northern ghettos,
and successes grew harder to come by, many were ready to
heed new voices. The victories of the South suddenly seemed
easy when measured against the jungle of poverty, joblessness
and crumbling family life of the slums. The ghetto seemed a
sinkhole of despair, and some of its most despairing members
rose up in violence in a score of cities—from Harlem in 1964
to Watts in 1965 to Chicago's West Side in 1966. There was a
prophetic sameness to many of these riots; very often they
were touched off by the police shooting of a Negro suspect, or
even the mere *rumor* that such a thing had happened. But
clearly they marked Whitey and his agents—the police, the
landlord and the storekeeper—as the enemy. And they spawned
another and far uglier war cry: "Burn, baby, burn!"

Radicalism, of course, was nothing new. On the far extremist fringe, the Black Muslims and their leader, Elijah Muhammad, had been preaching black separation for some years.
Now, ominous new black nationalist groups began to form, or
emerge from hiding. Some of these seemed to be more concerned with the pomp and circumstance of racial pride than
anything else. In Watts, for example, a bald little man named
Ron Karenga started a movement known as US (pronounced
like the pronoun, not the country). Karenga and the men of
US wear "bubas" modeled after the capes of African tribes-
men, children drill on weekends in T-shirts emblazoned with
a growling lion, and Swahili words and bongo drums punctu-
ate the group's meetings. Setting forth his creed, Karenga says

that "we have only one power left—to disrupt things." But groups such as US seem like mere child's play compared with others whose avowed aim is to get Whitey, or The Man, or The Beast, or whatever the common enemy might be called. Proliferating under such names as RAM, Uhuru, and Black Flag, they are shadowy organizations, manned by shadowy men and commonly said to be storing arms, studying the black art of municipal disruption, even poring over diagrams of city electrical systems to find the likeliest points of sabotage. They have never been taken very seriously, but the lengths to which such extremists can go was shown when three members of a group known as the Black Liberation Front were seized in a bizarre plot to blow the head off the Statue of Liberty, as a supreme gesture of contempt for whites. Perhaps the best known is RAM (for Revolutionary Action Movement), whose guiding spirit has been Robert Franklin Williams, a former NAACP chapter head who fled to Cuba to escape a North Carolina kidnapping indictment. From Cuba (he later moved on to Peking) Williams wrote tracts describing in great detail how Negro urban guerrillas can make use of fire and acid bombs, put sand in the gas tanks to immobilize public vehicles, lay booby traps in police telephone boxes and puncture oil storage tanks with armor-piercing bullets. Williams' own creed: "America is a house on fire. FREEDOM NOW, or let it burn, let it burn!"

Compared with inflammatory pronouncements like these, the black power cry of Stokely Carmichael and Floyd McKissick sounds almost tame. The black power champions are not interested in going back to Africa, or setting up a separate black state in the United States. They are not stockpiling guns. They say they don't hate the white man, they just distrust him. And they don't want to shoot him—unless he shoots first. Yet black nationalism and black power essentially have the same basic appeal to human emotion—to the Negro's desperate need for pride in his race and pride in himself. Thus at a time of divergent leadership and diverging ideologies, the critical questions become: What do the great masses of Negro Americans think of their leaders? What course do they want to follow?

To get directly at the question of leadership, the *Newsweek* survey asked Negroes to rate those who have generally been recognized as in the forefront of the Movement, whether they are activists or popular symbols, moderates, liberals or extremists. The following table, which also gives the 1963 ratings of those who appeared in *Newsweek*'s earlier study, illustrates the results:

HOW NEGROES RANK THEIR LEADERS

Rank and file Percentage approving			Leadership group Percentage approving	
1966	1963		1966	1963
88	88	Martin Luther King, Jr.	87	95
71	79	James Meredith	35	81
66	80	Jackie Robinson	58	82
64	68	Roy Wilkins	62	92
56	60	Dick Gregory	65	80
54	X	Charles Evers	68	X
53	62	Ralph Bunche	49	87
48	64	Thurgood Marshall	81	94
47	X	James Farmer	70	X
44	51	Adam Clayton Powell	49	52
35	X	A. Philip Randolph	83	X
33	X	Whitney Young, Jr.	70	X
22	X	Bayard Rustin	53	X
19	X	Floyd McKissick	35	X
19	X	Stokely Carmichael	33	X
12	15	Elijah Muhammad	15	17

NOTE: X—not on 1963 list.

Clearly, Martin Luther King remains the preeminent leader; where it is possible to make the comparison, every other leader has slipped since 1963. And Stokely Carmichael and Floyd McKissick come in near the very bottom of the list. True, King himself has slipped somewhat with the leadership sample, and these men also rate Carmichael and McKissick higher than does the rank-and-file. In part, this is because they are more likely to have heard the names of the newcomers—the recognition factor, in other words. But it also is a reflection of the fact that the leadership group is a great deal more impatient and willing to turn to the new militants like Carmichael and McKissick. In another question of the survey, 43 per cent of rank-and-file Negroes say the pace of the revolution is too slow, but an overwhelming 82 per cent of the leadership group feels the pace is not fast enough.

It is interesting to note, however, that the leadership sample is demonstrably more sophisticated in how it looks on some highly respected, but less spectacular, figures in the Movement. The leaders, for example, rate such men as A. Philip Randolph, Whitney Young, Jr., and Bayard Rustin much higher than does the rank and file. Conversely, they rank James Meredith much lower, recognizing perhaps that he is more of a popular symbol than a real motivating force. The case of Meredith, in fact, is unusual. Meredith himself was included in *Newsweek's* sample of 100 leaders, but in the course of being questioned, he insisted over and over that he did not regard himself as a leader, that he felt he would lose his real identity with the masses if he became a recognized leader. Yet in the estimation of most Negroes, he stands just below Martin Luther King himself.

On the next general question of tactics, King's nonviolent doctrine again comes out on top. A majority of 59 per cent of all Negroes are committed to nonviolence as the primary instrument of their revolution, and there is very little variation among different income groups or geographic locations (except that endorsement is highest, at 73 per cent, among middle- and upper-income Negroes of the South, lowest at 48 per cent in the leadership sample).

These figures by themselves do not tell all of the story, however. For the *Newsweek* survey shows clearly that a fair number of Negroes are intrigued by the vision of stature and pride embodied in the slogan, black power. It is true that they reject almost out of hand the extreme racist groups: only 5 per cent favor the black nationalists and 4 per cent the Black Muslims (and these small numbers obviously overlap). But fully 25 per cent of rank-and-file Negroes favor at least the idea of black power, and the appeal of the slogan is even greater (31 per cent) among young Negroes. Moreover, roughly half the leadership sample expresses some interest in black power.

What is quite clear from the poll is that black power—however magnetic it may be as a slogan—is still a fuzzy doctrine to most Negroes. In the survey, Negroes themselves found all sorts of ways to define the term. To some it means "self-identity"; to others it means "take over everything"; to still others, it means "colored people are tired of being pushed around." One of the leadership sample, New York psychology professor Kenneth Clark, even suggested waggishly: "It's the civil-rights version of the Watusi." Indeed, the leadership group went to some lengths to explain its interest in black power, being careful to make the point that they do not endorse it if it means violence and destruction. As Mervyn Dymally, a California state legislator from Watts, put it: "As a positive force—yes. Black power to be anti-white, to be destructive, to burn—no."

Precisely to try to clear up some of the confusion over the meaning of black power, the *Newsweek* survey put one of its major tenets to the test with this question: Should Negroes give up working with whites and go it alone to get what they want? Here the response of the Negroes is sharp and clear. By a resounding 81 per cent, rank-and-file Negroes all over the country reject the notion. Surprisingly, young Negroes are even more committed (by 84 per cent) to cooperation with whites than their elders. And in the leadership group, only 6 per cent favor a break with whites (to 81 per cent against). Even so, the sense of racial pride remains strong in many Negroes. In the survey Negroes were reminded that whites outnumber them by roughly 10 to 1, and were asked if they wouldn't lose in any all-out test against whites. Among rank-and-file Negroes, 27 per cent agree that they would lose, but very nearly half (49 per cent) do not agree at all. This inner feeling of superiority, regardless of the obstacles and the odds, is stronger among ghetto Negroes of the North (54 per cent) and strongest of all (56 per cent) among urban Negroes of the South, who over the years have fought most of the battles. But on this point, the Negro leadership group, more acutely tuned to the numerical reality of the Negro's position in America, splits sharply with the rank and file. Fully 61 per cent of the leaders agree that their race would lose any head-to-head test with whites. Only 14 per cent disagree. Even more realistically, some leaders recognize that if the Negro revolution ever reaches such an apocalyptic climax as black against white, no one would win and society itself would be the loser. As Martin Luther King answered the survey: "Both whites and Negroes would lose. Racial clash would disrupt Western civilization. . . ."

AS THE CONFUSION over the meaning of black power shows, the dialogue of the civil-rights movement has become infinitely more complex than it was just a few years ago. Then the Negro's leaders were—like so many boxers—more concerned with jabbing for weaknesses in the white racial barriers, and asking for admittance. But inevitably there were those Negroes who began probing for new meanings in their struggle and seeking new solutions. To some of the black nationalists it has seemed that the white man is an intractable enemy, hardly worth talking to any more, certainly not worth the ultimate indignity to the Negro of having to deal with him from a position of inferiority. Bitter playwright LeRoi Jones was quoted in *Life* Magazine: "I don't think it is necessary to make anything clear to the white man except perhaps that most of the world would be better off if the white man didn't exist." In the angry extremist view, men like King, Wilkins and Young are Uncle Toms, gullibly playing into the hands of whites who soothe them with sweet talk, and occasionally hire a Negro who looks as if he won't offend anyone. One of the most articulate spokesmen for the far-out wing is Dan Watts, who gave up a promising career as an architect with a white firm to publish the extremist *Liberator* in New York. Watts is convinced that the only answer is more long, hot summers to force a final confrontation with the white power structure. That, he said in a CBS documentary in 1966, will either bring on meaningful negotiations, or else the whites "will march us off to concentration camps, led by Louis Armstrong playing 'We Shall Overcome!' and blessed by Martin Luther King as we go through the gates."

The real problem, says Dan Watts, is that the white man simply does not understand that the Negro is serious. "You tell a white man that you love him and he believes it; but you tell a white man . . . 'I'm getting ready to slit your throat,' he just can't believe it."

The extremist creed of final confrontation with Whitey finds some acceptance among ghetto Negroes, especially the bitter young men who slouch on the street corners, their hair held flat against their heads with black kerchiefs. In Harlem, hundreds of these have banded into a loose amalgam of street gangs known as the Five Percenters,* whose principal mission seems to be to prey on white students and school teachers. But the far-out groups have not attracted any large following, and even their leaders concede that they played hardly any role at all in such riots as the ones in Watts and Hough.

The black power cry of CORE and SNCC, which concentrates less on the depredations of the white man and more on the latent assets of the Negro, has some overlapping dialogue with the extremists; indeed, both wings have steeped themselves in the writings of the late Frantz Fanon, a psychiatrist born in Martinique who believed that Western man is too decadent to emulate, and that fighting for one's freedom can have a therapeutic effect. High priest Stokely Carmichael has gone about the country cajoling his race to stand up straighter, to be proud, be exemplary. "We've got to say to our little chil-

---

* The name comes from the notion that 85 per cent of Negroes form a directionless mass, while 10 per cent are Uncle Toms, leaving only a militant 5 per cent to shape the destiny of the black man.

dren, you're beautiful," he once told a rally in Harlem. "With your black, nappy hair and your broad nose and your diaper hanging, you're beautiful. We've got to say it to ourselves." Carmichael exhorts his people to love and respect each other; he tells them they must stop "cuttin' each other on Friday and Saturday nights," they must stop "hustlin' off each other," they must drop "drinkin' that cheap rotgut wine and that cheap whisky." If this is his racial plea, Carmichael stresses also the need of the Negro for economic and political power—especially political.

Carmichael learned the lesson of political power well when he went into Lowndes County, Alabama, for SNCC in 1965 and conducted a successful registration drive among the rural Negroes; so successful, in fact, that the Lowndes Negroes formed their own Black Panther party and put up a slate of candidates for the election of November 1966 (they were, however, soundly defeated). At the time, Stokely Carmichael seemed the unlikeliest sort of operative for the Negro cause in the Deep South. Born in Port of Spain, Trinidad, in 1941, Carmichael moved with his family to Harlem when he was eleven years old (later they settled in the Bronx) and grew up in the swinging world of New York. Attending Bronx High School of Science, he read Karl Marx and took up with young Socialists, later went on to receive a degree in philosophy from Howard University in 1964. When he plunged into civil rights work in the South, Carmichael carried with him a clipped Eastern accent and a set of freshly pressed clothes.

But Carmichael learned fast. Trudging dusty roads to convert the placid sharecroppers of Lowndes County, he soon acquired a pair of rumpled dungarees, began dropping his "g's" and fell into the "he don't" vernacular. And what he saw appalled him. In the Black Belt of Alabama he came face to face with the numbing fear, the sense of inferiority that long years of segregation had ground into the black consciousness. Nothing, he felt, epitomized this more than when one Negro voted for a white sheriff, explaining, "We aren't ready to have a colored sheriff. The white folks wouldn't like that a bit."

Later Carmichael was to explain: "Black power means that in Lowndes County . . . if a Negro is elected tax assessor, he will be able to tax equitably and channel funds for the building of better roads and schools serving Negroes. If elected sheriff, he can end police brutality. . . . On the state and national level, it means that black people can say to white authorities, 'We need X million dollars to fix our roads, and we have X million votes behind us.' Without power, they can only say, 'Please, we need it'. . ."

As a direct result of his reputation of voting registration successes in Alabama, Carmichael in the spring of 1966, and then only 24 years old, was elected chairman of SNCC in a surprising upset victory over John Lewis, 26, a Chicago civil-rights worker who had headed the group since 1963. A bit earlier in the year, Floyd McKissick, then 44, a lawyer and a former NAACP youth chairman, succeeded James Farmer as head of CORE. Also a disciple of political muscle, McKissick joined forces with Carmichael to promulgate the message of black power during the Meredith March.

Stokely Carmichael, the more flamboyant of the two, got much of his feeling for racial pride from his origin in Trinidad, where the 96 per cent Negro majority runs the stores, mans the police and does not consider itself exploited.* Black power did not spring full-blown from Stokely Carmichael's brain. He borrowed tactics from James Forman, the former executive director of SNCC, and ideas from Robert Moses, the murky, moody intellectual who directed SNCC's so-called Summer Project of 1964, when hordes of college students from the North went down to Mississippi to help in a massive voter registration drive (Moses later drifted away to pursue "black conscious" concepts of his own in the South; believing—as does

---

* A number of the most militant new Negro leaders share Carmichael's West Indian background: Lincoln Lynch (associate director, CORE) born in Jamaica; Roy Innis (chairman, Harlem CORE) born in the Virgin Islands; Ivanhoe Donaldson (director, New York office of SNCC) born in Jamaica; Cortland Cox (SNCC field secretary) lived in Trinidad.

James Meredith—that he will lose his identity with the masses if he is a recognized leader, Moses changed his name to Robert Parris, substituting his middle name for his last name). But, as he flitted about the country speaking to crowds and appearing on television, Carmichael was incomparably the most compelling apostle of black power. A man with a quick pleasant smile and flashing white teeth, hunch-shouldered and easy in manner, Carmichael went about half-wheedling, half-demanding, but always conveying a sense of urgency. In quieter moments, his definitions of black power sounded cooler than the slogan itself. "Too often," said Carmichael, "the goal 'integration' has been based on a complete acceptance of the fact that *in order to have* a decent house or education, Negroes must move into a *white* neighborhood or go to a *white* school. What does this mean? First of all, it reinforces among both Negroes and whites the idea that 'white' is automatically better and that 'black' is by definition inferior. Such situations will not change until Negroes have political power—to control their own school boards, for example. With the achievement of such control, Negroes can become truly equal—and integration (is then) relevant. . . . 'Pro-black' has never meant 'anti-white'— unless whites make it so."

But while black power was supposed to sanction violence only in self-defense, Carmichael's sometimes bitter, angry use of the phrase made many whites—and some blacks as well— wonder. And Carmichael seemed to belie his own words in the Atlanta riot of September 1966. Atlanta is an image-conscious city that has prided itself on its peaceable race relations. Its silver-haired mayor, Ivan Allen, Jr., moreover, has been an enlightened supporter of the civil-rights cause. Yet Atlanta Negroes quickly gathered in angry crowds when a white policeman shot and wounded a fleeing Negro suspect (the old pattern). Carloads of police quieted the mob, and the matter might very well have ended there if Stokely Carmichael had not appeared on the scene. Sensing the hostility of the mob, Carmichael announced that he would return and "tear this place up." What came next was a seething riot in which hordes of young Negroes attacked the police with bricks and bottles, and Mayor Allen himself was toppled to the pavement (he was, however, unhurt). And hardly had peace been restored before Carmichael and SNCC were under attack. Carmichael was arrested (for the twenty-eighth time in the civil-rights struggle) on a charge of riot and released in $1,000 bond pending trial. Publisher Ralph McGill, a staunch defender of SNCC in the past, charged from the front page of his Atlanta *Constitution* that "SNCC is no longer a student movement (or) . . . a civil rights organization. It is openly, officially committed to a destruction of existing society. . . ." Police chief Herbert Jenkins of Atlanta put it more succinctly. "SNCC," said Jenkins, "is now the Nonstudent Violent Committee."

CERTAINLY THE ONSET of black power produced sharp birth pangs for its principal advocates. At SNCC, defeated chairman John Lewis abruptly quit, as did most of the white workers, leaving the organization almost totally black (for all its noise, SNCC is a relatively small group of about 135 workers). After the Atlanta riot, Julian Bond, SNCC's young public-relations director, also walked out. Never well-heeled to begin with (SNCC has paid its field workers a salary of $20 a week), both CORE and SNCC were reduced to serious financial straits as white sympathizers deserted in droves. And despite all the efforts of black power's champions to explain it in reasonable terms, to many whites and Negroes it still smacked of rabble-rousing. As A. Philip Randolph, the venerable president of the Brotherhood of Sleeping Car Porters, observed: "The term black power is an unhappy term. It has overtones of force and it does create a sense of antagonism." Nor did this kind of feeling vanish when the black power adherents began substituting the term "black consciousness." For Atlanta provided a chilling case of an eye-for-an-eye philosophy on the part of SNCC, as well as convincing evidence that SNCC, when it chooses, can generate an organized assault with almost military precision.

The rise of black power, however, served to point up the shifting nature of the revolution. Elder statesman Bayard Rustin has called it a shift from "protest to politics." A. Philip Randolph, the co-leader with Rustin of the Grand March on Washington in 1963, sees it as an evolutionary process. While declaring his unalterable opposition to violence, Randolph told the *Newsweek* survey that "I think the Movement needs various wings, it couldn't go very far with a monolithic civil-rights movement. The new generation is not thinking in terms of the old generation. (Black power) is a natural outgrowth of the movement." While there were still many battles to be won in the rural South, the revolution also was shifting to the urban ghettos, where more than half the Negroes live and where the battlegrounds are infinitely more precarious. And, finally, the new generation of militants had driven the civil-rights organizations into separate, hostile camps.

Arrayed on the right against CORE and SNCC are the old-line NAACP and the Urban League, powerful and wealthy organizations that have manned and bankrolled the struggle for years past. Their leaders, Roy Wilkins of the NAACP and Whitney Young, Jr., of the Urban League, are skilled practitioners of the possible; they are as impatient as any Negro, but long experience has convinced them that reversing three centuries of subjugation is not a task that can be accomplished overnight. Somewhere in the middle is Martin Luther King, ever fearful that the cause may fall into unscrupulous hands, and anxiously trying to preserve a common front.

That there has been some disenchantment with the older generation was clearly shown in the *Newsweek* survey, when Negroes were asked to rate the efforts of the major civil-rights organizations (as distinguished from rating their leaders). On this score, both the NAACP and the Urban League show some slippage from the 1963 study. The NAACP has dropped from a 91 per cent favorable rating in 1963 to 81 per cent among rank-and-file Negroes (the leadership sample gives it a 72 per cent favorable rating). The Urban League is down from 54 per cent to 50 per cent (but the leadership sample gives it

58 per cent). Martin Luther King's SCLC comes off better, showing only a one-point decline from 56 per cent to 55 in the estimation of the rank and file, and getting a healthy 74 per cent rating from the leadership group (the relatively low rating of SCLC by the rank-and-file is probably explained by the fact that King has such overwhelming personal stature that many people—white and black—do not realize that his home base is SCLC). On the other hand, both CORE and SNCC have risen in the estimation of Negroes, though not enough to show any clear-cut trend. CORE has gained only one point, from 59 to 60 per cent, among rank-and-file Negroes since 1963 (the leaders give it 65 per cent). SNCC has jumped from 18 to 44 per cent (53 per cent with the leaders) but there is almost certainly some distortion here. In 1963, SNCC was a comparative newcomer and its low rating of 18 per cent undoubtedly was caused by lack of recognition among the Negroes; hence its real gain between 1963 and 1966 is probably less than indicated.

Even so, the threat of black power and its sharp challenge to the whole early ideology of the Movement caused the old-line leaders to fight back. In July of 1966—a month after the Meredith March—Martin Luther King took a seven-column ad in *The New York Times* to condemn black power and plead for the preservation of nonviolence. Said King: "Surrounded by an historic prosperity in the white society, taunted by empty promises, humiliated and deprived by the filth and decay of his ghetto home, some Negroes find violence alluring. They have convinced themselves that it is the only method to shock and pressure the white majority to come to terms with an evil of staggering proportions. I cannot question that these brutal facts of Negro life exist. I differ with the extremist solution." King went on to say that nonviolence has achieved significant victories for the Negro, and remains the method that can succeed. "The 'Black Power' slogan," he said, "comes not from a sense of strength but from a feeling of weakness and desperation."

If King's message had any calming effect on the boiling

leadership conflict, it wasn't noticeable. As the fitful summer of 1966 wore on, black power became more talked about than ever. And with riots erupting all over the place—in Lansing and Detroit, Michigan, in Pompano Beach, Florida, even in the lush desert oasis of Palm Springs, California—a new and even more ominous danger to the civil-rights cause arose. This was the so-called white backlash.

The evidence of a crumbling movement, of progress thwarted and good will eroded, was clearly so critical that just before the 1966 national election a group of civil-rights leaders headed by A. Philip Randolph, Bayard Rustin, Roy Wilkins and Whitney Young, Jr., issued a manifesto of their own, "Crisis and Commitment." This document condemned rioting and demagoguery, reprisal or vigilantism, and reaffirmed the faith of the signers in democratic processes as the method, the Negro revolution and integration as its goal. But it also took special note of declining public sentiment and the possible consequences: "We cannot ignore the signs of a retreat by white America from the national commitment to racial justice. This trend can be disastrous to the nation's, as well as the Negro's, welfare if it is not checked, if our forces are not rallied and if the hard, demanding job of building lasting public support is not pressed forward now. It can be worse than disastrous for the generation of younger Americans, white as well as black, who would then indeed face a future without viable idealism." One curious sidelight of this pronouncement was that Martin Luther King, still struggling to preserve a united front in the Movement, did not sign it, though he later announced publicly that he supported the views expressed in the declaration. SNCC and CORE simply shrugged.

ANY ASSESSMENT OF the chauvinistic new philosophy of black power must conclude that—as the *Newsweek* survey showed—it is out of step with the views of the majority of Negroes. Some civil-rights observers see it as no more than a psychic phase the Negro must pass through, a groping for **group** identity before he moves on. Another question is whether the new philosophy has real substance. The quest for political power may work in Negro backwaters of the South, or even on that future day when blacks outnumber whites in some of the major cities of the North. When it's a case of whites outnumbering blacks, the black power policy planners grow vague, and the fact is that on the national level the Negro is outnumbered by ten to one. Stokely Carmichael says, "We don't want help." But to black power's opponents, the simple mathematics of the situation is the strongest evidence that the black man needs the white man's help. Bayard Rustin has observed: "Obviously, one-tenth of the population can't bring about solutions in a society where problems are solved by Congressional vote. To talk about black power is not realistic."

Realistic or not, it *has* seeped into the Movement, perhaps more deeply than the older generation of Negro leaders cares to admit. As we have already seen in the *Newsweek* survey, a quarter of rank-and-file Negroes and nearly half of the leadership group are intrigued by the slogan. When they first began chanting the cry, even SNCC workers were amazed at the emotional fervor of the response from Negro rallies.

The real danger—as Martin Luther King and other leaders have plainly seen—is the explosive force that could be generated by talk of black power and shooting-back among Negroes grown weary and frustrated by delay. How long can they be expected to go on waiting for something that is never quite delivered? How long, after so many agonizing confrontations with white mobs and white police, can they be expected to turn the other cheek? During a candid moment on the Meredith March, even Martin Luther King confessed that ". . . it is becoming increasingly more difficult to sell the nonviolence concept to a tired and abused people."

Perhaps the most revealing part of the *Newsweek* survey was the graphic illustration of just how large the danger is, and where it lies. It is perfectly true that the majority of Negroes remain committed to nonviolence as the primary strategy of revolt. But nearly a third of rank-and-file Negroes are angered at the tactics of the white police. More than a third think Watts-style rioting has helped the Negro cause more than it has hurt, and a small but explosive minority of 15 per cent (and that is 3.2 million Negroes) stand ready to join the fighting. Moreover, the majority of all Negroes think there will be more riots. The following table provides a breakdown of the results of the survey:

HOW NEGROES FEEL ABOUT RIOTS

	Total rank and file	Non-South	South	Under 35 years	Leadership group
Riots have helped	34	32	35	38	41
Have hurt	20	26	15	21	19
Made no difference	17	23	16	15	18
Would join riot	15	13	18	19	1
Would not join	61	62	59	57	75
Think there will be more riots	61	62	61	66	79
Will not be	8	7	8	7	2

NOTE: "Not Sure" answers excluded.

The interesting point here is that young Negroes under 35 years of age are demonstrably the most militant, and Southern Negroes are somewhat more belligerent than their Northern counterparts. Perhaps because of a better understanding of the disturbing forces at work in the Negro's revolt, the leadership group is the most convinced (by nearly 80 per cent) that there will be more riots, but also is the least ready to join. But whatever the differences, the potential for more trouble is there.

THE SPECIAL PROBLEM for responsible Negro leaders is how to contain the riot potential of the slums and channel the restless energy of the people there to constructive ends—and to do this, furthermore, without driving an even deeper wedge between Negro and white society. For they are acutely aware that the road from equality under the law to equality in fact can be

perilous in the extreme—if the major accomplishment is simply
to unleash more backlash. They knew that laws enacted and
gains made can be taken away, perhaps with far more ease
than they were won in the first place.

SNCC members often scoff at Martin Luther King's efforts
to preserve nonviolence, and mock him as "de Lawd" for his
spiritual approach to the hard business of achieving equal
rights. Yet there can hardly be any doubt that King—more than
any other civil-rights leader—bears the burden of finding the
path to the ultimate goal. It is to King, with his concept of
nonviolent protest, that black power has raised the sharpest
challenge. It is to King, as the foremost leader of his people,
that both blacks and whites will look for solutions.

Martin Luther King recognizes the awesome responsibility
that is his (and in private, at the end of a 20-hour day, sometimes wonders whether he will be physically equal to the
task). He also recognizes that the Negro's revolt has reached
a critical juncture where the victories get harder, and old
methods are becoming obsolete.

In King's view, the haphazard ways of the revolution—a
demonstration here and a demonstration there—must give way
to a highly organized effort directed principally at the evils of
the Negro ghetto. To do this, he proposes over the next few
years to organize the Negro slum dwellers in major cities
across the nation—into tenant groups, into neighborhood associations, into employment groups—in any direction where there
is a wrong to be redressed or an evil corrected. In this way,
he hopes to convince the ghetto Negroes that they have much
more to gain by collective action than by riot.

Actually, King's new concept is an outgrowth of his experience in Chicago during the summer of 1966, when he worked
with a host of strong local protest groups to mount an "end the
slums" campaign, culminated at Cicero in the Chicago housing
covenant. But King also appears to have borrowed directly
from the casebook of Saul Alinsky, the private Chicago organ-
izer who has made a highly successful career of building
minority protest organizations in the slums of major cities.

And like Alinsky, who freely uses harassment and agitation to gain his ends, Martin Luther King also believes that Negro demonstrations must go on. "There has to be confrontation so compelling as to force action from the white community," King told *Newsweek*. As his organizing drive progresses, therefore, he intends to put on demonstrations designed to produce the maximum of public attention. In this sense, Cicero was a classic, for it generated such a wave of white apprehension that King was able to win his point without staging the demonstration at all.

King is inclined to view black power as a passing phase or fancy. Yet his own discussions of the future make liberal use of the word "power," without the adjective "black." For in essence, that is what his organization plans mean; if Negroes organize a tenants' group and force even a few concessions from their slum landlords, they have exercised a power they never had before.

King believes that the task he has set is so enormous that all civil-rights organizations, including SNCC and CORE if they will, must join in. That is one reason why he has been careful not to repudiate the black power advocates openly; he wants, as he puts it, to "keep the lines of communication open" toward a reconciliation. For beyond the organizing of the unorganized masses of the slums, King has another goal in mind. Local protests and local demonstrations in America's cities will be directed toward specific local ills, but in their sum they will be directed toward winning finally a national effort to help the Negro. King remains profoundly convinced that the Negro can never win without white support, and that the major problem of the ghettos can never really be solved without massive government intervention. But he also is profoundly convinced that only a united effort on the part of the Negroes can carry the day—militant and aggressive, yes; violent and divisive, no.

"In Livin' Black"

"I REALIZED I WAS BORN BLACK *when I went to elementary school and they told me about Dick and Jane and Bow Wow and Spot and all that crap and I knew that wasn't me."*

Those bitter words were spoken by Jennifer Lawson, a slim, taut, 20-year-old Negro girl on the staff of the Student Nonviolent Coordinating Committee. Jennifer is one of the new generation of tuned-in, turned-off SNCC workers who preach black power, read the third-world (i.e., Negro world) writings of Frantz Fanon and shout defiantly to the white man, "Your job is to try to understand us."

It turned out to be rather difficult just to get to meet Miss Lawson, much less understand her. SNCC's financial plight has been such that it even charges for interviews with its staffers. Newsweek in the summer of 1966 was obliged to pay $50 before Miss Lawson could consent to talk. When she finally did, it was obvious that Jennifer is an angry young woman who sees everything in black and white.

"Columbus discovered America," she said in the edgy, strained way of many SNCC people. "That's white supremacy talking, see. Why should a Negro be taught that Columbus discovered America (when) somebody was already here? When a white person hits the scene then, bang, the whole thing is discovered, gets civilized. When civilization goes West, that means white civilization goes West. If you understood and accepted another civilization, there wouldn't be any need for that word civilization. That's one of your words—civilization. It means white."

A graceful girl who holds her head proud, Jennifer wore her hair in the frizzy "natural" style much favored by girls in the militant wing of the Negro Movement. She had on gold wire earrings and the loose shift dress that is practically a uniform for SNCC girls.

"All whites might not be racists," she snapped in a parting shot at the enemy, "but they all support white supremacy."

Jennifer was born and raised in Fairfield, Alabama, a tough steel-town suburb of Birmingham where her father ran an auto repair shop (she has two brothers, one in college and one in high school). She shrugs now at her early life, as if it hardly matters anymore: "I lived in my community . . . an Italian across the street ran a grocery store, took money back to the white community."

Jennifer was bright—so bright that she was often a step ahead of her teachers. "Some classes I didn't pay attention," she said, "and sometimes I wouldn't go to class. I'd sit down on my front porch looking out at the world—observing." She graduated from high school fourth in a class of 106 and won a scholarship to Tuskegee University. "The great white father gave me a scholarship for being the smartest nigger in Alabama," she sneered.

She majored in biology and chemistry, but quit in her second year, feeling that her studies were irrelevant to the plight of the Negro. "A Negro college student is stepping on a lot of black people," she said, "because the reason Sally didn't go is because she wasn't smart. She was lazy and stupid and ignorant and they're using me to make that point because if I can make it then there's nothing wrong with the system. It's just wrong with Sally."

Miss Lawson joined SNCC in 1964 and has worked on the development of the Black Panther political party among the Negroes of Lowndes County, Alabama. She has also used her considerable talents as an artist to illustrate a SNCC booklet called "Us Colored People." Are the illustrations in color? "In livin' black," she snapped.

In common with other SNCC workers, Jennifer has a habit of hurling defiant answers back in a questioner's teeth:

On Christianity: "Yeah. Christianize me and colonize me. Make me a slave and bring me your Jesus. It would have been interesting if Jesus lived today. He would be an agitator and the TV networks would work out a special interview with him."

On the U.S. Constitution: "The Constitution said I was three-fifths of a person."

On integration: "There has been integration for years. Half the children in my community are half-white."

The SNCC rhetoric has become one of anger, impatience, painful sophistication and utter black loyalty. Basically it is a don't-let-the-whites-define-our-terms-for-us philosophy in which words are distorted from their traditional use and familiar definitions become caricatures. Jennifer Lawson, in fact, makes it rather plain that she does not really level with whites when she talks to them. "I'm just a good actress," she said with a mock-smile, implying that she would be more open if the whites were capable of understanding anything the Negro says to them.

Yet Jennifer Lawson obviously believes very deeply. The

curl of anger vanished from her lips and her eyes took on a radiant glow when she talked of the black people, and their need for unity. In a warmer mood she recalled a favorite poem that ends with the words, "Let a race of men come forth."

"I sort of like that," she said. "I think that sort of says it."

CHAPTER 4

The Negro and Politics

THERE WAS A TIME when the Negro vote in the United States was considered a negligible factor—taken for granted in some cases or bought in others with money placed directly in the hands of the right white politicians. That day is no more. Today the Negro vote in America has become the most independent in national politics, showing larger shifts between parties from one election to the next than any other group in the electorate. In fact, if the next Presidential election in 1968 should be close, the Negro vote could very well tip the balance.

Since 1960, more than one million Negroes who never before had seen the inside of a polling place have registered to vote; on a nationwide basis the Negro registration totals seven million and by an overwhelming 8 to 1 these Negro registrations are Democratic. Indeed, by all the traditional ground rules of American politics, the Negro vote should normally be counted in the hip pocket of the Democratic Party. Races for Congress in most Negro districts are in the no-contest category. Short of their running a racist from the South for President, the Democrats appear incapable of losing a majority of the Negro vote in any national election in the foreseeable future.

At first glance, the Negro vote in 1964's landslide for Lyndon Johnson over Barry Goldwater made no difference at all in the final outcome. Johnson could have given away all the ballots cast by Negroes and still won the election by a clear-cut, 54-46 per cent. In 1964, the Negroes were not the balance of power by any stretch of the imagination. Yet the Negro vote in 1964 shifted more than any other part of the entire electorate. It soared 20 full percentage points from the 75 per cent cast for John F. Kennedy in 1960 to a monolithic 95 per cent for Johnson four years later. Surely, this is the closest to a unanimous vote ever cast by any 10 per cent of the population. The 20-point shift in the Negro vote was more than twice that for white voters; Negroes moved more decisively and in greater numbers from 1960 to 1964 than any other group in politics.

Two years later, in the 1966 election, Negroes proved their independence with an entirely different kind of voting pattern. This time 25 per cent—one in every four—swung away from the Democratic line and voted Republican for the U.S. Senate or for governor. The white part of the electorate in the same races shifted no more than eleven points, or less than half the rate of the Negroes.

The following table illustrated just how volatile and how independent Negro voting had become by the mid-1960s:

ESTIMATES OF NEGRO VOTE FOR MAJOR OFFICE 1960–1966

| | Voted Democratic | | |
	Governor-U.S. Senate 1966	President 1964	President 1960
	%	%	%
Nationwide	70	95	75
East	57	95	75
Midwest	82	96	78
South	69	95	71
West	95	97	78

Although still strongly Democratic, Negro voters have now shown that they can be highly selective in their ballot choices. In the State of Maryland in 1966, after having voted monolithically for Lyndon Johnson by 94 per cent two years earlier, Negroes gave the Democratic racist candidate for governor, George P. Mahoney, only 6 per cent of their vote. In Massachusetts, Negroes went from 6 per cent for Barry Goldwater in 1964 to 83 per cent for Republican Edward W. Brooke, the first Negro to be elected to the U.S. Senate since Reconstruction. In New York, Negroes switched from 92 per cent for LBJ to a slim 53 per cent for Frank O'Connor, the unsuccessful Democratic candidate for governor in 1966.

In Michigan, the Negro vote went from 4 per cent for Goldwater to 34 per cent for George Romney. In Arkansas, it went from 14 per cent Republican in 1964 to 71 per cent GOP for Winthrop Rockefeller. In Georgia, Negroes switched from 96 per cent for Lyndon Johnson to only 18 per cent for segregationist Democrat Lester Maddox two years later.

The independence and selectivity of Negro voting can be observed not only between elections, but also within states themselves. In the Old Dominion of Virginia, bad blood has existed for many years between the conservative Byrd machine and the rising Negro community. In the July primaries of 1966, moderate William Spong upended incumbent Senator A. Willis Robertson and took over the leadership of a new moderate wing of the Democratic Party of Virginia. Senator Harry Byrd, Jr., was also nominated to succeed his father in the same primary by a narrow margin.

In the general election the following November, Virginia Negroes showed just how selective they could be: 91 per cent cast their ballots for moderate Democrat Spong, but only 19 per cent for conservative Democrat (Byrd). Spong won easily, while Byrd was hard pressed. The difference clearly was the Negro vote. An incredible 72 per cent of all Negro voters in Virginia split their tickets on Election Day 1966.

The vote pattern in Alabama that same day showed more of the same. Moderate U.S. Senator John Sparkman won 71 per cent of the Negro vote as a Democrat. But racist Lurleen Wallace, running against a die-hard segregationist Republican, Rep. James Martin (thus presenting Negroes with a Hobson's choice), was able to gain no more than 33 per cent of the Negro vote.

In 1966, Negroes proved they could cast from 6 to 94 per cent of their vote for Democrats running for major office. The difference was based wholly on the candidate being offered. The issue was almost always the same: Would the candidate help or hurt the cause of civil rights?

Negro vote selectivity can be shown in no better way than in the following breakdown of how Negroes cast their ballots in 1966 by four types of candidates who ran: moderate Republicans, conservative Republicans, liberal Democrats, and segregationist Democrats:

NEGRO VOTE FOR DIFFERENT TYPES OF CANDIDATES (1966)

| | Voted ||
	Democratic	Republican
Type of Candidate:	%	%
Republican moderate	62	38
Republican conservative	86	14
Democratic segregationist	26	74
Democratic liberal	81	19

The message to the two major parties from the Negro electorate is crystal clear. Negroes are saying to the Democrats that although it is inconceivable that a majority of them will not vote Democratic, the difference between an all-out, pro-civil rights candidate for President or governor or the U.S. Senate and one who might drag his feet on the issue is as much as 25 per cent of the total Negro vote. To the Republicans, the Negroes serve similar notice: a conservative or segregationist GOP nominee for major office will lose a close election, while a moderate can be elected by the swing Negro vote.

To Democratic segregationists Negroes are saying, in effect, that party label will not mean a thing, that they will be unified almost to a man against a segregationist irrespective of party allegiance.

Fundamentally, this is one vote for one issue: civil rights. It is in the tradition of Samuel Gompers' political credo of rewarding your friends and punishing your enemies. It is a vote that no army of ward heelers can deliver. Yet it will deliver itself more massively than any machine ever attempted. It will be a vote that can shift independently for President, governor, Congress, or for mayor in any city where Negroes have a sizable share of the vote.

Forewarning of the sensitive selectivity of the Negro vote came in the election of liberal Republican John V. Lindsay as Mayor of New York City in 1965. Negroes make up 14 per cent of New York City's electorate. Jews constitute 30 per cent of the city's vote. White Protestants, Lindsay's own group, are the smallest minority in New York, weighing in at a slender 8 per cent of the vote. Republicans in New York City are also a small minority, coming to no more than 25 per cent of the registered vote. The enrolled Liberal Party membership, the other party backing Lindsay, is no more than 8 per cent of the registration.

In order to win, Lindsay had to crack two Democratic bastions: the Jewish and Negro vote. His opponent, Democrat Controller Abraham Beame, was himself a Jew, and New York has never had a Jewish mayor. New York's Negroes had just voted 96 per cent for Lyndon Johnson a year earlier.

Because of his outstanding civil rights record in Congress, Lindsay was able to expect that he could boost the Negro vote to 27 per cent by August, a spectacular gain of 23 percentage points over Goldwater's dismal showing. But at this figure, Lindsay still would have lost the election. He needed to achieve better than 40 per cent of the Negro vote to win.

By mid-October, with hard campaigning in the Harlem, Bedford-Stuyvesant, Jamaica, and South Bronx Negro ghetto areas, Lindsay had closed the gap among Negro voters and had risen to 39 per cent.

With one week to go, Lindsay edged up to 42 per cent of the Negro vote and forged ahead of Beame in the race for the first time city-wide. Then President Johnson endorsed Beame and the Lindsay surge in the Negro districts came to a quick halt. Vote switching back to Democratic regularity began to take place with five days still to go to election.

Lindsay changed all his campaign plans and went all out for the Negro vote. Lindsay caravans rolled fifteen hours a day, prowling block by block through the slum neighborhoods. He carried with him the pen that Lyndon Johnson had given him for his part in helping pass the Civil Rights Act. He waved the pen at every stop.

The Reverend George Lawrence of Brooklyn, Martin Luther King's representative in New York, toured with Lindsay and introduced him at each stop. Lawrence's introduction went like this: "Out in Queens, where the white bigots live, they are writing on the walls that Lindsay is a nigger lover. Well, I want you to know right here and now that we're going to show the —— bigots we know what's what. We're going for John Lindsay for Mayor. Why? Because when they write on those walls that he's a nigger lover, they're telling the truth, every word of it."

Lindsay's last act in that election was to go on a Negro radio station between 1 and 2 A.M. Election Day and invite calls from listeners. For the first ten minutes, the phones were almost silent. Then the calls began to pour in, until all the wires in the small station were jammed. It is estimated that close to 10,000 calls were received in the dead of night, all from Negro listeners wanting to know what Lindsay would do about rats, about no heat, about holes in the walls, broken windows, and garbage bags and urine in the hallways where they lived.

Election night, the Lindsay vote among Negroes reached 44 per cent, enough to insure his margin of victory by a narrow four percentage points. Overnight, he had put a new face on the Republican Party with Negroes in the North.

BECAUSE OF THE WAY the black population is distributed, 91 per cent of the Negro vote in America is concentrated either in the eleven states of the Old Confederacy or in the metropolitan big cities of the North and West. Therefore Negroes have to make or break it politically in the South and in the big cities.

In both power centers, Negroes are on the move.

The task in both the cities of the North and the states of the South is how to translate concentrated numbers of Negroes into viable political power. In the South, the problem is how to convert existing numbers into registered voters. In the Northern cities, the numbers themselves are jumping upward as though jet propelled. Not only is the Negro birth rate higher than that of whites, but Negro migration to the cities continues unabated. In city after city, Negroes are moving closer to that magic moment when they will constitute a majority of the entire electorate. In fact, the magic number for political control need not be 51 per cent. Anything over 40 per cent is close enough for Negroes to have the major voice in determining the political power of a city.

Here are the major cities of America where, by 1970, the Negro population will reach the critical level of 40 per cent or more of the electorate:

> Washington, D.C.; Richmond, Va.; Gary, Ind.; Jacksonville, Fla.; Baltimore, Md.; Detroit, Mich.; Newark, N.J.; St. Louis, Mo.; New Orleans, La.; Nashville, Tenn.; Trenton, N.J.; Birmingham, Ala.

By 1975, the cities in which Negro voting power is likely to grow to the pivotal 40 per cent or more include:

> Atlanta, Ga.; Memphis, Tenn.; Oakland, Calif.; Chattanooga, Tenn.; Cleveland, Ohio; Winston-Salem, N.C.; Jackson, Miss.; Savannah, Ga.; Mobile, Ala.; Portsmouth, Va.; Baton Rouge, La.; Philadelphia, Pa.; Camden, N.J.; Chicago, Ill.; Columbus, Ohio; Cincinnati, Ohio.

By 1980, Miami, Kansas City, Indianapolis, Charlotte, Houston, and Dallas will join the same ranks. Farther off in the future are Los Angeles, Buffalo, Louisville, Akron, Jersey City, and Sacramento.

The idea of city-wide Negro preponderance, however, is still only vaguely talked about. As late as August, 1966, the Congressional Quarterly concluded: "Election of Negroes as mayors of large cities was possible but still probably far off in nearly all cities."

Yet it was an open secret on Capitol Hill that perhaps the major reason for Congressional reluctance to give home rule to Washington, D.C., was the fear that the city's 60 per cent Negro majority would elect a Negro as its first mayor, despite reassurances that a white liberal would probably achieve that honor.

And in Cleveland in 1965, a Negro State Representative, Carl B. Stokes, came within one percentage point of being elected mayor. At the time of the election, Negroes made up 37 per cent of the city's population and 32 per cent of the registered vote.

Carl Stokes was an attractive young state legislator of 38, who had been voted the outstanding man in Ohio's lower house by his colleagues. He had sponsored fair housing legislation, but had also taken a firm stand against excesses on the part of some of the more militant parts of the civil-rights movement. For example, in 1963 during the legislative session in Columbus, Stokes took a hard line opposing civil-rights sit-downers who had invaded the floor of the Ohio House of Representatives. Stokes was excoriated by the demonstrators, but he was unyielding in his opposition to what he felt was carrying militancy too far.

When he ran for mayor of Cleveland two years later, he was given virtually no chance at all of winning. Stokes was one of four candidates—three Democrats and one Republican. His chief opponent was incumbent Mayor Ralph Locher, a rather colorless candidate of the regular Democratic machine. The Republicans felt that Locher might be in trouble and entered their first county-wide office holder in 30 years, Ralph J. Perk, the Cuyahoga County Auditor. Perk ran as a GOP liberal and against party bossism, stumped on the streets, and went all out for Negro rights and progress. The fourth candidate was Ralph McAllister, a conservative Democrat and former school board president, who made a not very veiled appeal for a white backlash vote by repeating, "I refused to be pushed around," in explaining why he took a firm stand against Negro sit-ins and civil disobedience.

Locher's troubles began to emerge when, against weak opposition, he lost all of Cleveland's twelve Negro wards in the primaries. Stokes, described at the time as "personable and handsome, the most articulate of all the candidates," campaigned across the city in every ward, even though he knew his strength was centered in the east side wards where the Negroes live. In all neighborhoods, however, Stokes made the same speech: "I offer a program for all of the people. My program is leadership, something City Hall now lacks. I recognize the grave problems before the city, finances, urban renewal, better policing, the need to stop street attacks. I hope that I can be accepted in white areas for what I am—Carl Stokes, candidate for Mayor. I would hope that the sheer fact of birth would not be a limiting factor in whether Carl Stokes can become Mayor." He never backed down on his strong civil rights advocacy, and was proud of his support from Americans for Democratic Action and the United Freedom Movement.

In the end, Stokes achieved 36 per cent of the vote and Locher 37 per cent, a difference of just 2,143 votes out of close to a quarter million cast. But an election post-mortem showed that Stokes received 97 per cent of his vote from Negroes and only 3 per cent of his total from white voters, despite his pleas to be judged as a man rather than as a Negro.

At the time Carl Stokes ran in Cleveland, the Negroes made up only one-third of the electorate. By 1970, they will be close to the magical 40 per cent mark. And the chances are that Carl Stokes, still a young man in politics, will be heard from again in racially-tense Cleveland. One thing is certain about Cleveland and the other cities of America where Negro political power is moving up—any candidate who is in trouble in the Negro wards is likely to have a dim political future, and whether he is a Democrat or Republican won't make a particle of difference.

The other center of Negro political thrust is the South, where half of America's black population still lives.

A year after Carl Stokes had been counted out in Cleveland, a young 33-year-old Korean War veteran, Lucius Amerson, was elected the first Negro sheriff in Alabama since Reconstruction days. He scored his victory in Macon County, where Negroes make up 84 per cent of the population. Amerson won by one percentage point, 44-43 in the Democratic primary in May 1966. In the run-off four weeks later, Amerson took the Democratic nomination with an absolute majority, and in November was swept into office with two-thirds of all the votes cast.

Amerson put together his majority by striking a moderate balance between the intellectuals at Tuskegee Institute and the rank and file of Negro working people. Before he achieved his striking breakthrough, Negroes had gained two out of five City Council seats in Tuskegee.

But Amerson had to overcome two facts of life for a Negro political candidate in the deep South. In his county, the U.S. Census last counted 2,818 white people of voting age. But the voting rolls of Macon County show that 4,997 whites are registered. This is called "100%+" enrollment. It means that there are almost twice as many whites registered now as were counted by the Census in 1960. It means that a white man's vote in Macon County literally counts twice as much as a Negro's. This condition prevails in no less than 36 of Alabama's 67 counties. Even with this bloated white registration in Macon County, by the summer of 1966 Negroes finally outnumbered whites on the rolls by a 7–5 margin.

Lucius Amerson also had to contend with scurrilous charges

and not very subtle threats over his running. One charge, widely circulated, was that he had been put in jail for beating his 25-year-old wife six months before the primary. Amerson outlasted all of the handicaps and is Macon County Sheriff today. As an elderly Negro remarked right after the primary, he would "feel a lot easier" now dealing with the law where he lives.

In that same election, the Negroes of Alabama won another notable victory in nearby Dallas County. This county became a landmark in the civil rights struggle because its county seat was the site from which the 1965 Selma freedom march was launched. Dallas County's most notorious citizen was Sheriff Jim Clark, who had taunted rights marchers verbally and had scattered them with mounted police. In many ways, Clark became a symbol of the brutal determination of Deep South whites to use any and all means to thwart the Negro revolution. He was the southern white counterpart of Frank Hague's boast of the 1930s, "I am the law."

A year after Sheriff Clark became this symbol, he was no longer the law. In his place was a white moderate by Alabama standards, J. Wilson Baker, who not only welcomed Negro support but in fact advocated peaceful demonstrations. In the end, Baker needed every last Negro vote in Dallas County, winning by a narrow 51–49 per cent, a total of 507 votes.

In Dallas County, Negroes are a majority of the voting-age population, but a minority of the registered vote, despite major efforts of civil-rights groups to put Negroes on the voting rolls. The defeat of Sheriff Jim Clark is therefore all the more notable, for it proves that Negroes can successfully form a coalition with whites in the Deep South and win by backing a white candidate, even when the Negroes are not a majority of the electorate.

In sharp and direct contrast with Negro voting successes in Macon and Dallas counties, they met decisive defeat in nearby Lowndes County, where Negroes make up 73 per cent of the voting age population.

Lowndes County had been heralded by SNCC and other black power advocates as the wave of the future in Negro political organization. Stokely Carmichael made his early reputation in Lowndes by organizing the Black Panthers, an all-Negro political party dedicated to complete separation from the whites.

The Black Panthers did not enter the Democratic primary in Alabama in May of 1966, but rather ran their own candidates for sheriff and tax assessor in the fall elections. Both candidates of the Black Panthers lost by an identical 58.5–41.5 per cent margin.

"Coalition's no good," Carmichael told *Newsweek* when he took over SNCC leadership in late May. " 'Cause what happens when a couple of Negroes join in with a bunch of whites? They get absorbed, that's what. They have to surrender too much to join. . . . Black people got to act as a black community, and the Democratic and Republican parties are completely irrelevant to them."

A closer examination shows clearly that without the fanfare of separatism, without the extravagant claims of accomplishment before the fact, a much more effective organizing job was done by integrationist Negroes in Macon and Dallas counties than in Lowndes. At election time, only 52 per cent of Lowndes Negroes were registered, compared with 62 per cent in Macon and 70 per cent in Dallas. What is more, in the election itself, fully one Negro voter in six in Lowndes broke with the Black Panthers and voted for a white candidate.

In Dallas and Macon counties, Negroes kept their claims down and essentially played coalition politics. They spent their energies far more productively by getting Negroes out to register and then to vote. They worked with the Democratic Party locally and are now close to control in both counties. In Lowndes, the Negroes must now regroup, repair their damaged ranks, and still face law enforcement officers who were elected as segregationists. In Macon and Dallas, the law is on their side. For the first time since Reconstruction, they will receive a fair shake. A national symbol of white racist extremism, Jim Clark appears finished. And the luster of Stokely Carmichael, whose early claim to fame was his work in Lowndes County, was certainly dimmed.

In fact, it is fair to conclude that easily the biggest shot in the arm the Negro voting surge in the South received was from the Voting Rights Act of 1965, signed into law by President Johnson on August 6, 1965. Simply but forcefully, the law suspended all literacy tests and other discriminatory tests for voting, directed the Attorney General to go to court to test the constitutionality of the poll tax, extended civil and criminal protection to qualified persons seeking to vote, and provided for assignment of Federal examiners to conduct registration and observe voting.

In due course, the Supreme Court did outlaw the poll tax, ending a device that had stripped millions of Negroes of their voting rights. Along with the courts, the President and Congress had placed the full weight of the Federal government behind the cause of Negro exercise of the franchise to vote.

By mid-summer of 1966, Federal examiners had poured into 41 counties in Alabama, Louisiana, and South Carolina. According to the statistics of the Voter Education Project of the Southern Regional Council, the impact of the Federal examiners was decisive. In Alabama, for example, where there were no examiners or special Voter Education Project drives, Negro registration continued to limp along at 45 per cent. Where the VEP went in alone without the Federal examiners, registration soared to 58 per cent. But where the examiners went to work without the VEP, registration climbed to 64 per cent. Finally, in the counties where both the Federal examiners and the Voter Education Project drive worked together, Negro registration soared to 70 per cent.

By the end of 1966, Negroes were spurting to close the voting gap of 100 years in the Deep South. The gains were spectacular in many states. Here is the change in statistical terms, compared with the results reported in the *Newsweek* survey of 1963:

POTENTIAL NEGRO VOTE IN SOUTH

	Negro percent- age in popula- tion	Negro percent- age of regis- tered voters	1966 Negroes registered	1963 Negroes registered	Increase in Negroes registered since 1963	Eligible unregis- tered Negroes	Per- cent- age of eligible Ne- groes regis- tered 1966	Per- cent- age of eligible Ne- groes regis- tered 1963
	%	%					%	%
Mississippi	42	25	139,000	25,000	114,000	283,000	33	6
South Carolina	35	21	191,000	94,000	97,000	181,000	51	25
Louisiana	32	18	242,000	152,000	90,000	272,000	47	24
Alabama	30	17	246,000	82,000	164,000	235,000	51	17
Georgia	28	17	290,000	186,000	104,000	323,000	47	30
North Carolina	24	12	281,000	216,000	65,000	270,000	51	39
Arkansas	22	16	115,000	73,000	42,000	78,000	60	38
Virginia	21	15	205,000	108,000	97,000	232,000	49	25
Florida	18	12	287,000	200,000	87,000	184,000	61	43
Tennessee	16	14	225,000	162,000	63,000	89,000	72	52
Texas	12	13	400,000	128,000	272,000	249,000	62	20

There are still approximately 2,500,000 Negroes of voting age in the South who are not yet registered. But the rate of enrollment has doubled in two years and the momentum is not likely to slacken. Nor are the efforts of the civil-rights workers and the Federal government in putting muscle into the drive.

Negroes are now 15 per cent of the South's voting population and soon they will be 20 per cent. But the impact of the increased registration and voting could already be felt in key elections. In the border states of Oklahoma and Tennessee in 1964, moderate Democrats won elections to the U.S. Senate on the strength of an overwhelming Negro vote.

In 1966, Ernest "Fritz" Hollings of South Carolina had to depend on an 89 per cent Negro vote to win the election to the U.S. Senate in a tight 52–48 per cent race with Republican Marshall Parker. Had Hollings been limited to the white vote alone, he would have lost by 55–45 per cent. A former

Governor, Hollings had been on many sides of the race issue. In 1962, he made an abortive run for the Senate against the late Senator Olin D. Johnston. Hollings pitched his entire primary campaign to a pledge that he would carry on in the tradition of Senator J. Strom Thurmond as a champion of states rights and segregation. He lost, 62–38 per cent. By 1966, Hollings had moderated somewhat, and, in fact, was thought to be encumbered by two charges his Republican opponent made against him: that he was a longtime friend of Robert Kennedy (which made him a Kennedy man) and his alleged efforts to win the Negro vote. If Hollings had lost, it would have been attributed to his Kennedy ties and his "softness" on the Negro issue.

But Fritz Hollings won in South Carolina and by any measure, he has the Negro vote to thank for it. And he may well have to cultivate that vote in any future elections, for potentially, one in three Palmetto State voters is going to be black.

But the most spectacular victory for Negroes in politics happened in a state almost devoid of Negroes—Massachusetts. In 1966, a 47-year-old Negro, Edward W. Brooke, won election to the U.S. Senate by an overwhelming 61–39 per cent margin over Democratic liberal Endicott Peabody. Roughly 2 per cent of the population in Massachusetts is Negro.

Yet Brooke stands as the first member of his race to sit in the U.S. Senate since Reconstruction, and he is the first Negro to achieve major office in this country in modern times. Brooke is a calm, handsome man who bears no scars of white prejudice and wears no racial hearts on his sleeve. "I know the dreadful discrimination and bigotry which many American Negroes have suffered," he has said, "but honestly I cannot claim that this has had any shattering effect on me."

The son of a government lawyer, Brooke grew up in Washington, where his middle-class family was comfortably off and determined to overcome the deprivation of segregation. When they couldn't buy tickets for concerts or the opera in the segregated theaters of Washington, Brooke says, "My mother simply took me to New York to Carnegie Hall or the Metropolitan." After graduating from Howard University, he was

inducted into an all-Negro infantry unit, and ended World
War II behind the German lines with Italian partisans. There
he met Remigia Ferrari-Scacco, the Italian girl who is now his
wife and the mother of his two teen-age daughters. During his
campaign, Brooke made no effort to downplay his white wife
in potential backlash areas; instead he pointedly made her a
political asset. Sometimes speaking in her native language, she
campaigned for him through some of the Italian-American
districts where white prejudice against him might have been
deepest.

Brooke carried the Italian vote on Election Day. He swept
greater Boston, making a particularly impressive run in the
suburbs. Symbolic of Brooke's identity with the suburbs was his
moving his own family from the Negro ghetto neighborhood
of Roxbury to the upper-middle-income, fashionable white
suburb of Newton. He had vacationed for a number of summers at "in" Martha's Vineyard.

Many had believed that Brooke would fade in the stretch
in 1966, a victim of inflamed racial feelings that were catching
fire in white communities across America. He had no guarantee that he would even receive the small Negro vote outside of
Boston. His public pronouncement on the civil-rights question
was this: "Boycotts, sit-ins, demonstrations don't achieve the
desired consequences. . . . On the contrary, they merely inten-
sify the resentment of the population at large and undermine
the best interests of the Negro community. . . . The Negro
must win allies, not conquer adversaries. If we reject the legal
road and use fire and sword, we will confuse those we are
trying to persuade and destroy our own program."

For such sentiments, the diametric opposite of those of
Stokely Carmichael and certainly no echo of Martin Luther
King, Brooke has been labeled an Uncle Tom by some of the
militants in the civil-rights movement. Yet on Election Day,
Brooke won 83 per cent of Massachusetts' Negro vote, some
72 percentage points better than Barry Goldwater's showing
two years before.

In fact, Brooke scotched a possible double play of white
negative reaction and Negro opposition by taking a tack in his

campaign similar to that employed by John F. Kennedy on the Catholic issue in the West Virginia primary back in 1960. Brooke said late in his campaign, "If I am to lose this election because of whites who will hold against me that I am a Negro, then I am prepared to lose on this issue. Or if I lose because I refuse to go along with the advocates of black power in the Negro community, then I am prepared to lose because of that, too."

Middle-class Edward Brooke in the end shamed white Brahmins, white Catholics, and slum-dwelling Negroes into voting for him as a man. He is a loner in the Republican Party, a loner to the civil-rights movement, and a loner to the Negro people, having married a white woman. He has been described "as white as a black man can be," but he can be counted upon to vote moderate to liberal in the Senate, to support civil-rights legislation and to be a potent force in moving the Republican Party back to the mainstream of American politics.

The conversion of the Negro 10 per cent of the country into a powerful, well-knit, political force is still in its early stages. Registration in the South and split-ticket voting in the North are beginning signs of a new-found sophistication.

The *Newsweek* survey attempted to find out at the grass roots level just how active Negroes are politically compared with whites. It should be pointed out that for the vast majority of Americans, political participation means voting and not much else. Here, Negroes still lag 15 points behind whites, but are closing the gap rapidly.

Participation in politics beyond voting shows that Negroes are on the move. The following table compares Negro political activity with that of whites:

POLITICAL ACTIVITY AMONG NEGROES AND WHITES

	Negroes	Whites
	%	%
Written or spoken to Congressman	13	18
Worked to elect a political candidate	12	11
Given money to a candidate or political party	11	17
Belong to a political club	10	12

While the Negroes have participated less in all these political activities than whites, except to work for a candidate, their showing must be classified as significant and impressive. For this performance in the political vineyards has to be judged against the enormous handicaps of education and lack of money under which Negroes labor. The day might not be far off when Negroes will be more active than whites in politics on the precinct level.

It is perfectly apparent that Negroes are now excited by what they can achieve through politics and, what is more, they like the process itself. As a young Negro lawyer in the Bronx put it, "Politics is where the action is and there's a big payoff waiting there for the Negro people." John Miller, a civil service worker in Cincinnati, saw the ultimate reward when he said, "I feel that maybe someday I'll see a colored President."

But the Negroes have no thought of trying to form their own party; most are committed to working through the two major political parties. This sentiment has grown over the past three years:

HOW NEGROES SHOULD OPERATE IN POLITICS

| | Total Negroes | | Leaders |
	1966	1963	1966
	%	%	%
Mainly as separate group	7	9	10
Mainly in existing parties	74	67	59
Both (volunteered)	6	8	17
Not sure	13	16	14

Thus the 7 to 1 margin of 1963 against a Negro third party swelled to 11 to 1 by 1966. These results in themselves are ample testimony to the fact that most rank-and-file Negroes simply do not buy the separatism voiced by Floyd McKissick and Stokely Carmichael.

The 30-year-old wife of a bus driver in suburban St. Albans in New York City said, "Even though they treat us like it, we shouldn't be separate. We should be with them. If we want to be equal to them, we shouldn't make ourselves separate." Mrs. Mary Kemp, a housewife in Buffalo, chimed in, "If we were to work separate, we would defeat our purposes. One thing we're trying to prove is that we can work together. So there's no reason to work separate." Clivis Mahone, Jr., a 56-year-old laborer from Louisville's West Central district, summed up, "Anywhere there's a third party, there's always confusion. Look, we're trying to get equal rights. So it would be a bad thing to have our own political party. We have to get along with everybody and politics makes the laws we are trying to get."

Negroes simply cannot find any logical connection between separation in politics and an end to segregation and discrimination in their lives. After having had their votes bought and counted in advance for so many years, after having seen political promises broken for so long, they are convinced that their only salvation is to use their new-found political muscle right within the two major political parties.

Commitment to major parties, by and large, means commitment to the Democratic Party. By 1966, Negro registration in the Democratic column totaled 79 per cent, compared with 10 per cent Republican, and 5 per cent independent. The remaining 6 per cent failed to express a view in the *Newsweek* survey.

More significant than mere enrollment, however, is the expression of faith Negroes give to the Democratic Party as the political organization that will help them:

WHICH POLITICAL PARTY WILL DO
MORE FOR NEGROES?

	1966	1963
	%	%
Democrats	69	63
Republicans	3	4
Other parties	*	*
No difference	14	18
Not sure	14	15

NOTE: * Signifies less than 1%.

All things being equal, the Negroes will give Democrats the benefit of the doubt. Part of the reason goes all the way back to the Great Depression. Joe Blackman, 38, an unemployed laborer in the Watts section of Los Angeles, said, "The Democratic Party has proven itself. When President Roosevelt became President, things got better for the Negroes." Many more recall another, more recent President—John F. Kennedy. In Bastrop, Texas, Theodore Alexander said: "I can remember when Kennedy took office. I noticed he started helping the colored people so much."

But the pro-Democratic sentiment is also a reflection of the deep distrust Negroes have for Republicans. The wife of a longshoreman in Jacksonville, Florida, had a long memory. "I look back to when Hoover was in there and put the panic on us," she said. Mrs. Earle Harris, a 62-year-old housewife in St. Louis observed: "I have to believe what I've seen. There's an old saying that pie crust is meant to be broken and that's what the Republicans have done with their promises." Mrs. Pearl Margetto of St. Louis added, "The Democrats seem to know that it takes money for people to live—and the Republicans don't think that." A service worker, James Auston, in upper New York State, summed up: "The Republicans always put the money in their pockets. They don't invest it in people, don't help the Negroes."

The cross the Republicans bear among Negroes is a big one. The memory of Barry Goldwater far outweighs the memory of Abe Lincoln. It is obvious that the Republicans have to carry the burden of proof with Negroes that they stand for equality and civil-rights progress. No more than 3 Negroes out of every 100 now assume that the Republican Party is friendliest to their cause. It is a safe assumption that any GOP candidate starts off close to the zero mark when he begins to solicit Negro votes.

What is more, the Republicans have not yet developed national figures of sufficient stature to match the magic drawing power of two very current Democratic names: Lyndon Johnson and Robert Kennedy. At a time when Johnson has been bumping along the shoals of widespread public discontent, he receives overwhelming praise for the job he is doing from Negroes.

In November 1966, Johnson's job rating dipped lower than at any time since he took over the reins at the White House, down to 43 per cent approval. Yet almost 9 out of every 10 Negroes still expressed confidence in the job he was doing. Without Negro support, President Johnson's standing would be almost 2 to 1 negative among the American people.

Shirley Scruggs, a housewife in Pontiac, Michigan, was typical. "I like the plan he has on the war on poverty and his placing a Negro in his cabinet," she said. Laurence Lanier, a dyesetter in Louisville, added, "He's covered it all as President of the United States, and, remember he has had to survive the lashes of Vietnam, civil rights, and keeping up with two daughters." Elderly Dan W Matthews in Decatur, Alabama, said slowly, "He seems to be a very calm and cool-headed executive. He has tried to push the civil-rights movement. I'm for him."

But while the Negroes appreciate what Lyndon Johnson has done, they can never quite forget his martyred predecessor, John F. Kennedy. So deep is the effect of the Kennedy name on Negroes that by 60–40 per cent Negroes would prefer to see Robert Kennedy run for President in 1968 than Lyndon Johnson.

Negroes mourn the loss of President Kennedy very deeply, as do most Americans. But for Negroes, Kennedy's time will also go down as the time the great revolution of the 1960s began. He was part of that time to them. A. Philip Randolph's eulogy to Kennedy still stands as the most eloquent spoken by any Negro: "The call of history in this hour of trial by fire is for Negroes in particular and America in general to march forward toward the goal of human dignity and social and racial justice, to honor this man whose place in history will be next to Abraham Lincoln—the greatest President this country has ever known."

But for all of their devotion to the Johnson record and the Kennedy memory, American Negroes by the latter part of the

1960s were prepared to guard their voting commitments with care. Just about one Negro in every two was ready to kick over the political traces and vote for a Republican, if the right man came along and if the Democrats seemed to be taking his vote for granted. For Negroes were all too well aware that they had already separated the Deep South from the border states. They could point to Republican and Democratic moderates in Tennessee, North Carolina, Arkansas, Virginia, Kentucky, and Oklahoma—all making open and even urgent appeals for the Negro vote. They could also show some localized progress in the Deep South, albeit painful and slow. But most of all, Negroes could demonstrate that in the big cities of the North and West, they were becoming increasingly selective. And these big cities of the big states are where presidents are made or broken.

In 1964, Lyndon Johnson didn't need the Negro vote to win. But 1968 looks more and more like 1960 than 1964. Every poll shows Johnson is in a nip-and-tuck struggle to gain another term in the White House. In cold, statistical language, if Johnson is behind 52–48 per cent with the white electorate, the Negroes can give him a 51–49 or even 52–48 per cent victory, as they did Kennedy in 1960.

On the day in October 1960 when John F. Kennedy asked the Governor of Georgia to release Martin Luther King from jail there, Lyndon Johnson was campaigning in the boondocks of central Pennsylvania. He called up on the telephone to give this message to Robert Kennedy: "If you talk to Jack today, please tell him this about that King business in Georgia. Tell him he should go ahead and do it because it's the right thing to do." And then as an afterthought, the man who was to become Vice President and then President added, "What's more we're gonna need all their votes we can git come this election."

If the Republicans hedge on the civil rights issue in 1968, if they nominate anyone even remotely resembling Barry Goldwater, then the Democrats can count on as much as a 90–10 split in the Negro vote. But if the GOP turns to a moderate

candidate, one who has been four-square on the rights question, then Johnson again will need "all their votes he can git."

For with the electoral college system constituted the way it
is—with Negroes concentrated in the pivotal industrial states,
and where all of a state's votes can go one way or the other, if
a man wins that state by only one vote—Negro national political power reaches its zenith of effectiveness in a close election.
It is a safe bet that the Democrats and probably the Republicans will both go all out for the Negro vote in 1968, as though
their political lives depended upon it. The Negro vote could
well be the thin thread of life for whoever wins in 1968.

"When Will They Ever Learn?"

IT WAS DURING CHICAGO'S *riot-torn summer of 1966 that Agene Beach, a burly Negro patrolman, waded into a sneering crowd of his fellow black men on the teeming West Side and began rounding up the ringleaders. Cries of "Freedom" and "Police brutality" burst from the mob, but Beach was undeterred. He hauled seven men out of the crowd and hustled them off to jail, explaining later that "black or white, it doesn't matter to me. If a man breaks the law he's going to be arrested. If I couldn't do it this way with a clear conscience, I'd be the first to turn in my badge."*

Probably more than any other class of blacks, Negro policemen stand as the symbol of white law and white authority in the streets. And theirs is the fundamental conflict between sworn duty and sympathy for the aspirations of their race. Beach, a tough, proud man in his mid-30s who has been on the Chicago police force for half a dozen years, has resolved that conflict in the only way he sees possible: he's a cop first and a Negro second. "If it was my wife who broke the law," he told a Newsweek *interviewer, "I'd arrest her, too."*

Perhaps the circumstances of his life have helped Beach reach that detached view, for he is a self-sufficient Negro who, when off duty, is far removed from the struggle in the streets. The son of a Mississippi farm hand who came North to work in the steel mills, Beach was co-captain of the basketball team at Chicago's Du Sable High School (a school noted for its outstanding cage teams), rose to the rank of petty officer dur-

ing a hitch in the Navy in the 1950, and was bent on becoming a lawyer until he ran out of money and joined the police force. In 1953 he married his wife Verda, a slender, striking girl who was born in the Chicago slums but whose quick intelligence drove her to become a teacher. Beach's $7,500 salary plus his part-time work as a landscaper and his wife's $8,000 wage as a grade-school teacher add up to a solid middle-class living. They dwell in a comfortable three-flat building in a quiet integrated neighborhood on Chicago's southeast side; they drive two cars; their two young daughters play on peaceful tree-shaded streets. They are, in fact, buying the building they live in for $34,500.

Sprawled in his spotless, tastefully furnished home, Beach has the dispassionate sound of a white moderate when he discusses the plight of his race. He sees the major problem as "misunderstanding and little contact between Negro leaders and Negroes, and between Negro and white." Yet Beach has no intention of shrinking from the tough duty of the West Side. "I could have put in for a transfer nearer home," he said. "But I like helping people and working with them, and so I think I'll stay there."

What he has seen in the streets has convinced Beach that Martin Luther King's nonviolent approach is the proper one, and he has little use for black power. "It's a riot term," he said flatly. "It means violence. Some persons are now exploiting the civil-rights movement and the riots were the first example of this I've seen here. When they came pouring out of their homes to riot, they wanted just one thing. They wanted to loot. Some ran around shouting 'Freedom' and things like that, but they were opportunists. Eighty per cent of the rioters were good people urged on by people like that."

In the gut world of the cop, Beach has run into Negroes who expect a Negro cop to give them favored treatment; he has had to turn deaf ears to the taunts of rioters to "come on and join us." Normally, he said, he can reason with his people in rou-

tine police matters. But the Chicago riots were something else again. "The people become mindless. In such a situation you can't reason." Recalling his seizure of the seven ringleaders, Beach explained: "I used whatever force was necessary to arrest them. Then, of course, you get cries of police brutality. It's so easy for them to say that. Where does that leave us? If someone fights with us or throws a bottle, are we supposed to stand there and take it?" Beach's squad car took a bottle through the front windshield, and only the spectacles his white partner was wearing saved him from eye damage. "Police brutality is an out for a riot," Beach declared. "I'm not saying that sometimes some police don't get out of hand. But you have to hit back if you are hit."

If Beach is the thoroughgoing professional, hardened to his duty and the plight of his people, his wife Verda, who teaches social science courses in an all-Negro school, is considerably more idealistic. Beach once taunted her: "You'd go up to an offender and say he's really a good boy and pat his head."

"I might do that," Verda replied. "You're a policeman and think like a policeman. I think like a social scientist. I work with those types of kids, too, you know. I can see what's wrong with them."

Beach, cruising through the squalid West Side neighborhoods in his blue-and-white squad car, can also see what's wrong. Teenagers lolling on the sidewalks give him a bored stare, or a hostile glance and a curse. "I have to rely on myself and my partner," he said. "One minute one of those kids might be saying, 'Help, save me.' The next minute he may be aiming a brick at you."

Once a small Negro child picked up a piece of bent pipe and pointed it at Beach like a gun as he drove by. "When will they ever learn?" Beach sighed. "I've got a job to do. All they have to do is behave. It makes you wonder, doesn't it? Do you think that kid is training now for the day when he's old enough to fight me?"

CHAPTER 5

White Attitudes: Political Cross Fire

THE SUREST RULE IN POLITICS or physics is that force will produce counterforce. After 100 dormant years, American Negroes are beginning to march toward real political power. But with each forward step by Negroes, white discomfort and unease mounts, too.

The classic case of point and counterpoint in Presidential politics was the incredible victory of Harry S. Truman in 1948. Faced with open rebellion within his own party, Truman appeared to be a sure loser to Governor Thomas E. Dewey of New York, the rising Republican who had made a strong run against Franklin D. Roosevelt in wartime 1944.

Because Truman had taken a strong position on behalf of civil rights for Negroes, Southern Democratic conservatives organized the Dixiecrats, and nominated a young segregationist governor from South Carolina, J. Strom Thurmond, for the Presidency. Many thought this doomed Truman, for he would need every electoral vote from the traditionally Democratic South.

Not to be outdone by their Dixie counterparts, the Northern left wing of the Democratic Party also splintered off to form the Progressive Party, and ran former Truman and Roosevelt Cabinet member Henry Wallace for President. Dewey had seemed invincible running against Truman alone. Now with no fewer than three opponents, Dewey logically had to be considered a shoo-in.

Then the reaction and the counter-reaction set in, sparked by an undaunted Truman who never gave up. Because the Dixiecrats had defied Truman over civil rights, Northern liberals and Negroes rallied to his banner. Because the Wallace candidacy challenged him on the cold war and labeled him as a reactionary or worse, moderates in the South, Midwest, and West took a second sober look at the Truman candidacy.

In the end, the election of 1948 turned into a vast Democratic Party primary, with Tom Dewey shunted more and more into a vacuum on the side lines. Truman lost four states and 39 electoral votes to Thurmond in the South, but won nine states with 109 electoral votes in the South and border states. Wallace cost Truman 101 electoral votes in four key states— Connecticut, Michigan, New York, and Maryland.

But the more conservative Midwest and West were not to sit by idly and watch Harry Truman chopped up by the left-wing radicals of the East and the racist radicals of the South. Truman amassed a farm vote that gave him the Midwest, and he literally swept every state in the Mountain and Far Western reaches of the country. The Negro vote put him over in the big populous states of California, Illinois, and Ohio.

Truman's election in 1948 proved that a strong stand on civil rights could trigger a most unexpected realignment of the electorate, but also that it could be good politics. In early October 1960, in Hyannis Port, Massachusetts, a veteran of the Truman campaign, Clark Gifford, advised John F. Kennedy and his brother Robert that a major effort must be put forth to win the Negro vote, for it might prove to be decisive.

Clifford was right. The Negro vote gave Kennedy Michigan, Illinois, New Jersey, and Pennsylvania, all of which proved to be his margin of victory. Once again, it had been shown that a strong stand on civil rights could be good politics.

In 1964, Lyndon Johnson, also a strong pro-civil-rights candidate, did not need the Negro vote to win. The "Solid South" of ancient Democratic tradition had now become the backbone of a states'-rights, pro-segregationist Republican Party. The notion of casting a ballot for the Democratic Party, because it was the party of one's granddaddy who had fought the War Between the States, died on the political battlefield of the rural Deep South in 1964.

The rural vote of Georgia, which had gone out of party loyalty to Democrat John Kennedy by 73–27 per cent in 1960, now went 57–43 per cent for Republican Barry Goldwater. Rural South Carolina, which had helped give Kennedy that state in 1960, slipped from 58 to 39 per cent Democratic.

Just as bitter-end Democratic segregationists wanted to punish border-state President Harry Truman in 1948, now Deep South whites wanted to show Texan Lyndon Johnson he could not turn his back on Southern racial traditions. Both protests ended up as a small minority on the losing side.

But the successive victories of Truman, Kennedy, and Johnson have left an indelible mark on the Deep South. The states of Georgia, South Carolina, Louisiana, Alabama, and Mississippi are now in open revolt against the commitment of the national Democratic Party to the cause of Negro rights. While there is much rationalization that their ideology is rooted in states' rights to resist growing encroachments of centralized power in Washington, or in a philosophic conservatism which wants to preserve the rights of the individual against monolithic government, the real heart of the resistance is race. The Deep South radicalism of the late 1960s is a last die-hard effort to preserve the system of racial segregation born of slavery, the Civil War, and its aftermath.

But it would be a mistake to suppose that segregationist sentiment in Alabama is the last gasp of a dying and archaic system; actually it is showing more strength than ever. For by the end of 1966, Alabama had routed a bid by the white liberals and moderates to win the Democratic primary, had elected its first woman governor in history, and had propelled George Wallace to the undisputed leadership of the conservative and segregationist wing of the Democratic Party.

The success of the Wallaces in Alabama can be traced directly to the white reaction to the Negro registration drive in the state. That drive reached an abortive first climax in the May primary for governor, when State Attorney General Richmond Flowers became the candidate of Negroes for the Democratic nomination. Flowers had stood for moderation in race matters, and had successfully blocked Wallace's efforts to legalize his own succession to another term. Flowers was the sworn enemy of Wallace power in Alabama.

After meeting defeat in his attempt to get the legislature to change the state's constitution so that he might run for governor again, Wallace struck out on a bold and brazen tack of nominating his wife, Lurleen, for governor. He never made any bones about the fact that he would be the de facto chief executive of the state if she were elected.

But despite the reluctance of more than 4 Alabama voters in 10 to have a woman governor, Lurleen Wallace was never the issue at all in that election. Nor was the question ever one of whether Alabama would take a moderate or extremist course in race relations or in its politics.

Rather, the issue was whether or not the Negroes would be allowed to take over political control of Alabama. The embodiment of this Negro challenge became Richmond Flowers. And in the end, Flowers was reduced to the Negro vote in the primary and almost no white votes at all. He won 94 per cent of all Negro votes cast, but less than 3 per cent of the white vote.

Lurleen Wallace won an absolute majority of the vote in the primary against her ten opponents. Her election was synonymous with the preservation of rule by the white majority. The moderates in Alabama politics had lost their power base.

So great was the Wallace sweep that no part of Alabama was left untouched. A pre-election survey of voter sentiment in late 1966 recorded the high esteem now achieved by the Wallaces. More than 8 in 10 Alabamians had high praise for the record of George Wallace as Governor, in contrast to a similar 8 in 10 who gave Lyndon Johnson negative marks. Better than 70 per cent of the state said it would vote for Wallace if he were to run for President in 1968 as an independent candidate.

In fact, the big win for Lurleen Wallace in the primary settled the November election right then and there. Her opponent, Rep. James Martin, a Goldwater Republican who had come within 5,000 votes of unseating moderate Lister Hill for the U.S. Senate in 1962, had his conservative thunder completely stolen by the Wallaces. By Election Day, Alabamians had concluded by 3 to 2 that in a choice between a plain Goldwater conservative and a states'-rights, ultra-segregationist conservative, they would take the latter.

The vote for Lurleen Wallace in Alabama was a mandate from the white majority for George Wallace to undertake a national campaign to capture the Democratic Party and reshape it in the image of the Wallace philosophy. The heart of this credo reads that Negroes never had it so good (by a margin of 2 to 1 in the *Newsweek* survey, these people do not think Negroes are discriminated against in Alabama), that Negroes should be put in their place, and that race relations should be a matter totally for the states to decide. The decision by Governor Wallace to refuse all Federal education money, in order to avoid the accompanying order to desegregate schools, received a hearty endorsement from 86 per cent of Alabama voters.

What motivates the white Alabamians is simply this: They feel that they are willing to say out loud what they believe other whites really think but won't talk about. This is that the Negroes want to go too far and that whites had better reassert their control and supremacy.

White segregationists in the South have not forgotten three primary elections in the spring of 1964, when Governor Wallace made dramatic forays into the Democratic Presidential primaries in the states of Wisconsin, Indiana, and Maryland. In the first two states, Wallace won 33 and 30 per cent of the vote, and in Maryland he soared to 43 per cent. While in all of the states he had only token opposition and the vote outcome had no bearing on the actual Presidential nomination, the Wallace runs were impressive and his vote count substantial.

There is no doubt from surveys during those primaries that the Wallace support came from white people who wanted to express a protest against the Negro revolution. They could do it without serious political consequences, for these primaries obviously were not for keeps.

But the early 1964 Wallace primaries exposed for all to see the potential cross fire which racial tensions could touch off in politics. In Indiana Wallace barely achieved 30 per cent of the vote, but he swept the steelworker precincts where the descendants of Eastern European immigrants live, in East Chicago, Hammond, and Gary, with close to 70 per cent of the vote. In Maryland, where Wallace rose to 43 per cent, the Alabama governor took a majority of 56 per cent among Catholic voters.

Much has been written about the so-called "white backlash" in the big cities of the North. The assumption is that this vote is a straight-out, one-to-one counter-reaction to the Negro drive for equality in education, jobs, and housing. White people in Alabama make the assumption of others that northern "backlash" steelworkers of Gary could be interchanged with their fellow-union members in Bessemer.

But there is a vast and critical difference between the two. In the Deep South, segregation has been a way of life for a century. When Negroes are able to sit anywhere on buses, can eat in any restaurant, attend an integrated first-grade class, work side by side with whites on the job, the change is sharp and dramatic.

It is different in the East Chicagos and the Hammonds of

the North. There it is commonplace for Negroes to jointly use public facilities, for schools to have Negro and white students, and certainly for white and black workers to labor side by side.

All Northern white minority groups have tasted bitter discrimination themselves in their own recent past in education, jobs, and housing. They have been called "Polacks," "Wops," "Hunkies," and worse, as they have grown up. Most of all, they have been discriminated against by the immigrant groups who arrived in this country a little ahead of them. As each generation of immigrants made it and were able to move out of their own ethnic ghettos, as they climbed the economic ladder, they in turn scorned "the base degrees by which they did ascend," as William Shakespeare so aptly put it. The byword of the ethnic jungles of the big cities of the North always was that one had to scrap and claw his way up and out of the ghetto.

Therefore, when Negroes turn to quite different measures—the enforcement powers of government and mass public demonstrations—the sons and daughters of the immigrant groups resent it. When asked about it in surveys, 61 per cent of these minority-descended people say that Negroes are getting a better break than their own fathers and grandfathers received as immigrant outsiders. More directly, nearly 2 out of every 3, 63 per cent, feel that Negroes aim to take over white jobs, and more particularly their own.

Finally, when Negroes take dead aim at integrated housing, the white urban minorities see their own homes and neighborhoods threatened. This feeling of impending insecurity ironically stems more from the incursion of an "out" group on the home territory of an "in" group than it does from racial origins as such. The older Irish and German immigrant minorities heaped great scorn upon their Southern and Eastern European counterparts who arrived in the United States much later.

The bulk of the white people who live in the neighborhoods and work at the jobs and send their children to the schools, where Negroes would like to see the barriers of discrimination fall, happen to be Catholic. If they were of some other ethnic origin, the resultant reaction and ultimate political cross fire would probably have been the same as that which became visible in 1964 and was to continue into the late 1960s. It is a matter of record that the Catholic Church in the United States has, almost without exception, taken an all-out position in support of integration and the major aims of the civil-rights movement.

But when Catholic priests have urged their parishes to make a show of tolerance in racially tense neighborhoods in the cities of the North, the response of their flock has usually been something less than enthusiastic. Socially, as they have progressed from unskilled to skilled employment, the white Catholic minorities have measured their upward climb with pride. Generally, they have been in no mood to share the better things of life with newcomers, particularly if they are black.

Politically, these descendants of immigrant minority groups make their home in the Democratic Party. Catholic voters tended to stray from the Democratic reservation as far back as 1940 when many opposed the interventionist policies of FDR's foreign policy. Many came back in 1948 in response to the threat to Harry Truman from Henry Wallace's Progressive Party.

But rank-and-file Catholics trooped back to the Democratic Party in the election of 1960, when they had a chance to help elect the first Catholic President, John F. Kennedy. The embodiment of all the style that they would like their own sons to have, a four-square advocate of the Democratic Party tradition of helping the underdog, Kennedy was able to bring the Catholic vote back to 2 to 1 majorities, compared with no better than the even split Adlai Stevenson had achieved in two Presidential elections running.

In 1964, Lyndon Johnson raised the Democratic majorities among Catholics to an even greater 72 per cent, higher than at any time since the heyday of Al Smith and FDR back in the heart of the Depression. But the Catholics did not rally to

Johnson in 1964 because he stood resolutely for civil rights. On the contrary, Johnson won the Catholic vote mainly for the same reason he won the American people: he stood for peace and orderly domestic progress against an opponent who worried people that he was trigger-happy and would roll back the clock at home.

Unnoticed in the Johnson landslide of 1964, however, were signs of a fall-off of the vote among some of immigrant-descended groups. In Pennsylvania, the Polish vote was down 5 points from the Kennedy high of four years earlier. In industrial areas of Illinois and Ohio, the Polish vote showed the same signs of softening. But the sharpest breaks of all were in two states—Indiana and Maryland—in the same neighborhoods where George Wallace had polled such a handsome vote earlier the same spring. In Indiana's Polish precincts, the Johnson vote was 7 points lower than that for Kennedy.

IN 1966, THERE WAS NO state-wide major election in Indiana by which to measure a trend. But in Illinois, the Polish and Eastern European precincts showed a precipitous drop of 17 points in the Democratic vote from two years before, and a full 22 points off the high-water mark of 75 per cent registered for Kennedy six years earlier. In Ohio, Polish precincts plummeted to 44 per cent Democratic in the contest for governor there, off 39 points from 1964 and 45 below JFK's showing in 1960. The drop in Pennsylvania's Polish precincts was not as precipitous, but still fell 7 points below Johnson's showing and 12 below Kennedy's mark.

The defections from the Democratic Party of the late-arriving Catholic minorities are crystal clear in state after state. The question is how much of this is due to civil-rights crossfire reaction and how much to other reasons.

A nationwide survey in late 1966 yielded the answer. Voters across the country were asked if they would be upset by Negroes moving into their neighborhoods, and, if so, how upset they would be:

HOW WHITES FEEL ABOUT NEGROES MOVING
INTO THEIR NEIGHBORHOODS

	Total Nation	Irish- Catholic	Italian- Catholic	Polish- Catholic
	%	%	%	%
Would be:				
Upset	52	59	62	79
A lot	24	36	24	40
Some not a lot	16	21	24	15
Only a little	12	2	14	24
Not upset at all	*48*	*41*	*38*	*21*

Similar results were obtained in answer to another question asked in the same survey—whether people felt uneasy for their own personal safety because of racial violence that might occur on their streets:

FEEL PERSONALLY UNEASY ABOUT RACIAL VIOLENCE

	Feel uneasy	Don't feel uneasy
	%	%
Total nation	*44*	*56*
White Protestants	38	62
Catholics	52	48
Jews	29	71
Irish-Catholics	47	53
Italian-Catholics	69	31
Polish-Catholics	67	33

There is no doubt at all that the Catholic minority groups were feeling the press of civil-rights incursions more than others in 1964 and in 1966. In the racially tense areas in and around Chicago, 89 per cent of the people descended from Eastern European stock said they would be upset if Negroes moved into their neighborhood, while a rather startling 58 per cent reported that they would be upset "a lot" if that happened. In Michigan, 62 per cent of the Catholic voters said

they felt "uneasy personally as a result of racial violence."
Even in California, where Catholics, other than those of Mexican origin, are more assimilated than in the big Eastern states,
65 per cent reported the same feeling of uneasiness as a result
of the riots, compared with 54 per cent of the adult population
as a whole.

If this discomfort did exist, a further question is whether it
reflected itself in the voting. It is not enough simply to report
that the Catholic Democratic vote went down in Michigan
from 75 to 52 per cent or in Ohio from 72 to 43 per cent or in
Connecticut from 69 to 55 per cent or in New Jersey from 67
to 37 per cent.

The key to measuring the impact of the racial issue on white
Northern minority groups in statistical terms is to look for
what happened to *both* the Negro vote and the Catholic vote
in the same election. For example, there are some states in
which the Democratic decline in 1966 was substantial among
both Negroes and Catholics. In these cases, there might have
been some white reaction against Democratic candidates over
civil rights, but because of a comparable drop in the Negro
vote, obviously there were other reasons for the decline in
Democratic fortunes. Here are such general drop-off cases:

| | Democratic Vote | | | |
| | Negro vote | | Catholic vote | |
	1966	1964	1966	1964
	%	%	%	%
Massachusetts (Gov.)	40	94	41	74
New Jersey	68	95	37	67
Pennsylvania	75	96	50	69
Ohio	69	98	43	72

In contrast to these four, however, are four other key states
in which the Negro vote held for the Democrats, but the
Catholic vote fell off sharply. In these situations, it can be said
with fairness and with statistical soundness that the net losses
for the Democrats centered on a white cross fire over civil
rights:

CROSS-FIRE STATES

| | Democratic Vote | | | |
| | Negro vote | | Catholic vote | |
	1966	1964	1966	1964
	%	%	%	%
Connecticut	95	98	55	69
Michigan (Senate)	86	96	52	75
Illinois	90	98	46	62
California	96	98	52	71

In Connecticut the Democratic fall-off in the race for governor in 1966 did not prove fatal to incumbent John Dempsey, for he was able to make up these losses with substantial showings in normally Republican and white Protestant suburbs and small towns.

In other states, the Democrats were not so fortunate and the effects of cross fire were damaging, if not a pivotal reason for defeat. In California, for example, the successive riots in Watts, San Francisco, and then in Oakland, close to election time, had a devastating effect on Governor Edmund G. "Pat" Brown's chances for re-election. A survey just before that election revealed that 52 per cent of California's voters believed the 1965 Watts riots had been handled badly, and these people voted 2 to 1 for Ronald Reagan.

In fact, the California outcome could have been foretold on the single issue of race alone. The state divided down the middle 50–50 over whether Brown had been too willing to yield to minority-group demands. Those who felt he had been "soft" on racial matters voted 9 to 1 for Brown. This is not to say that Ronald Reagan's vote was derived exclusively from a racial reaction. However, the facts do prove that 3 out of every 4 people who voted for Reagan found it easier to do so because they felt they could register a protest in varying forms to the riots and racial unrest that had taken place.

In the Michigan contest for U.S. Senator between Robert Griffin, the Republican, and G. Mennen Williams, the Democrat, the civil-rights issue again foretold the ultimate outcome. On the direct question of who would do a better job of controlling riots and racial unrest, Griffin won over Williams by 61–39 per cent. Negroes picked Williams 86–14 per cent. White Protestants selected Griffin 67–33 per cent. Both of these results paralleled normal party divisions. But among Catholic voters, who had been 75–25 Democratic in 1964, Griffin was preferred on the racial issue 52–48 per cent. This foretold the 23-point drop for Williams among Catholics in this race.

In Illinois, racial feelings ran high because of the summer crisis over open housing in Chicago. A high 34 per cent of all whites in the state reported that they would be extremely upset if Negroes were to move into their neighborhoods. With the pivotal Eastern European group, this number soared to 58 per cent. One voter in every 3 criticized incumbent Senator Paul Douglas for being too radical on civil rights. Again, among the Catholic group it was 1 in every 2. On the other hand, by 4 to 1, Illinois voters did not feel that Charles Percy was too strong for open housing, although he had taken a position in favor of such legislation for multiple-dwelling units. In the end, the Negro vote held relatively firm for Douglas, but the Catholic vote dropped off sharply, heavily affected by the racial cross fire.

In Illinois, California, Michigan, and in other key industrial states of the North, the civil-rights issues may well tear apart the traditional big-city Democratic Party coalition of minorities in future elections. John F. Kennedy won the Presidency by bringing back record numbers of Catholic minority voters to the Democratic fold and by raising Democratic majorities among Negro voters. To say that this Kennedy coalition is in trouble is a vast understatement.

Part of the reason is that many of the Catholic minorities live directly in the path of the Negro surge for greater opportunity. Another reason, however, is that there seems to be a kind of chemical reaction between the two groups—Catholic and Negro—in their voting patterns, which in times of civil-rights crisis will often make them veer in opposite directions.

This pattern of cross fire is no better shown than in another Northern state where things went directly opposite for the Democratic vote in the 1966 election:

CROSS FIRE IN MARYLAND

| | Democratic vote | |
	1966	1964
	%	%
State-wide vote	41	66
Negro vote	6	94
Catholic vote	66	70

The difference between Maryland and the rest of the Northern states, of course, is that the Democratic candidate there was George P. Mahoney, a contractor who had won the gubernatorial nomination on the racist platform, "Your Home Is Your Castle." Negroes left the Democratic line wholesale, as did white suburban residents in Montgomery County across the line from Washington, D.C. But Catholic voters centered in suburban Baltimore County and in the city of Baltimore stayed with Mahoney in numbers paralleling the strong run made by George Wallace in the spring of 1964 in Maryland.

One other recent election provides an interesting study of the racial cross fire in American politics. That was the New York gubernatorial election of 1966. For one thing, it was a four-way race between Nelson Rockefeller on the GOP line, Frank O'Connor for the Democrats, Franklin D. Roosevelt, Jr., for the Liberals, and Paul Adams on the Conservative ticket.

But the election was also beset by a referendum in New York City over a civilian review complaint board, which Mayor John Lindsay had established to handle civilian complaints against the police. The Conservative Party and the Patrolmen's Benevolent Association, the policemen's union, petitioned and obtained a public referendum. The review board was defeated by 3 to 2 on Election Day.

The air of New York was heavy with racial tension all through the campaign for governor in 1966. A survey taken a week before the election showed that 80 per cent of the people of the state thought the Negroes were moving too fast in their quest for progress, 56 per cent were worried about Negroes moving into their neighborhoods, and a rather high 38 per cent believed that many Negroes are committed to violence in their struggle.

Among the people who believed that Negroes are not bent on violence, Rockefeller led O'Connor. Among those who thought Negroes were committed to a course of violence, O'Connor held a lead of 11 points. Among white people who expressed no concern about Negroes living in their neighborhood, Rockefeller led O'Connor by 7 points. Among whites who said they were extremely concerned about Negroes moving in where they live, O'Connor led Rockefeller by 49–31 per cent, or an edge of 18 points.

The election itself proved out these survey results:

CROSS FIRE IN NEW YORK STATE

	Democratic vote	
	1966	1964
	%	%
State-wide vote	38	68
Negro vote	53	92
Catholic vote	57	64

Democrat Frank O'Connor's big losses were incurred in the vote of Negroes, who worried about his seemingly half-hearted endorsement of the civilian review board. By contrast, the Catholic voters, a high 58 per cent of whom felt uneasy on the streets due to racial violence, held relatively well for the Democrats, considering the four-way race and the overall 30-point drop for the Democratic Party state-wide in the vote for governor.

The New York election shows, of course, that having a racial cross fire at work does not always prove out a victory for the side of the whites who are most aroused on the issue. On the contrary, with New York's relatively liberal and moderate electorate, it was impossible to win on such an issue. And in Maryland, it was the Negroes who joined with the racial moderates in the Washington suburbs to put across moderate Republican Spiro T. Agnew for Governor.

What New York and Maryland clearly show is that if the Democratic Party in the North tries to trim, or even give the impression of trimming, on the Negro-rights issue, it probably will end up losing elections and giving birth to a vigorous, moderate, and enlightened Republican Party in the process.

The South now appears to have been split in two. In the Deep South, the Republican Party has been committed to trying to be more conservative and more segregationist than the states'-rights Democrats. But it seems highly unlikely that the Republicans will be able to outdo the George Wallace-led Deep South Democrats.

In the South outside of Alabama, Mississippi, South Carolina, Georgia, and Louisiana, things appear to be changing rapidly. In Arkansas and Tennessee, Republican racial moderates were elected to major office in 1966. In Virginia, the first moderate Democrat won election to state-wide office in nearly half a century. In the ring of states outside the Deep South, many voters appear to want to join the rest of the country in rejecting the racial extremism of George Wallace and Strom Thurmond.

Despite Wallace's strong runs in the 1964 primaries in the North, when surveys pit him as an independent against Lyndon Johnson for the Democrats and either Richard Nixon or George Romney for the Republicans, the Alabama segregationist does not do well; he is able to capture no more than 10 per cent of the nation's vote. He would cut deeper into the Republican than the Democratic vote. Even in the South, Wallace would run third in a Johnson-Nixon-Wallace race. While George Wallace might be capable of carrying his own state of Alabama and neighboring Mississippi, he would be hard pressed to win Georgia and Louisiana and might well lose South Carolina.

There is an undercurrent of reaction against the Negro

surge in America and it is reflected in the changing politics of the latter half of the twentieth century. On a national basis, the Negroes will remain pivotal in their vote because they are strategically located for Presidential elections. But on a local level there will be casualties among moderates who have stood up for Negro rights during periods of stress and tension.

But just as there is some reaction and cross fire resulting from the Negro drive for political power, there is every indication that Americans are not about to panic into a crusade behind George Wallace to maintain the racial status quo. In an odd way, the Wallaces serve as the leaveners to the Stokely Carmichaels politically. The old coalition may be changing beyond recognition, but the essential stability of the center in American political life is likely to remain intact.

"Whites Can Be So Nasty"

ARCHIE CALVIN EPPS III, *born in the steamy Negro community of Lake Charles, Louisiana, is a man who has made his way very well in the white world. He is the assistant dean of Harvard College, supervising relations between the college and such public programs as VISTA and the Peace Corps. From his rooms in Leverett House Towers he tutors students interested in Negro history and literature. He is also the assistant conductor of the Harvard Glee Club, and as head of the Leverett House Opera Society has produced such operas as* Don Giovanni *and* Così Fan Tutte.

A graduate of Talladega College in Alabama—"a good liberal arts college with an integrated faculty"—Epps is a cultivated man of nearly thirty who also took graduate work in social relations at Harvard. But he has never forgotten, indeed is proud of, his humble beginning.

"A very strong influence was my father," Epps told a Newsweek *reporter in 1966. His father earned a certificate entitling*

him to be a school principal in Louisiana, but was too proud to yield to white authority and chose instead to drive an ice wagon. "He was penalized for his pride," said Epps, "as Negroes were always penalized for it and still are today. The lesson he drew, and taught me, was a kind of heroic notion of life in which you didn't allow one setback to discourage you."

Epps has never been discouraged, but he has had to search long and hard for his own place in society.

"I had my own phase of being angry at whites," said Epps. "That was about two years ago. The whole question of how I got caught up in it is complicated. I suppose it was sheer anger at the killings of civil-rights workers. I just became increasingly aware of the day-to-day insults that the Negro had to deal with, and still has to deal with. It was always such an ordeal to go to a restaurant. Whites can be so nasty in little ways."

Epps was a coordinator of the March on Washington of 1963 and once locked arms with other Negroes in protests against the Boston school system. He invited the late black nationalist leader Malcolm X to lecture at Harvard and has compiled a book of his speeches there.

Yet Epps has now tempered his views. He professes the greatest respect for Martin Luther King and the strongest faith in nonviolence. "I don't see why nonviolence and black power should be mutually exclusive," he said. "I don't think Negroes should react to whites from the wounded side of our experience, but from the other side—to believe in the possibilities of the brotherhood of man. Gosh, I wish we could do that."

His ambivalence has caused some anguish for Epps at Harvard. "The expectations people have of me here—one is that I will, or should, lose my Negroness and just become a gentleman, or that I should gratefully accept this opportunity that Harvard has bestowed on me. And the Negroes here want me to be very much the Negro activist. I'm under no pressure *from the administration to take any particular view. I must find my own way. One must retain the right to do that."*

Epps believes that the basic problems of the Negro are two-fold: "One is the predicament of the Negro masses, who have not been allowed to improve their condition. The second aspect is the failure of the Negro middle classes to assist the Negro masses to improve their lot. They . . . by and large served their own self-interest . . . and must, in part, be blamed for the failure of the government to conceive radical programs to deal with the Negro problem."

In this context, Epps sees Roy Wilkins of the NAACP as a man who "is out of touch with the masses of Negroes." But is Epps too? "I'm in touch only as an intellectual," he said. "My life is that of the Negro middle class. But my parents always taught me to have a sense of public service. I hope I don't have a sense of noblesse oblige *about it."*

For the moment, Epps considers it his mission to help the Negro students at Harvard to understand that they must compete on the basis of ability. "Liberal white students are afraid of criticizing a Negro, because they don't want to offend him," he said. "A Negro should expect criticism of his intellectual performance, just as other students do." But Epps also has lingering doubts whether it is all worthwhile. "I wonder," he said, "whether the integrated experience at Harvard really changes the mind of a person who comes here. At Harvard, it's the thing to be liberal and tolerant. It's not so easy in society."

CHAPTER 6

White Attitudes: The Age-Old Dilemma

BY THE LATE 1960s, the Negro revolution was getting under the skin of millions of white people in America. Whites were beginning to realize that the surge of Negroes for freedom and equality was not a passing phase that could be appeased by a single generous or moral act and then would not be heard from again.

By now, the persistent and unyielding efforts of Negroes to roll back barrier after barrier had led 85 per cent of all white people to feel that the pace of civil-rights progress was too fast. Only a year before, the number who had felt Negroes were moving too fast had been 49 per cent. A year before that, only 34 per cent of all white people felt that way.

A housewife in Dayton, Ohio, exclaimed, "Oh, they are so forward. If you give them your finger, they'll take your hand." Sandra Sayle, a 22-year-old commercial artist from Arlington, Virginia, said, "They're asking for too much all at once. They should try the installment plan. People don't adjust that quickly." A 55-year-old man in Port Huron, Michigan, added,

"They are trying to force themselves on us." A housewife in California was cryptic, "Rome wasn't built in a day. They've come from cannibals in a short time." A toolroom machinist in Wood River, Illinois, was revealing, "It's like a dog you keep tied up for a long time. Then when you let him loose he goes everywhere, every which way. He doesn't know how to act. He goes overboard."

The early tactics of the sit-ins, the chanting demonstrations, and the dramatic marches had always made whites nervous. Back in 1963, the orderly and dignified March on Washington had been favorably received by no more than half the white people of the country.

But by late 1966, 85 per cent of all whites had come to the conclusion that the demonstrations were hurting the Negro cause. It was almost as though every time defiant Negroes came into the homes of white Americans on television, millions of white people leered right back at the tube.

A Joliet, Illinois, housewife expressed it for many, "When I see on TV these demonstrations it makes me think of them as savages." A young mother in Garland, Texas, sized up what she saw this way, "I'd say 90 per cent are a bunch of nuts— yelling because they don't have anything better to do." In Houston, another woman thought she was being kind when she said, "Most of the poor souls that march don't know what they are marching for." A man from Rochester, New York, added, "Someone starts something going and then they all march."

A small minority of white people disagreed. A steelworker in Hellertown, Pa., saw the demonstrations as serving a useful purpose, "Some people must see action before they believe a problem exists." A worker from Harper Woods, Michigan, said, "The demonstrations have sort of begun to chop at an awfully thick tree."

But the white people who still held any sympathy for the tactic of demonstration were harder and harder to find. Whites felt that they no longer needed to be reminded of the 100 years of discrimination against Negroes. The growing feeling is that demonstrations just stir up trouble, lose friends for the cause among white people, make people fear Negroes, are a sign of irrational impatience, and suggest violence.

The first cousin to the demonstration in the eyes of most white Americans is the riot. And while Negroes tend to justify, explain, and even defend the riots, by a nearly unanimous 76 to 5 per cent (19 per cent not sure), whites feel the wave of riots in every part of the country has hurt the Negro cause.

White people are willing to admit that restlessness and frustration emanating from slum crowding, a lack of jobs, and poverty, contribute to the tinderbox condition in which a riot can be sparked. Mrs. Muriel Senseman, a Cleveland Heights, Ohio, housewife, said: "They're tired of being the underdog. This country is very prosperous, and too many Negroes have not shared in this prosperity." A toolroom machinist in suburban Chicago thought the riots had the effect of jogging complacent white people loose from a lack of sensitivity to the plight of Negroes. He said, "They're clamoring to show us how we've been treating them. You don't miss electricity until the wires go down. So you don't pay attention to the colored person until he riots and jars you with a picture of yourself you don't like."

Such calm and cool reactions were few and far between in the *Newsweek* survey. The reaction of most whites to the riots is high fury and indignation. Many attribute the outbreaks to subversive elements, Communists, or worse. A housewife in California said, "It's the Communists behind them. They'd never have the guts to do it without the Communists." These were other comments: a juke-box serviceman in Chicago, "They hear about what they're gonna get for free and it doesn't show up so they bust things up like a bunch of little kids"; a policeman who has been on the line in Chicago, "Some drunks get out of hand, and everybody pitches in to join the fun"; a foreman down the street from a riot, "I feel the gangster element stirred up a situation so they could loot"; a 68-year-old widow in Moscow, Idaho, "They should be treated like the Jews and put in a country of their own. They are egged on by the Communists"; a Milwaukee machinist, "Instigators are probably paid to get it started and then it snowballs like in Watts"; Dan Foster, Jr., of Jacksonville, "They want power—not only want to be in the show but want to run it, too"; the wife of a service worker in Columbus, Ohio, "I think they want to make slaves of the white people."

All in all, the riots have evoked from a majority of whites a reaction that Negroes are not stable in character, want black power to the exclusion of white power, and have an avaricious tendency to want something for nothing. It is hard to conceive of a set of episodes better designed to bring forth from white people all their worst possible prejudices about Negroes than the riots.

Changes in white attitudes are one major impact of the riots. But white reaction goes deeper than that. One in every 2 white people (57 per cent in the big cities) now report that they feel personally unsafe on the streets as a direct result of the riots. This personal unease adds a dimension of personal security to the racial struggle which had not been present earlier.

In turn, this dimension of safety on the streets has placed the local police squarely in the middle of the civil-rights struggle. Negroes are highly critical of police, implying that they tend to have double standards for whites and Negroes and employ brutality against them.

White people sharply disagree with Negroes about the police. By a wide 6 to 1 margin, whites believe policemen help Negroes much more than they abuse them. For every white person who believes the police practice brutality against Negroes (17 per cent) there are more than three (58 per cent) who vigorously defend the police. A Midwesterner of Italian descent put it this way, "If cops are going to be tough, they'll be tough with everybody. I grew up in 'Little Italy' so I know. If a cop's mean, he's mean, and color has got nothing to do with it." A machine operator in Venice, California, said, "I think there should be more police brutality, more martial law.

Then they would have more respect for the law. Martial law is shoot now and ask questions later."

The 3 to 2 vote in New York City in 1966 to eliminate the civilian review complaint board was far more a reflection of people's anxieties over their own personal safety than an out-and-out anti-Negro vote as such. But the riots have triggered a connection in many white minds between growing crime and racial agitation.

And the resultant white reaction can be highly personal, especially among women. A housewife in Dayton, Ohio, told the *Newsweek* survey, "I'm never sure of the Negro. I can't read their faces because they have no expressions to me on their faces. I just don't want to be close to one." Another housewife in West Orange, New Jersey, said, "People have become afraid of Negroes. When you see them in groups you think they're going to start a riot."

With this sharpening of the cleavage between the races, it is hardly surprising that by 3 to 1 whites feel that Negroes are asking for more than they are ready for.

If this decisively negative reaction of white people to the demonstrations and riots were the entire story of white America's feelings about the Negro revolution, then this country would be a powder keg of racial tensions ready to explode at a moment's notice. As a Washington newspaperman put it, "If white reactions to the riots were the whole picture, why we'd be well on our way toward putting our own President Verwoerd in the White House."*

But the reactions of white America are not a simple, one-dimensional matter. As Gunnar Myrdal pointed out almost a quarter of a century ago, a deep dilemma and ambivalence besets white people in this country.

In the *Newsweek* survey, by better than 2 to 1, whites believe that Negroes are discriminated against:

* Hendrik Verwoerd, as South African Prime Minister from 1958 until his assassination in 1966, was the foremost exponent of that country's much-criticized *apartheid* policy of racial segregation.

ARE NEGROES DISCRIMINATED AGAINST?

	Discriminated against	Not discriminated against	Not sure
	%	%	%
Total Whites	61	28	11
East	62	25	13
Midwest	70	20	10
South	39	47	14
West	64	28	8

Even in the white South, substantial numbers of white people recognize that discrimination exists against Negroes. When asked to spell out the areas of inequality, whites come up with a roster not dissimilar to that volunteered by Negroes: the lack of job opportunities and a poor chance to get ahead in employment, housing and slum conditions, segregated schools, social isolation.

A white schoolteacher in Texas said, "They should have moved a long time ago—about a hundred years to be exact." And a farm manager in Coal City, Indiana, added, "As they get educated, they will learn how to get along. But now they have to fight back and strike out and rebel—even get unruly. But what can we expect? They've been pushed too far."

Nor are most Americans unmindful of the deleterious effect of discrimination against Negroes on the reputation of the United States abroad. Fully 7 in every 10 people believe that our racial problems at home have hurt this country abroad. Often the American people are accused of being insular and oblivious to what other peoples of the world think. To the contrary, as a nation the people of the United States are highly sensitive, and most are aware that a majority of the world's peoples are colored, not white.

White America is capable of understanding what it is like to be a Negro. When they are asked what it would be like to be a Negro living in America in 1966, the four main strands of white reaction were these: resentment and belligerence, an inclination to be tough and pushy; a sense of being something less than a person; a feeling that one's ego had been destroyed; and a fate worse than death.

A retired woman in California said, "I think it would be terrible to be a Negro. I just couldn't stand it. Suppose I went into a restaurant and they wouldn't serve me. It would be awful." A laborer in Michigan expressed a strong reaction, "If I was colored, I'd feel like I didn't belong. Like a dog. I'd be hurt and bitter against the whites. I'd take revenge." A Pennsylvania housewife, "It would hurt, especially to see your child hurt. I was a foreigner as a child because I'm Polish, and I know how cruel people can be." A farmer's wife in Kansas, "It would be very humiliating. If I was a Negro, I would commit suicide."

One of the incredible marks of affluent America in the late 1960s was that it had the capacity to put itself in the shoes of the Negro, but at the same time continued to play the role of discriminator. Some rationalize it all, like the businessman in Seattle who said, "It would be pretty bad to be a Negro." Then, as an afterthought he added, "But, after all, they aren't like white folks. I don't think it bothers most of them." A laborer on the West Coast said, "They're only a hundred years old in civilization and expect to catch up, and we been civilized for thousands of years."

The point is that most whites do not often think of how it would be to exist as a Negro. For most whites quickly find themselves caught up in the throes of a dilemma over their own emotional prejudices and what the impact of such white attitudes is on life as a Negro. It is a vast overstatement to say that white people in America suffer from a guilt complex over the treatment accorded Negroes. They know discrimination exists. Most believe it wrong. But along with overeating, not getting enough exercise, not taking part in community activities, not watching safe driving rules on the highways, and a whole host of other imperfections in their daily lives, whites find it difficult to brood over the plight of the Negroes without becoming depressed and unhappy.

So most Americans would just as soon admit to the injustices accorded Negroes, and move on to a pleasanter subject.

Yet whites also have a sense that discrimination is wrong and that the Federal government should put its full weight behind the elimination of injustice. As a consequence, thumping majorities of white people support legislation giving Negroes equal voting rights (91 per cent), the right to a fair jury trial (87 per cent), non-segregated use of buses and trains and airlines (87 per cent), and integrated education (72 per cent).

It has been argued that it is relatively easy to favor civil-rights legislation, but much more difficult to abide by the impact of these new laws in one's daily life. And there is much truth in this.

But white America feels rather keenly that profound and even sweeping changes have occurred in white society on the race issue over the past three years. The *Newsweek* survey recorded many of these changes by asking an identical series of questions of whites in 1963 and again in 1966:

WHITES ASSESS ROLE OF INSTITUTIONS
IN RIGHTS STRUGGLE

	1966	1963
	%	%
National Administration		
Helping Negroes	85	84
Keeping Negroes down	4	6
Not sure	11	10
Congress		
Helping Negroes	74	46
Keeping Negroes down	5	15
Not sure	21	39
U.S. Supreme Court		
Helping Negroes	71	73
Keeping Negroes down	4	7
Not sure	25	20
State Government		
Helping Negroes	65	54
Keeping Negroes down	5	13
Not sure	30	33

	1966	1963
	%	%
Railroads, Bus Companies		
Helping Negroes	64	46
Keeping Negroes down	8	27
Not sure	28	27
Local Government		
Helping Negroes	58	44
Keeping Negroes down	8	16
Not sure	34	40
Retail Stores		
Helping Negroes	58	45
Keeping Negroes down	12	25
Not sure	30	30
Business Corporations		
Helping Negroes	55	32
Keeping Negroes down	13	29
Not sure	32	39
White Protestant Churches		
Helping Negroes	54	50
Keeping Negroes down	11	16
Not sure	35	34
The Professions		
Helping Negroes	54	48
Keeping Negroes down	11	15
Not sure	35	37
Catholic Church		
Helping Negroes	54	57
Keeping Negroes down	6	5
Not sure	40	38
Restaurant, Hotels, Motels		
Helping Negroes	52	24
Keeping Negroes down	19	49
Not sure	29	27
Labor Unions		
Helping Negroes	51	41
Keeping Negroes down	16	26
Not sure	33	33
Real Estate Companies		
Helping Negroes	30	22
Keeping Negroes down	34	44
Not sure	36	34

The striking fact in this inventory is that with the single exception of real estate companies, white America is convinced by more than a majority that the major institutions in the country are helping rather than retarding Negroes.

W. F. Schnell, a 65-year-old retired machinery dealer from Moscow, Idaho, summed up a lot of white feeling when he said, "The Negro hasn't given all these civil-rights laws a chance to work."

Basically, white people believe that the fair and right thing is to help rectify the years of racial injustice. But a great deal of this feeling is quite akin to giving to the local Community Chest. If you do it once a year, you are helping give the needy a boost. After all, tokenism is quite enough, considering that each and every family has plenty of problems of its own to look after.

It is obvious, of course, that Negroes are not prepared to agree that tokenism is enough. It not only may not affect their lot a bit, but it may also give the white man an easy way to get off the hook. For example, a white minister in Nashville interviewed in the *Newsweek* survey said quite casually, "Negroes are in better shape than they ever were. We haven't hurt them any. Been good to them, I think."

People with views such as these feel they are being fair-minded on the civil-rights question. In fact, this kind of up-standing white citizen is positively outraged at the tactics of the Ku Klux Klan. When asked if they thought the Klan did more harm or more good for America, by 7 to 1 a cross-section of white Americans answered more harm. They went on to characterize the KKK as made up of "terrorists" (48 per cent), "white Southerners" (41 per cent), "sick people" (31 per cent), Communists (29 per cent), "poor white trash" (23 per cent), "bad people" (19 per cent), and "bigots" (16 per cent). When asked who opposes the KKK, they answered "red-blooded Americans" (50 per cent) and "good people" (50 per cent), followed by "Negroes" (49 per cent) and "patriots" (37 per cent). Percentages added to more than 100 per cent because few white people had only one word to describe the Ku Klux Klan.

In the South, opposition to the Klan runs nearly 4 to 1. It is perfectly apparent that people who think they are decent-minded Americans are as much against the KKK as they are against the Negro riots in Watts or Hough or Hunter's Point. In fact, many white people equate the two with expressions of equal disdain.

Some of the same strands of ambivalence are evident when whites discuss civil rights and education. The Commissioner of Education has pointed out that progress in school integration over the past few years has been token at best. Yet there has been a sharp change in the white assessment of the quality of education for Negroes over the past three years. Back in 1963, by 48 to 41 per cent, whites agreed that Negro children received an education inferior to that obtained by whites. In 1966, however, a rather substantial 54–36 per cent majority had changed their minds and viewed Negro education as being just as good as white children receive.

Whites make it abundantly clear that they have no deep aversion to Negro children going to the same school as their own offspring. By better than 3 to 1, they deny the claim that white children's education would suffer with Negroes in the classroom. Even white Southerners now share this prevailing view.

Yet when confronted with another question which asked if they feel Negro children would be better educated in integrated classrooms, white Americans, by over 2 to 1, feel that this would not be the case.

This last view, of course, is at sharp variance from the U.S. Supreme Court in its historic 1954 decision, when the Court concluded: "To separate them (children in grade and high schools) from others of similar age and qualification solely because of their race generates a feeling of inferiority as to their status in the community that may affect their hearts and minds in a way unlikely ever to be undone."

White Americans say to the tune of 72 per cent that they

approve of the Court ruling outlawing segregation in education. But it is equally true that most whites are not ready to do anything to help bring about integration in the schools.

The education issue, in fact, is closely tied to the housing issue. Where it has been tried, busing children of one race to another part of a city or town has, for the most part, either not worked out well or has been greeted with downright hostility —not all of it white, either. Educators point out that integrated schooling will not arrive in America until integrated housing and integrated neighborhoods exist.

Of all the issues confronting white and black America, housing in the late 1960s has easily become the most explosive. When asked about it directly, a majority of 58 per cent of all whites in the *Newsweek* survey said they would be upset by Negroes moving into their neighborhood, and this figure rises to 76 per cent among whites living in the areas where Negroes would like to move.

A retired policeman in Asheville, North Carolina, said, "It would tear me up! The Negro is inferior and utterly impossible to live with as neighbors. I can't even stand to think about it!" A chain grocery-store manager in Chicago explained, "If they were well behaved, it wouldn't bother me. But they are usually dirty and bring rats and bugs. They ruin a neighborhood." A 71-year-old woman in Ohio had heard stories: "You hear so many people say things about them. They act trashy and mean. I don't want to mingle. I'll stay with my color and they should do the same." A 38-year-old housewife of Hyde Park, New York, said, "Wherever they go they make a mess of everything. They have no pride in their home. They make a ghetto of it." Mrs. Elias Olvera, a housewife in Joliet, said this: "They're dirty. They get housing projects and in two years they look like dumps."

The feeling on housing is so strong and so passionate that even the majorities of the public that back legislation in Congress to outlaw discrimination in most other areas of life balk at an open-housing bill. When Congress did not pass President Johnson's recommended legislation on open housing in 1966, it was an election year. The evidence clearly shows that a majority of white Americans by 52–48 per cent opposed such legislation. This directly parallels the feelings of white America about having a Negro as a next door neighbor—most would not like it.

Even the people who say they don't mind if Negroes move into their neighborhood almost inevitably voice some reservations about it. A whole series of "if's" emerged from the more tolerant whites in the *Newsweek* survey. Negroes are welcome, they say, if they have the same standards as others in the neighborhood, or if they can afford the cost of the proper upkeep, or if they are "clean and nice."

The apprehensions among whites over integrated housing center on a whole cluster of dire expectations: social contact will lead to troubles; property values will be lowered; the neighborhood will soon be inundated with Negroes and there won't be any whites left in it.

Time and again, interviewers in the *Newsweek* survey brought out the ultimate concern over integrated housing: that it would lead to intermarriage. James P. Rudy, a salesman in Lewistown, Pennsylvania, said, "I have nothing against Negroes—as long as it doesn't get too personal like dating and marriage." The wife of a skilled worker in Salt Lake City added, "Races should stay and breed with their own. It's the end result that bothers me—a white marrying a Negro."

White attitudes slowly but discernibly are moving toward greater acceptance of the idea of integration in employment, education, and the use of public accommodations. But the overwhelming view of white America toward miscegenation remains intractable. In 1963, 90 per cent of all whites would object to their teenage child dating a Negro. Three years later, 88 per cent felt the same way. In 1963, 84 per cent would be upset by a close friend or relative marrying a Negro and in 1966, 79 per cent said they would look on such an eventuality with a fair amount of horror.

Obviously, the question of intermarriage was remote for most Americans as a matter of practical possibility. However, it should be noted that a *Newsweek* survey among white college students found that over one student in three would have no objection to marrying a Negro, and one in two would not mind dating a member of another race. If there were any real signs of greater acceptance of social contact with Negroes it was almost all among the better educated, among the sons and daughters of the affluent rather than the less privileged.

In fact, the entire civil-rights issue in America by the latter part of the 1960s was dividing white people in a quite unexpected way. To be sure, the gulf is wide between Negroes and whites in terms of the pace of progress, the tactics of the revolution, and even the ultimate objectives of how far integration should go. In addition, the white South still lagged behind the rest of the country in holding out against the inevitability of desegregation. But more and more, the Deep South was being isolated from the border-state South. These divisions between Negroes and whites, between the North and South all are 100 or more years old.

But the newer cutting edges are part of another revolution which is taking place in America. In 1966, an estimated 53 per cent of all high-school graduates went on to college. The number of students in college rose from 1.4 million in 1939 to nearly 6 million by 1966. In 1940, the number of households with incomes of $10,000 and over annually was 2 per cent. By 1966, the number had swelled to 24 per cent of American homes.

Even discounting the loss of value of the purchasing power of the dollar, there has been an explosion in major proportions in the United States in education and in income. This has given rise to a new and growing and dynamic affluent segment of society.

By 1975, the number of people earning $10,000 and over a year will be greater than those who earn under $5,000 a year. America is clearly on its way toward becoming the first mass affluent nation in the history of the world.

Back in the heart of the Depression of the 1930s, when the less privileged in society were a clear majority and the privileged were a small and highly select group, the pressures for social change came almost entirely from the lower-income masses. To be a member of the privileged sector of society automatically gave one a vested interest in the status quo.

Civil-rights leaders talk in terms of the 1930s when they describe their struggle against the "white power structure" or the "establishment." They represent the most underprivileged 10 per cent, whose aim is to share the fruits of abundant America on a more equitable basis. All of their objectives converge on this central goal: political power to make certain that the leverage of government power is used to alleviate their plight; economic power so that they may pull themselves up by their bootstraps to live better lives and to open the doors of greater opportunity; educational power to enable them to earn more and to gain an equal footing with whites.

The underprivileged in an affluent society tend to feel alienated from the mainstream, the power centers. As more people receive an education and move into higher income brackets and achieve more comforts and greater mobility, those who are left behind become embittered.

In the group earning under $3,000 a year in the United States, only one-third are Negro and two-thirds are white. The War on Poverty has been widely advertised for what it can do in the Negro ghettos of the big cities, how in the end it will relieve the pressures triggering riots.

Yet the War on Poverty has never been sold to the American people. By a 5 to 4 margin, most Americans are critical of the anti-poverty program, mainly because they feel it is too rife with politics. Negroes, on the other hand, favor the program by 5 to 1. However, the most bitter reactions against the War on Poverty come from whites in the $3,000 and under group. By 70–30 per cent, these low-income people believe the program is designed to aid Negroes and won't help them because their skin is not black.

In fact, by the end of 1966, alienation was far greater among low-income whites than comparable, low-income Negroes. A series of statements, many of them old shibboleths, was read off to a cross-section of the public:

EXTENT OF ALIENATION

	Total public	Negroes	Low-income whites
	%	%	%
Sometimes feel that:			
Rich get richer, poor get poorer	48	49	68
What you think doesn't count much	39	40	60
People in power don't care about us	28	32	50
Other people get lucky breaks	19	35	37
Important events in world don't affect me	18	12	26
Few understand how I live	18	32	36
Nobody understands problems I have	17	30	40

While Negroes are far more alienated than most whites, low-income white people are in turn much more alienated from society than Negroes. A key indication is the category "important events in the world don't affect me." Negroes feel less that this is the case than even affluent whites. The reason: Negroes have come to believe correctly that the civil-rights issue is one of the great crises America and the world has faced. And civil rights is their issue. They, the Negroes, are what it is all about.

The net result is that low-income Negroes possess an abundant quantity of hope about their future, while low-income whites feel quite hopelessly caught up in the forgotten backwash of society.

But the division between low-income Negroes and whites goes even further. Low-income whites also have a deep and abiding aversion to seeing Negroes get ahead. Part of the reason is that the less-privileged whites feel that their own plight is sorely neglected. Another reason is that misery loves company and they dislike seeing Negroes make progress when they are standing still. Still another reason is that people always take some solace in seeing others whose lot is worse than their own. As America emerged from the mid-1960s, low-income whites found their Negro scapegoats slipping away.

As a consequence, the heart of resistance to change in racial matters in the United States rests squarely among the low-income whites. Now they are the most ardent advocates of freezing the status quo.

In direct and sharp contrast to low-income white views on civil rights are the more enlightened and even advanced attitudes of the affluent one quarter at the top. These better educated and more privileged white people feel most deeply about the necessity to make progress to achieve equality for Negroes.

The following table illustrates the deep cleavage which is growing between low-income and affluent whites on the subject of the Negro revolution:

WHITE ATTITUDES TOWARD NEGROES

	All whites	Low-income	Affluents
	%	%	%
Negro housing worse than whites	65	46	69
Negroes are discriminated against	60	46	78
Negroes laugh a lot	56	66	49
Negroes smell different	52	61	45
Object to Negroes living next door	51	54	41
Negroes have looser morals	50	56	46
Sympathize with Negro protests	46	24	57
Negroes want to live off handouts	43	53	33
Object to having Negro child to supper	42	51	29
Negro education worse than whites	40	27	58
Object to trying clothes Negroes tried on	31	44	21
Object to using same restrooms as Negroes	22	36	14
Object to sitting next to Negro in movie	21	31	11
Object to sitting next to Negro on bus	16	25	9
Object to sitting next to Negro in restaurant	16	26	8

The stereotyped beliefs about Negroes are firmly rooted in less-privileged, less-well-educated white society: the beliefs that Negroes smell different, have looser morals, are lazy, and laugh a lot. Willingness to have contact with Negroes is far less among poor whites, whether it is a matter of using the same public restrooms, or going to a movie or a restaurant, trying on clothes in a store, or living next to a Negro. The less privileged also fail to see that Negroes receive poorer education or housing than whites, and, in fact, a majority of poor whites don't even think Negroes are discriminated against.

The affluent group is right at the opposite pole from the unaffluent. They hold least of all with the old stereotyped beliefs, voice the least objections to contact with Negroes, and feel most keenly the heavy toll discrimination has taken on the lives of Negroes.

It is a fair conclusion that the gulf between the affluent and unaffluent segments of white society in America is now as wide as that between Negroes and the unaffluent whites, between the Deep South whites and the Negroes. If there are two races in this country poles apart on the race issue, then it is equally true there are two white societies just as far apart.

The implications of this central finding are far-reaching. For the future lies clearly with the growth of affluent society. The thrust of education, mobility, and rising incomes will produce fewer backlash whites and far more affluent whites.

It has been claimed that higher-income white people can afford to hold more enlightened views about the Negro quest for equality and justice because Negroes are no immediate threat to the more privileged groups in white society. It certainly is a fact that people who live in $40,000 and above homes are not about to be inundated by Negro migration. But it should be pointed out that Bronxville, New York, and Deerfield, Illinois, and Grosse Pointe, Michigan—all among the most affluent communities in America—have been beset with fierce racial controversies over the past few years. Such communities contain prejudice but they also contain powerful forces for change.

The line of reasoning that the more privileged have bought their way out of the oncoming path of the Negro revolution also ignores a critical element: the role of education in raising the levels of understanding among whites. It can now be proved that a college education tends to make a person more international in his outlook, more tolerant of nonconformist views, and more aware of injustice to Negroes.

It became popular in 1966 among the Stokely Carmichaels and the Floyd McKissicks to tell the white liberals that their role in the civil-rights movement had become peripheral at best. In terms of the direction of the civil-rights organizations, such a conclusion was correct. Negroes in the future will command the line organization jobs and decision-making in the Movement. Liberal white contributions will be monetary and advisory at best.

But in a much broader sense, the civil-rights movement will depend more than ever before on affluent white society. For the only way in which the 90 per cent white majority will ever make a frank confrontation with itself to tear down the barriers of reality that still stand in the way of the fruition of Negro aspirations is for large numbers of whites to press for change in white society.

The instrument of government is powerful and still the major force in white society that Negroes must depend upon. But the support and impetus and pressure on government and upon all white institutions must come from the better educated, the more privileged, the affluent whites, or it will never come at all.

It is no happenstance that in the *Newsweek* survey, it was a Washington banker who said, "Negroes are only human. The general tone that has been ingrained into the white American is that he is a shade better than other people of the world. He can't get over the shock that he is no better or worse." An affluent lawyer on the North Shore of Chicago, living in one of the most prosperous suburbs in America said this, "If we had no march on Selma we would have had no civil-rights law. If we didn't have the sit-ins, nothing would have been done in behalf of the Negro." A prominent television newscaster in Chicago observed, "It makes no difference to me what a person's color of skin is. If he wants to move into my neighborhood, I would not object to it. The reactions of . . . unscrupulous real estate men would concern me more." And a businessman in a fashionable suburb of Detroit, said, "Their brains are the same. It's not like some brains are black and some are white."

The impact of education and rationalism is having a telling effect on white society in America, struggling as it is with its own emotions and conscience on the question of civil rights. The new alliance could well put the Negro—the least privileged—and the affluent whites—the most privileged—on the same side, as progenitors of change. Perhaps the greatest irony of the entire Negro revolution is that it has become a catalyst that is forcing white America to search its soul and seek out new solutions to an ancient injustice.

"Be Not Afraid"

THE TEMPERATURE HAD REACHED 96 *degrees one muggy Sunday morning in July of 1966 when the ancient green Buick pulled away from the courthouse square in Marion, Alabama, and headed out of town on State Highway 14. Inside were the Rev. Liona Langford, a circuit-riding Negro preacher, his wife Nannie, and the three youngest of their thirteen children— Edna, a poised 15-year-old in a white cotton dress and new high heels; Robert, 13, dressed in a black suit with a clip-on tie; and bouncing energetically on the back seat, Kenneth, 6, also in a dark suit with a clip-on bow tie.*

As the Buick swung off the highway onto a red-dirt road running back into the tall pine, cotton and corn country of Perry County, it sputtered and died on a steep grade, a broken fanbelt whanging against the hood.

The Reverend Langford, who had already delivered one sermon that day, got out and shook his head in disgust. But a battered Ford came by and Langford struck a fifty-cent bar-

gain with its two Negro occupants to carry him and his family to his next stop, the Simpson Chapel, six miles out of Marion.

A solemn, unsmiling man in his late 50s, Langford waited patiently in the small concrete-block church while the women and children of the congregation took their places (only four men were present) and his daughter Edna distributed cardboard fans, courtesy of the Tubbs Funeral Service in Marion.

"Sometimes we forget that God made us for a purpose," Langford began his sermon in a flat monotone. "Sometimes fear overtakes us. Probably it is hard to forget this fear, especially when I am in danger as an individual.

"At night sometimes I become so frightened I turn to childhood prayers. Remember the one that starts: 'Now I lay me down to sleep'? Sometimes I recite this—I don't know about you—because I'm so afraid in these times of peril.

"But there is always His voice who comes to me and tells me: 'Be not afraid, it is I.'"

The congregation stirred restlessly. There was really no need to tell them what the peril was. It was The Man, the white man who had ruled their lives for generations. In the rural South it has always been thus; in no other place in the United States has the Negro been so fear-ridden, so subservient. And it has often been the worrisome task of the Negro's church to guide him and counsel him in the strange new quest for freedom.

The Reverend Langford makes it plain in his sermons that he puts his fundamental trust in God. But he recognizes that there are also times when the Negro must act on his own. In 1965, accompanied by Martin Luther King, he led a march on the courthouse in Marion, to protest the police killing of a Negro demonstrator. A gentle man who has little taste for violence, Langford was deathly afraid. "I sure wouldn't want it to happen again," he told a Newsweek reporter who visited him in his spare parsonage behind his home church, Zion Chapel, *in Marion. "We walked toward the jail. The state highway patrol chief asked the sheriff what he wanted the state troopers to do, and the sheriff said, 'Get 'em.' They came running into the crowd swinging billy clubs. It's a wonder I survived."*

The march seemed to accomplish little at the time, yet it may have accomplished much. "Marion will never be the same," said Langford. "It may appear the same on the surface, but deep down the white man knows he can't keep things the way they were."

Guiding his flock has required a great deal of personal sacrifice from Langford. A good many Negro pastors in the South eke out an existence by taking on weekday jobs like farming, or barbering. But Langford has refused to do this; he spends much of his spare time accompanying his parishioners in their dealings with white men, to quiet their fears. As a result he makes only $65 a week from his various parsonages and his wife is obliged to can voluminous quantities of peas, tomatoes and jellies against the inevitable wintertime when the donations at the churches fall off. Eight of his children have gone to Michigan to seek factory work and a better life in the North.

What does he counsel his people? "All I want is for my people to lose their chain of fear," he said. "They have the ballot now, but some won't use it. They come to me and say, 'If I vote, The Man will fire me or get me off his place.' I'm not looking for any change unless the people of Alabama themselves do what is necessary."

As a simple rural preacher, Langford does not profess to know what the answers to the plight of his people may be, but he is certain that they must be found. "In my opinion, change must come, and rapidly before it is too late," he said. "I see a gleam of light. But we need something more to relieve the tension. The Negro should be welcome in America as an individual, and he is not."

CHAPTER 7

The Negro Family

SLAVERY AS IT EXISTED in America more than a century ago was an ugly stain on the bright promise of the New World that may never be fully erased. Human bondage itself was bad enough. By the hundreds of thousands blacks were wrested from their homes in Africa, stripped and branded, and ferried in festering, death-ridden slave ships to America, where they were whipped from their beds into the cotton fields of the South by daybreak, whipped at their work under the hot sun, and driven home again like cattle by night. But the degradation did not stop there. The Negro slaves in America were regarded as chattels, with no more status under the law than animals. They could not be taught to read or write, nor could they even meet with each other except in the presence of a white man. More important, from a sociological point of view, marriage was not recognized, and many Negro women were simply ordered by the slave master to mate with men for whom they had little or no emotional attachment. On top of that, women and children could be—and continually were—

143

sold off for the further enrichment of the slaveholder. The inevitable result was an almost non-existent family life among the Negro slaves; indeed there is every evidence to suggest that many slave owners openly promoted the breakup of the Negro family, so that the engulfing waves of imports from Africa could never unite in rebellion.

Today some authorities contend that the tattered fabric of Negro family life, surviving to this day principally among ghetto Negroes of America's great cities, is the single most important problem facing the black man—far more basic and critical than his need for better education, jobs, and housing. Some even go so far as to suggest that the Negro's struggle for equality can never really succeed unless and until his shattered family structure is repaired.

The principal exponent of this view, or at least the man most prominently identified with it, is Daniel Patrick Moynihan, a former Assistant Secretary of Labor under Presidents Kennedy and Johnson. One of the new breed of young men who bring considerable social consciousness and training to public life, Moynihan, in March 1965, produced for the White House a pamphlet entitled *The Negro Family: The Case for National Action** that was at once a devastating portrait of the Negro family, and the sharpest kind of challenge to current thinking about the so-called Negro "problem."

Wrote Moynihan:

"At the heart of the deterioration of the fabric of Negro society is the deterioration of the Negro family.

"It is the fundamental source of the weakness of the Negro community at the present time.

"There is probably no single fact of Negro life so little understood by whites. The Negro situation is commonly perceived by whites in terms of the visible manifestations of discrimination and poverty, in part because Negro protest is directed against such obstacles, and in part, no doubt, because these are facts which involve the actions and attitudes of the

* U.S. Government Printing Office, Washington, D.C. Price: 45 cents.

white community as well. It is more difficult, however, for whites to perceive the effect that three centuries of exploitation have had on the fabric of Negro society itself. Here the consequences of the historic injustices done to the Negro Americans are silent and hidden from view. But here is where the true injury has occurred. Unless this damage is repaired, all the effort to end discrimination and poverty and injustice will come to little."

Moynihan then proceeded to back up his contention with some impressive government statistics. Nearly a quarter of all urban Negro marriages eventually break up, he reported, compared with about 8 per cent of white marriages. At any given time, some 36 per cent of young Negroes are living in broken homes. Similarly, nearly a quarter of Negro births are illegitimate (vs. about 4 per cent for whites) and the true figure may well be higher; one confidential survey in Baltimore showed that 62 per cent of first-born Negro babies in 1965 were illegitimate. And—a critical point—nearly a quarter of all Negro families are headed by women.

Moreover, in another study to be published this year by the Federal Government, Sociology Prof. Daniel O. Price of the University of Texas reported that "significant increases" can be expected over the next few years in the number of Negro families headed by women. Price based his estimate on the fact that Negro women tend to stay in school longer, and have a far better record than men in finding good jobs (many of them as schoolteachers). "If the Negro is to be integrated into American society as an equal member," Price concluded, "it seems that greater efforts must be made to improve the status of the Negro male."

Actually, these portraits of the unstable, matriarchal character of Negro society broke no really new ground. Nearly three decades ago, E. Franklin Frazier drew much the same sort of picture in his classic study of the Negro family,* and the basic problem has long been recognized in academic circles. The

* The Negro Family in the United States, The University of Chicago Press, 1939.

chilling part lay in the estimates that the problem is worsening. Moynihan, for one, did not contend by any means, that all, or even the majority, of Negro families have deteriorated. Like Frazier before him, he found a rising middle-class group of Negroes that is steadily growing stronger and more successful. But he also found a widening gulf between these Negroes and the disadvantaged lower classes. "By contrast," Moynihan wrote, "the family structure of lower-class Negroes is highly unstable, and in many urban centers is approaching complete breakdown."

Obviously this was potent stuff, and the Moynihan Report, as it was more popularly called, very soon became explosively controversial. Moynihan himself had recommended that the Federal government do nothing less than adopt a brand new national policy, directing all its energies toward a new national goal: the establishment of a stable Negro family structure. And President Lyndon Johnson seemed to embrace the idea when he delivered a speech (drafted in part by Moynihan) at Howard University on June 4, 1965. Said the President: "Unless we work to strengthen the family, to create conditions under which most parents will stay together—all the rest: schools, and playgrounds, public assistance and private concern, will never be enough to cut completely the circle of despair and privation." There was even talk that the President planned to use the Moynihan Report as the government's official analysis of the Negro problem at the White House Conference on Civil Rights scheduled to be held in June of 1966.

Yet despite this impressive send-off, the Moynihan Report now entered upon a curious and perilous kind of odyssey. For one thing, the very existence of the report and the name of its author were not acknowledged by Washington for some months after the report's completion. The first tentative story on it was leaked to *The New York Times* on July 19, 1965, and the first comprehensive summary appeared in the August 9 issue of *Newsweek* in that year. And very soon author Moynihan found himself under attack from some elements of the press, the Negro civil rights groups and even the government (because Moynihan's conclusions stepped on the toes of those Federal agencies concerned with public welfare). He offended many liberals, to whom the goal of integration is far more important than an abstraction like family stability. But plainly, Moynihan's report caused the greatest anguish to the Negro community itself, for at the very time when the Negroes were pressing hardest to overcome white resistance, the report seemed to place most of the onus for his troubles on the Negro himself. Conceivably, it could be an excuse to slow down integration— a convenient "out" for the white man. Martin Luther King saw this very clearly when he stated: "The danger will be that problems will be attributed to innate Negro weaknesses and used to justify neglect and rationalize oppression." Such civil-rights leaders as Bayard Rustin, John Lewis and Floyd McKissick also joined in the condemnation. Privately, some ideologists in the Negro protest movement even insinuated that Moynihan had forsaken his liberal background to become an out-and-out racist.

The upshot was that the White House said no more about the matter, and the question of the Negro family was dropped from the agenda of the June White House Conference on Civil Rights (the Moynihan Report was not even among the Conference's official working papers). Having left the government in July of that year (to be an unsuccessful Democratic contender for City Council president in New York), Daniel Patrick Moynihan retired to write a book on the Negro family and to become director of the Harvard-MIT Joint Center for Urban Studies.

SOCIOLOGISTS ALWAYS GO BACK to slavery as the root cause of Negro family problems, though precisely why slavery in America was "the most awful in the world" (to use one expert's description) is not so clear. Nowhere else were slaves regarded as mere chattels without status in society. Authorities in the field are fond of pointing to Brazil, where slavery developed under a feudal Catholic society in a much different way than in America. In Brazil the slave could legally marry, and his family was not broken up for sale; he had at least some independence of action, and he could earn money to buy his freedom. Thus today the Brazilian Negro—while often poor and relegated to menial jobs as are Negroes in the United States— nevertheless enjoys complete acceptance in his country's society. Stanley M. Elkins, in his comparative study of slavery,* suggests that without a feudal tradition and an all-powerful church, American slavery was ruled by the profit motive— with the Negro the loser.

Yet slavery was only the beginning of the Negro American's troubles. With emancipation, a Negro family structure began to emerge, but in a far different form from that of the American white family. Under slavery it had been the practice of profit-minded slaveholders to accord Negro women somewhat preferred treatment, since they were the childbearers who could produce more slaves (another reason was that many white masters liked to dally with the Negro women themselves). The net result of this, as E. Franklin Frazier has pointed out, was to elevate women to the dominant role in family and marital relations—the beginning, really, of the Negro's matriarchal society. Emancipation when it came in 1863 served only to accelerate this trend. Under the profusion of Jim Crow laws that flourished in the South during Reconstruction, it was the Negro male who was most humiliated and driven to subservience. The threat of being lynched if he so much as sassed a white, eroded the Negro male's manhood, and it certainly inhibited his emergence as a strong father figure in the Negro family. So it was that Negro society entered the twentieth century already bearing the seeds of its own destruction—only to encounter another circumstance that all but completed the process for many Negro families. This was the urbanization of the Negro.

Urbanization has also been a phenomenon of white society in this country, but the Census figures for the Negroes are dra-

*Slavery, The University of Chicago Press, 1959.

matic. In 1910 there were 7.1 million Negroes living in rural areas of the United States and only 2.7 million in the cities. By the 1960 Census, that picture had changed completely; there were 13.8 million Negroes living in the cities and only 5.1 million on the farm. The effect of urbanization, in many large cities, was to pour wave upon wave of rural Southern Negroes into the grinding poverty and numbing despair of the slums. Already ill-equipped for their role as family leaders, many Negro fathers simply fled rather than face the fresh cultural and economic pressures of the slum. Left behind were mothers who were forced to work to feed their children, and who inevitably were tempted to promiscuity, spawning more children to grow up in fatherless homes and perpetuate the whole unhappy cycle.

Moynihan has observed: "Almost every wretched thing that pops into your mind when you think of the Negro ghetto is traceable to the condition of the Negro family. I'm not talking about all Negro families, but only the poorest. Even after allowances are made for differences in socio-economic status, the crime rates among Negro males are twice those of whites. The conclusion of any number of researchers is that a principal reason is the early absence of the father in so many poor Negro families." Indeed, Moynihan suggests that one source of racial strife in the slums is the failure of fatherless youths to adjust maturely to authority—that and their need to demonstrate their manhood. "One of the tragedies of life in the slums," he says, "is that so much of the aggressiveness exhibited there is really intended as reassurance for troubled young men who are not at all certain that they really are tough."

Newsweek's survey of Negroes clearly reinforces this bleak view of the Negro downtrodden. Illegitimacy is certainly not the easiest kind of subject to tackle by direct questioning. But 63 per cent of the rank-and-file Negroe sample admit they know someone who is an unwed mother, and 24 per cent admit that this someone is close to them, possibly in their own family. The survey indicates that Negro high-school drop-outs may run as high as 27 per cent, compared with the national average of 10 per cent. And such is the matriarchal character of Negro society today that nearly half the Negroes sampled say that—whether or not the father is present in the home—the mother has the sole job of raising the children.

The Negroes themselves are scarcely entranced by this circumstance. A Negro woman in Louisville, Kentucky, told the survey: "The children are very bad. A mother can't do a man's job." And Mrs. Revonne Young of St. Louis, Missouri, said this: "Children seem to have more respect for their fathers—it could be the tone of their voice." Some Negro men also recognize that female discipline may have its shortcomings. "Mamas are too soft," said a Negro in San Francisco, California, "they hate to whip the kids." And Charles Shonron of Detroit, Michigan, observed: "The children behave better when the daddy say it. I'm not going to tell them but twice. The mother will say it about six times before doing anything." On the other hand, it is perfectly obvious that a great many Negro mothers perform miracles of self-denial and devotion to keep their families together at all. "If it were not for some mothers," a Negro woman in South Carolina said simply, "I don't know what would become of the children in many families."

TO GET A CLOSER LOOK at the Negro family structure, *Newsweek* in the late summer of 1966 dispatched reporters into big-city slums across the United States. In Atlanta, one of them found Charlie Belle Perkins, 39, a tall, slender mother of five living on Walnut Street, a narrow littered lane in the slum section known as Vine City.

"This isn't a good neighborhood," Charlie Belle told her interviewer softly as she brushed at the dirt-spattered hem of her polka-dot dress. "I don't like nothin' about it. I just can't do better." Mrs. Perkins came to Vine City from another Atlanta slum four years ago with the father of her three youngest children (she has two older children by a previous "arrange-ment" who live with a cousin in Athens, Georgia).

"To tell the truth," she said, "I never been married. The sec-ond one, he was nice, but he was just too hot-tempered. He drank and had lady friends, and whenever I'd complain he'd start knockin' on the kids and me. He put me out three years ago and to tell the truth I was glad to see him go. I never did want to marry him. I was mostly just afraid of him."

Pregnant at the time and with nowhere to turn, Charlie Belle moved into a three-room, gray-shingle shack that has no gas or electricity, sharing it with an elderly Negro woman who looks after the children while she works. Charlie Belle toils as a sorter in a laundry, for which she earns $35 a week. Of this she pays $10 a week for rent and most of the rest goes for food and clothing. "We eat mostly chicken backs and necks and wings," she said, adding wistfully, "Sometimes I buys the whole chicken." But working at the laundry has at least one advantage; several times a month she bundles the children's clothes into a shopping bag and takes them with her to be washed and dried for free. In between she washes their clothes on an old-fashioned washboard in the bathtub.

Home for Charlie Belle and her brood is a study in squalor that not many whites ever see. The kitchen has a stained sink hanging precariously from the wall and no other furnishings whatever save a woodburning stove. The matron of the house occupies a middle room and in the front room is Charlie Belle's domain, a bare-floored cubicle stuffed with three beds and a dresser.

"What I really want is a better place to live, a better environ-ment," said Charlie Belle. "I'd like a quieter place for my chil-dren to grow up." But she knows from her own experience that this may never happen. "My father left when I was very small and my grandmother raised me on welfare. I guess I just got the wrong start off. I guess where I went wrong was just stay-ing with them men and never gittin' married. But I love my children. I'd really like for them to have a father. I really think it would help them. I have a friend who comes around, and whenever he's here, they're just as nice as can be. But he's married . . ."

Also on a Walnut Street, but this one in Chicago's West Side ghetto, lives Mrs. Catherine Dandridge, a bustling woman of 45 who occupies a six-room apartment hard by the noisy elevated tracks. Mrs. Dandridge has been subsisting on Aid to Dependent Children funds since 1950, when her husband left her while she was pregnant with her first child. Unable to find a job, she went on ADC and subsequently bore six other children to a succession of men, the last one of whom stayed around long enough to sire three of them.

When *Newsweek* visited Mrs. Dandridge, she had found a job as a nurse's aide in a hospital for a take-home pay of $55 a week. The father of her last three children contributes $70 a month, and the Cook County Department of Public Aid $115 a month.

"The welfare department was giving me $125," Mrs. Dandridge complained, "But they kept figuring and figuring my budget until they figured it down." And she made it plain that her world is a world of everlasting reckoning of dollars and cents. "Buying seven pairs of shoes is something," she said. "I have to buy very cheap shoes, and then they all tear again in a month. But I don't have enough money to buy better shoes, even though they would last longer. The welfare people never pay your whole bill. My light bill runs about $11 or $12. They allow me about $7 or $8. Well, it don't matter what they allow. The bill still has to be paid. So I have to take it out of the food or clothing budget."

Mrs. Dandridge is very much aware that the children suffer most from her kind of life. Her teenage son will probably drop out of high school, she said, because she can't provide him any spending money. And her eldest daughter, who is twelve, bears the brunt of keeping the family going while her mother works. "She has to get them all ready for school," said Mrs. Dandridge. "Sometimes the littler ones are late or sometimes the older one is so busy with the younger ones or is so tired she is late. Then they get suspended, and they say I have to come in. Well, I'm working so I can't always go right in. I tried to explain that to the school but they won't listen. So the children have missed a lot of school." But the real fault, Mrs. Dandridge contends, lies with the welfare people. "They are always figuring my budget," she said. "They keep me dependent on them all the time. Because you're not making much money, they figure you're not supposed to live."

Newsweek also visited Negro families where the father was present and actively directing the destiny of his wife and children. In many cases the fathers and mothers in these families sprang from the same disrupted backgrounds as the broken families, yet somehow they had persevered. Why, is not easy to fathom—unless the answer is some innate sense of determination, or conviction.

Take the case of Alfred Foster, a brawny Negro laborer of 34 who lives with his wife and eight children in a dingy four-room flat on the same Walnut Street in Atlanta as Charlie Belle Perkins. Both Foster and his plump wife Jeanette, 30, come from homes that were broken up when they were children. As a result, Foster got no farther than the second grade in school, while his wife managed to hang on until the sixth grade.

Yet Foster has no thought of abandoning the struggle, and his fiercest determination is to see that his children stay in school. "I'd like for them all to finish high school," he said, "even if they can't go on to college."

When *Newsweek* visited Foster, all eight of his children were crowded into one room, furnished with two double beds and a cot. "We have two more rooms," said Mrs. Foster somewhat apologetically, "but we can't use them because the rats are so bad." The parents sleep in a remaining room that also serves as a parlor, its double bed and two cheap couches covered with flower-print covers. A battered gas heater sits in the mouth of the fireplace, and the mantel serves as a makeshift medicine cabinet. On a small dresser is a dime-store picture of President Kennedy and Jacqueline, and a can of Hot Shot fly spray.

"I'd like to get a house in some nice, quiet section," said Foster, echoing the sentiments of so many Negroes. "This place isn't fit for raising children." But Foster only makes $90 a week as a construction laborer when he can get work, and $47.50 of that goes for rent. As a substitute for better housing, he enforces a tight discipline on the children.

"You bet I'm strict," he said. "I'm about as strict as a poor father can be. I want my kids to be respectable and presentable wherever they go." The Fosters hold periodic family discussions "about doin' right," and the older children are obliged to report what they have been learning in scohol. "I don't know if what they're sayin' is right or wrong," Foster lamented. "All I can do is listen and say 'uh-huh.'" But he is determined that so far as it is in his power, his children will have their chance in life. "I got seven boys," he said soberly, "and I sure would like for one or two of them to be somethin'. I know they can't all make it, but if only one or two of them could be somethin'. . ."

IF THE PLIGHT OF THE NEGRO family is granted, the much larger question is what can be done about it. And on that score, unhappily, there are as yet no certain answers. For years, reformers have looked to education as the first hope of elevating the black man in America. But the massive study of U.S. education submitted by the Coleman group in 1966 went a long way toward dispelling that notion.

As we saw in an earlier chapter, Coleman was concerned primarily with finding out how well each pupil in the U.S. public schools "is equipped at the end of school to compete on an equal basis with others, whatever his social origins." On this score, he found that Negro children (and, it should be said, American Indians, Mexican Americans and Puerto Ricans as well) trail well behind the average white child both at the

start in elementary school and most of all in the final grade of
high school when the great majority are ready to go out into
the world on their own. But Coleman found additionally that
differences in school facilities, such as the number of books in
the library or the age of the buildings, count hardly at all in
the final result. Most of the variation in student achievement
lies within the same school; there is very little variation between schools. The implications of the Coleman findings are
all too clear. It hardly matters what school a Negro child goes
to. He starts school with a serious educational deficiency. And
as the U.S. public education system is presently constituted—
that is, largely segregated—almost nothing in his school experience overcomes that deficiency. Or as Coleman, cutting to the
heart of the matter, has put it: "The sources of inequality of
educational opportunity appear to lie first in the home itself
and the cultural influences immediately surrounding the home;
then they lie in the schools' effectiveness to free achievement
from the impact of the home. . . ."

Moynihan contends that the Coleman Report patently reinforces his own view of the Negro family. "This means simply
that the schools cannot repair the damage that is done within
the broken family," he said. It also appears to raise a serious
question about what direction the Negro struggle for equal
schools should take.

So long as the schools remain largely racially segregated and
culturally homogeneous, the Negro child's disadvantage is
merely perpetuated. If he always goes to school with his own
kind, he never has the opportunity to broaden his achievement.
Coleman and other educators have therefore suggested the
possibility of new kinds of educational institutions—perhaps
educational parks that would bring together pupils from all
walks of life and improve the achievement not just of the
minorities, but of all children. As for the Negro family problem, Coleman has proposed substituting an educational environment for the family environment of the disadvantaged—
by starting school at an earlier age and holding classes from
early to late in the day.

Moynihan, himself a product of a poor, broken family who was raised in Hell's Kitchen and other New York slums, also has called for programs to improve the level of Negro education. But it seems desirable to him to attack the family problem at its source. As part of a new national policy directed toward reweaving the fabric of Negro society, he has suggested, for example, that aid to dependent children, which can and often does encourage irresponsibility in the father and promiscuity in the mother, might instead be turned into family allowances that would encourage families to stick together.

Another angle of attack is already under way. This is Project Head Start, one of the most enlightened so far of the government's anti-poverty programs. The task of Head Start is to provide three-to-six-year-old children from the poorest of America's neighborhoods with educational, social and cultural training, as well as medical attention, precisely so they can enter kindergarten or the first grade of elementary school on a level with more privileged children. At the beginning of Head Start in 1965, more than a half-million children (not all of them, of course, Negro) participated in an eight-week summer session. In 1966 the program was expanded to include a year-round operation, with some 200,000 additional children taking part in this. Head Start has drawn criticism in the South and it has had trouble reaching children in the so-called "hard core" of poverty-stricken families, which unhappily includes many Negro families. A survey in late 1966 also showed that largely because of poor teachers or poor curriculum, the benefits of Head Start training can wear off quickly after the child enters school. But the survey also showed that Head Start creates an unmistakable "thirst" for knowledge; plainly it is a strong stride in the right direction.

Most encouraging now are signs that the Negro's foremost leaders—however abhorrent the Moynihan statistics may be to them—are beginning to acknowledge the problem. Roy Wilkins, executive director of the NAACP, reiterated to *Newsweek* that the majority of Negro families are "stable, law-abiding and God-fearing" (a point, of course, that Moynihan does not dispute). The Negro, said Wilkins, cannot be blamed for the condition in which he finds himself. But Wilkins went on to say this: "I think we're going to have to come to a consideration of Negro life and the Negro family structure. We can't go on covering the weaknesses of the Negro family." And Martin Luther King himself has said: "Family life not only educates in general, but its quality ultimately determines the individual's capacity to love. The whole of society rests on this foundation for stability, understanding and social peace."

Obviously there can be no easy solution to the human havoc wrought by centuries of discrimination against the Negro. Presumably what would be needed would be a program more massive than current anti-poverty measures—directed principally at stamping out the breeding ground of family strife in the big-city ghettos. And that surely is a task almost as formidable as ending discrimination itself. Perhaps the best evidence of this came in August of 1966 when a Senate subcommittee held hearings on the plight of American cities. A parade of Negro witnesses, some of them now distinguished men, spent many hours telling tales of the almost unrelieved iniquity of the ghetto—where stealing and cheating are not regarded as wrong, where children become dope peddlers in their teens, and where mothers sleep with the butcher or the grocer to get enough food for the family. The dimensions of the task was summed up by Arthur Dunmeyer, a product of New York's Harlem who has spent nearly half his life in reform school and prison. "You have," said Dunmeyer, "to tackle this problem by problem, individual by individual, block by block."

"All I Can Say Is I'm Sorry"

WEST FULTON HIGH SCHOOL *squats in decaying, colon-naded majesty at the crest of a blacktop hill in Atlanta's heavily Negro west side. Three years ago West Fulton was almost all white; now it is almost all Negro and bursting at the seams. Some 1,756 students jam every day into a school originally designed for 1,100. Many have to sit on the window sills, the radiators and the filing cabinets in their classrooms. Some rooms serve two different classes at the same time, with the teachers vying for attention and the students scribbling math and English exercises on the same blackboard. Even the library and the cafeteria have given way to classes.*

Overcrowded as it is, West Fulton is all the world to Roseann Pope, 21, a slight, attractive Negro who teaches 10th-grade English. Roseann has a natural empathy with her underprivileged, bored, hard-to-manage students, for she comes from their own environment. Born in Atlanta, she scarcely remembers her mother and never knew her father. "I think he died in jail somewhere," she told a Newsweek *interviewer in 1966. Roseann was raised by an uncle and aunt in Kentucky and attended Howard University, where she started out majoring in French but quickly switched to English education. "I did some research on the quality of Negro teachers," she explained, "and didn't like what I found. Many Negro students study one thing and take some education credits just in case. When they can't make it in what they want, the just-in-case becomes their profession. That's why you have second-rate teachers."*

Roseann is only in her first year as a teacher, and at the outset she was almost in despair trying to keep control of her restless charges ("Sometimes you practically have to stand on your head to keep their attention for five minutes"). But with infinite patience and tact she has won their respect and boasts that she has had to expel only two of the most obstreperous boys. And she has had to break up only one fight.

Roseann is well aware that, as the Moynihan and other reports have pointed out, Negro students carry a heavy handicap in their studies as a result of impoverished or broken homes. But she also thinks that Negro teachers—especially female teachers—may often aggravate the problem. "Some teachers will almost continuously call on the girls in their class to answer questions," she said. "How does this make the boys feel? Even if he studies he isn't called on. Over a period of time he gets the feeling that regardless of what he does, he won't be recognized. At home he has a henpecked father, and in school he's henpecked."

Roseann has found that home environment is particularly important when it comes to reading. Many of West Fulton High's students can read only at the second-grade level, and they never seem to improve. "We can have all kinds of reading labs and remedial reading courses and it won't make any difference," she said. "When the kids go home, they don't see anybody reading. They don't have any books or magazines in the home. Reading becomes something associated with the time they spend in school, when it should become a habit, like brushing your teeth."

By dealing gently with their mistakes and offering encouragement, Roseann has tried to build what she thinks her students need most: self-image. "Too many Negroes have been conditioned to being Negroes—to being nobody," she said. "They feel defeated. They feel they won't be able to get a job anyway, so why study? I try to convince them that everybody can't be an A student, but it's important to do the best they can."

Roseann feels quite strongly that she could use more help in her task. There should be smaller classes, she feels, more teaching materials, more blackboards, more audio-visual aids. "We don't need films made in the thirties that don't relate to the present problems," she complained. "They need to see Negro children in the films. And Negroes in better situations. Why show them all these films about poverty? They know what poverty looks like. They need to see and hear Negroes who have made it."

After hours, Roseann makes a practice of calling aside some of her problem students and delivering a special lecture that begins: "Do you realize that in two years you're going to be out of school? What are you going to do then?" Usually the response is a bowed head and a mumbled, "I don't know." But some resolve to do better. "They're perfectly honest about themselves," Roseann said. "Most of the time they just want attention. So many of them have six or eight brothers and sisters at home, or they have a job after school, and they just don't get any attention at home. I have one boy who works eight hours a day after school. I can understand why he might want to show off a little during school."

Roseann's overriding conviction is that the Negro children need an outlet for their latent talents, and she tries to provide it with a variety of outside projects. But inevitably there have been disappointments. As advisor to the school's drama club, she spent weeks drilling seven students for a production of the play, The Unguided Miss. *It had to be canceled when the auditorium was carved up to provide more classrooms. Rose-ann sadly apologized to her cast in these words: "For those of you who have been staying up late learning your parts, all I can say is I'm sorry."*

CHAPTER 8

A Home in the Service

SEVEN BATTALIONS OF U.S. MARINES were assaulting a North Vietnamese division in the hills of Quang Tri Province one hot July day in 1966 when a Negro soldier and a white soldier were brought before their commander for starting a fight with each other.

Nettled at this petty interruption of a deadly serious business, the commander—a Marine captain—stabbed a finger first at one man and then at the other.

"You aren't white, buddy," he barked, "and you're not black, either. Both of you are Marine green, and don't forget it."

This small episode in the midst of a flaming war points up a central paradox of the Negro American's search for equality. While Negro civilians struggle to overcome the antipathy and the prejudice of the white man in the streets at home, the Negro G.I. has found a haven in the U.S. armed forces. To be sure, racial discrimination can still exist on a man-to-man, low-echelon level of the armed forces, and it is still a harsh reality for many Negro servicemen when they venture off base. But it is safe to say that nowhere else in American society has the color line been so effectively blurred. In the services, the color of a man's uniform counts more than the color of his skin. All this began when President Harry S. Truman, with a stroke of the pen, abolished discrimination in the armed forces nineteen years ago. In July of 1948 he signed Executive Order No. 9981, which said in part: "It is the declared policy of the President that there shall be equality of treatment and opportunity for all persons in the armed services without regard to race, color, religion or national origin."

Some Negroes have suggested that the military could well serve as a model for integration in the rest of American society. Patently, though, the two systems—military and civilian life—are not analogous. The military is a regimented democracy whose very heart and soul is obedience to command through all ranks. Thus it is one thing to order desegregation in the armed services, and quite another to impose it on the amorphous mass of millions of white civilians. Even so, the U.S. military today serves as a useful and dramatic example in microcosm of how the Negro male can blossom and rise to his fullest potential when he is treated as an equal, and like a man.

To get at the Negro G.I.'s innermost feelings about his life in the service, about his sacrifice for a country that, in the main, doesn't accept him, and about the current struggle of his civilian counterparts for equality, *Newsweek* reporters in the summer of 1966 fanned out to military bases all over America, and deep into the jungles of Vietnam. Among the scores of Negroes in all ranks they talked to were some grizzled veterans who could remember well what the "old" military was like, before desegregation. One was M/Sgt. Ralph Tann, a 43-year-old recruiting supervisor at the Boston Army Base, who quit the Army in disgust in 1946, only to be recalled during the Korean War. "Negro units were getting the worst quarters and the worst equipment, and were considered a necessary evil by most commanders," Tann recalled. "They weren't permitted to fight; they were thrown into service and supply units."

Today there may be lingering remains of the old ways in some branches of the services and at some bases, but *Newsweek* found not too many complainers among the Negro G.I.s themselves. Instead it found a large measure of contentment, fulfillment and a zest for reaching higher goals. "You might say I'm military all the way," Air Force Capt. Randolph Sturrup, 27, told his interviewer as he fitted a white airman with false teeth in his dentist's office at Ellington Air Force Base near Houston. "I hope to make it for thirty years. It's a chance to improve yourself professionally." Staff Sgt. Seman Jenkins, a 13-year Air Force veteran also stationed at Ellington, said this: "In the service I have felt more a real part of the Great Society. I have been recognized as a man in every sense of the word."

Perhaps the best description of the change the services can bring came from Pvt. Luther Burke, 18, of Knoxville, Tennessee, a raw rookie who freely admitted he had been getting nowhere at home and spent most of his time hanging around with a street-corner gang.

"We would stand around," Burke recounted, "and when a white man would come by, we'd call him 'nigger.' That really gets 'um. Then we'd start prowling around looking for something to get into. I couldn't get a job other than washing dishes or shining shoes, so I didn't work much."

Then Burke's father persuaded him to join the Army in April of 1966; when *Newsweek*'s interviewer found him he was stationed at Fort Benning, Georgia. And Burke was already convinced that the black man gets a "square deal" in the U.S. Army. "I know he's treated better in here than he is in civilian life," said Burke. "In civilian life a Negro isn't judged for what he is. He's judged for being black. But when you're fighting, you're colorless." Once slack and out of shape, Burke was now hard-muscled and fifteen pounds heavier than when he entered service.

If the color line has become indistinct at bases in the United States, it has been all but obliterated by the smoke of battle in Vietnam. Over and over, Negro combat veterans in

Vietnam—and their white brothers-in-arms, too—testified that when the bullets are flying, when there is fighting to be done, color matters scarcely at all. Said Staff Sgt. James Davis, 26, the white leader of a Marine mortar battalion: "It does not make any difference to me if they are white, Negro, black or blue. We treat everybody the same, and we expect everybody to do his job." Pfc. Claude Weaver, Jr., a 22-year-old Negro who is an assistant squad leader in the First Cavalry Division, said this: "You get shot at, you get hit equally out here . . . and everybody knows it." Indeed, color may vanish so completely in the battle zone that Negroes themselves don't even think of it. Off the coast of Vietnam, Lt. (j.g.) Harold R. Wise, Jr., was genuinely startled when a *Newsweek* reporter asked if he felt any discrimination in the Navy. "I never thought about it . . . until you came aboard," said Wise. "I'm just one of the guys out here."

The Negro's status in the service is of special importance, because at mid-passage in the Negro revolution, Vietnam was an overriding national issue, and not all Negroes were convinced that their race was getting a fair shake in fighting it.

Newsweek's survey of rank-and-file Negro civilians established that they, like the Negro G.I., recognize the strides made by the armed forces in desegregating military life. By two to one they say Negroes get a better break in the services than in civilian life. They are even able to rate the various services, giving the Air Force the highest mark for its treatment of Negroes, then the Army, the Marines and finally the Navy (which until desegregation used Negroes mostly as mess boys). A majority of the Negroes approves of President Johnson's handling of the war, and only a minority of 18 per cent thinks the United States should pull out of Vietnam. Moreover, there is no question of where Negro civilian loyalty would lie if the United States got into another world war. Fully 87 per cent, compared with 81 per cent in *Newsweek's* 1963 study, say that their country is worth fighting for, even if it has not as yet granted them full equality. "America is the Negro's country, too," a woman college graduate from Cartersville, Georgia, told the survey. "She's not perfect, but we love her."

Yet that is not the whole story. The survey found that 43 per cent of rank-and-file Negroes think the draft laws are fair to Negroes, but it also found that a sizable 25 per cent do not think so. Moreover, disaffection with the draft reaches a thumping 58 per cent in the sample of Negro leaders, who are the opinion makers of the black community. In fact, the subject of the draft drew strong condemnation even from such temperate leaders as Martin Luther King, Whitney Young, Jr., and Bayard Rustin. "Segregated draft boards inevitably discriminate," said King. Both Young and Rustin felt that draft tests penalize the Negro for his environment and lack of education, casting those who are accepted into low-ranking, menial jobs. As Rustin put it: "A society first denies opportunity for education, and then judges the Negro entering any of the armed forces on the basis of education denied."

What are the true facts about the Negro's service to his country?

Negroes, who constitute 11 per cent of the nation's population, currently make up 9.5 per cent of all the armed forces—a figure that is obviously not out of line. But at the end of 1965, according to the last Defense Department study available, they made up 13.4 per cent of all the draftees inducted. And in Vietnam at the end of that same year, Negroes accounted for 12.5 per cent of all U.S. servicemen there—and 14.6 per cent of the battle dead. On an individual service basis, the Negro can come off worse. He makes up, for example, 13.9 per cent of enlisted men in the Army, which bears the brunt of combat. And he accounts for 22.1 per cent of the Army's enlisted dead.

If these figures seem disproportionate, there are explanations that—ironically—go back to the Negro's downtrodden status in American society. One reason why Negro draft numbers are high is that not nearly as many of them as whites get college deferments. In fact, many more Negroes might be in service if large numbers of them did not fail the induction tests. A special Defense Department study during an 18-month period from July 1964 to December 1965 showed that a whopping 67.5 per cent of 18-year-old Negroes failed the tests given for both draftees and enlistees (the comparable white figure was 18.8 per cent). The Defense Department study also revealed wide regional differences. In Washington State the failure rate of Negroes was only 25 per cent, but in South Carolina it was 85.6 per cent. In general, the Negroes fared best in the Middle West and Far West, poorest in the South. But the survey showed that Negroes still fall short of matching whites even in states where the educational opportunities for each are roughly equal. The conclusion of the study was that many schools have not yet overcome the environmental handicaps of the Negro, thus substantiating the view of the Coleman Report.

Military sources say that the major reason why there are more Negroes in Vietnam—and consequently more casualties—is that they volunteer for service there. Why? Because many Negroes, obliged to support poor families or relatives back home, simply need the extra money that war service can bring. They know that promotions to higher-paying ranks come faster in combat, and they are attracted by combat bonus pay, such as the extra $55 a month paid to paratroopers. There may also be another reason—again stemming from the Negro's status in American society—why he volunteers for hazardous duty: a need to prove himself. In Saigon a *Newsweek* correspondent reported: "Negroes tend to volunteer for tough duty in disproportionate numbers, as if they feel the need to prove their valor to themselves and to their race."

Whatever their reasons, the Negro G.I.s do not seem to see anything sinister in the fact that, percentagewise, they have carried a heavier share of the load in Vietnam. "Somebody's got to be here," shrugged Walter Foster, 32, an Aircraft Maintenance Helper Second Class on the carrier *Intrepid*. "We're all Americans." The Negro G.I.s also do not seem to resent the draft, recognizing as do the Negro civilians that educational handicaps play a part, but accepting that fact philosophically.

Some, with traditional service pride, even think that a taste of military life might do the complainers good. At Fort Ord, California, First Lt. Donald L. Holmes, a 30-year-old Army career man, told a *Newsweek* interviewer this: "A lot of these guys who just hang around poolrooms and street corners might get something out of the Army. Most of them wouldn't take an education if you offered it to them."

The truth, of course, is that Negro soldiers are no more enamored of war than white soldiers. They don't really want to be wounded, or killed. But they recognize that there is a job to be done, and they do not feel—as do many Negro civilians —that the black man has less to fight for in Vietnam. As Navy Chief Petty Officer Joseph Jones, commanding a group of Negro and white men at Da Nang, put it: "Most fighting men don't want to be here—not just Negroes. The only way you can look at it is that it is my country I am fighting for . . . whether you are black or white. It's my country, even if it is not perfect."

Perhaps because of his preoccupation with war, or because he is out of touch with events at home, the Negro G.I. exhibits a certain amount of malaise about the civil-rights struggle. Army Sgt. Joseph Connor in Saigon said: "The main thing is to do our job and get out of this damned country. Civil rights can wait, as far as soldiers are concerned." But the Negro servicemen admire Martin Luther King; like the Negro civilians, they tend to feel that his nonviolent approach is the right one. Almost to a man they reject the concepts of black power and black nationalism. As Navy Chief Petty Officer Joe Jones put it: "My people have been told all their lives that they are inferior. Now to have somebody tell them they are superior is a little silly. I don't think the black power movement will get far; most Negroes I know don't like it." From Navy man Walter Foster came this succinct dismissal: "Black power is a bunch of nuts."

It would be a mistake, of course, to assume that all is sweetness and light for the Negro in the armed forces, despite President Truman's order and despite all the undoubted progress that has been made. Privately, some Negroes complain that there can still be subtle forms of discrimination in the matter of promotions or work details or disciplinary punishment. Who can say, for example, what passes through a Southern white sergeant's mind when he confronts a work detail? Does he, consciously or unconsciously, hand out the dirtiest jobs to the Negroes in the detail? Some Negroes complain that they have received harsher punishment than whites for the same offense, or that they have been passed over in promotions when they felt they were superior to the white man who got the job. Often cited as evidence of discrimination is the comparative scarcity of Negro senior officers in the services, notably in the Navy and the Marines. One possible explanation advanced by Negroes themselves is that Negro officers too often are shunted into supporting or administrative posts, and don't get the command experience that leads to senior rank. Whatever the reason, Pentagon figures show that there is only one Negro general in all the services, Lt. Gen. Benjamin O. Davis, Jr., of the Air Force, who is also the son of a retired Army general. The Air Force has 16 Negro colonels and the Army 9, but the Marines have none, nor does the Navy have a single Negro officer of equivalent rank. The Army has 172 Negro lieutenant-colonels, the Air Force 61, the Navy 5 of equivalent rank, the Marines none. Indeed, the Negro seems underrepresented throughout the officer ranks. Of all white servicemen, 14.6 per cent are officers, but of all Negro servicemen, only 2.3 per cent are officers.

It is also true that Presidential fiat does not necessarily banish prejudice among all white soldiers. One Negro G.I. told of being assigned to a barracks that was otherwise all white. "I didn't have any trouble," he reported, "but I had to watch my step." In Vietnam, *Newsweek* reporters found two white soldies who said simply: "We're Southern boys. We don't mix with 'em." Occasionally there are tense moments between white and black in the services, sometimes in the heat of recreational games or in unguarded moments when a white will say something disparaging about the blacks in the presence of a

Negro. Most often, the Negro swallows his pride and allows the incident to pass.

But the Negro has a harder time trying to swallow the kind of treatment he may run into off base. Oddly enough, there is a sort of off-duty segregation even in Vietnam, where whites and blacks tend to seek out their own bars in Saigon, and to congregate in separate groups in rest camps. But this seems to be more personal choice than anything else. As one Negro G.I. chuckled: "We sometimes segregate ourselves from these white guys. We don't like their hillbilly music."

The story can be different in the States, especially the Southern states. Negro servicemen tell of the difficulty of finding off-base housing for their families, of finding a motel that will take them when they are traveling, even of finding an off-base barbershop that will give them a haircut. One Negro officer told of being denied gasoline in the South, but of having learned the trick of stopping when his gas tank was only half empty, so that if he was refused he had plenty left to get him to the next station. Others recalled the humility of having to separate from their white buddies and seek out a greasy spoon restaurant that would serve them, while their friends dined in a plush restaurant for whites. At Fort Benning, Georgia, rookie Luther Burke reported: "The signs are not around anymore, but they don't need them. The look them cats give you speaks louder than any signs they gonna put up." Burke would not leave his base, even on weekends, to frequent the gaudy, neon-lighted taverns and eating places lining Highway 27 into nearby Columbus, Georgia. "Man," he said, "I'm really afraid to leave the base. They almost killed one of my buddies in Phenix City (Phenix City, Alabama, is just across the Chatta-hoochee River from Benning and Columbus)." Burke's case may be extreme, but there can be little doubt that in areas where prejudice is still strong, the Negro serviceman's uniform is no guarantee that he will get better treatment off base.

There is, in any discussion of the Negro's role in the military, the touchy question of his performance under fire. In Vietnam, *Newsweek* correspondents encountered some white officers who were frankly critical of the Negroes. Said a white lieuten-ant-colonel in the special forces: "Negro officers have done a pretty good job as compared with Negroes in World War II and Korea. They are better qualified, better trained. But in spite of this, I would be reluctant to assign a Negro officer to lead a difficult counter-guerrilla operation. I don't feel that I could rely on his judgment in an adverse situation. I don't feel Negro officers have the tenacity or tiger instinct of some white officers."

Yet this same white officer admitted that it was a Negro officer who saved the day when the Special Forces camp at Pleime was under deadly assault in November of 1965. And the weight of the evidence is that the Negro—officer and en-listed man—has served with distinction in Vietnam; he is ad-mired for his physical stamina, his team play and his general performance under fire. No less an authority than Gen. Wil-liam C. Westmoreland, the U.S. commander in Vietnam, has said: "One of the great stories to come out of this war is the magnificent job being done by the Negro soldier."

Late in 1966, the U.S. Army published a book bearing heav-ily on the Negro's status as a soldier in World War II and his performance in combat.* One of a series of special studies by the Army's office of military history, the work was authored by Ulysses Lee, a Negro veteran of World War II who served for seven years as the Army's historical specialist on the Negro, and who is now a professor of English at Morgan State Col-lege. Lee finished his book some years ago, but the Army de-layed in publishing it, and in fact had some misgivings whether it should be released at all in the heat of the Negro's home-front revolution. For it could well feed the racial fires with its unvarnished recital of the Negro's poor treatment in World War II, as well as the shortcomings of some Negro troops in combat.

* *United States Army in World War II, Special Studies, The Em-ployment of Negro Troops.* U.S. Government Printing Office, Wash-ington, D.C. Price: $7.75.

It is important to remember, of course, that this was before the Truman desegregation order of 1948. Thus Lee recounts that Negro policy in the Army stemmed from post-Civil War practices, replete with Jim Crowism in the assignment of separate barracks, denial of promotions, and so forth. But in justification he writes that neither the Federal government nor the Army felt that in time of war the armed forces should take on the added task of setting a sociological model for the nation.

In military operations, discrimination wore another face: The great bulk of Negro troops were assigned to the humdrum tasks of building roads, driving trucks, or running bakeries and laundries (which for the most part they did very well). Those Negro soldiers who did get into combat were often poorly led by white officers who had little or no taste for the job and little or no faith in their men. At high levels of command, some officers thought the Negroes should not be committed to combat at all.

With all this, Lee does not attempt to gloss over the Negro failures that did occur in World War II. He recounts, for example, how the Negro 93d Infantry Division came to grief in the Pacific largely because a single company, encountering a handful of Japanese on Bougainville, panicked and began firing in all directions, killing and wounding some of its own men. After this and other incidents, Lee writes, the 93d was not again "employed for any tactical missions other than minor ones." Similarly he describes the frustrations and failures of the 92d Negro Division in Italy, where it repeatedly retreated from objectives and in some cases become so unruly that at least one unit was disarmed and placed under arrest.

In Lee's recital, there are tales of great individual heroism on the part of some Negro troops. He recounts how the 99th Fighter Squadron, the first Negro pursuit group in Italy, went on to great fame after some early combat troubles. He cites officer comment that what happened to elements of the 92d and 93d Divisions was no more than could happen to any green, untried troops. He comes back again to the question of poor leadership. But the real answer seems to be summed up best in a letter quoted by Lee and written in 1945 by the late Dr. Walter L. Wright, Jr., then the Army's chief historian. Wright wrote: "What troubles me is that anybody of real intelligence should be astonished to discover that Negro troops require especially good leadership if their performance is to match that of white troops. This same state of affairs exists, I think with any group of men who belong to a subject nationality or national minority consisting of underprivileged individuals from depressed social strata." So the real villain for the Negro in World War II was his blighted life, as it has been before and since. The special value of this episode, of course, is that it points up how things have changed with desegregation of the armed forces. Better trained and better led, but also more sure of himself, the Negro has performed outstandingly in Vietnam.

Today, Negroes themselves attest that any black man can probably find prejudice in the service if he goes looking for it. Undoubtedly some do—for officers who handle complaints from the ranks say that the majority of Negro gripes about unfair treatment prove, on investigation, to be unfounded. But there can be no doubt that many a Negro has found a home in the service, and the best evidence of that is the rate at which he re-enlists. In 1965 the re-enlistment rate for whites was 17.1 per cent. For Negroes it was 45.7 per cent.

The high re-enlistment rate of Negroes must certainly be a reflection not only of the superior treatment they get in service but of their disenchantment with the age-old pattern of discrimination when they get out. At Fort Ord, California, a *Newsweek* reporter found three career men who had gone through the experience of leaving the service, taking one look at civilian life and scurrying back in. One was First Lt. Donald Holmes, who enlisted in the Army in 1958 and left in 1961. "I had two years of college, I was articulate and well dressed," Holmes recalled. "I wanted to get out and get started. I had the drive, but not the outlet. I couldn't get the jobs and I could damn near tell why. It had to do with race. I'd call for an appointment about a job I knew was open, and when I'd get

there they'd say, 'I'm sorry, sir, this job is no longer open, but
we do have something in the janitorial field.' At twenty-five,
I saw no reason why I should accept a job as a garbage man.
I knew my potential was greater." Holmes re-enlisted after
only two months, went to Officer Candidate School and at
Fort Ord was a spit-and-polish company commander. Another
example was Sgt.-Major Garland R. Alston, a slight, 39-year-
old Negro from rural Arkansas who got into the Army in 1947
by eating bananas and drinking water all one day to make the
weight. He left in 1953 to work in Los Angeles as a furniture
and appliance salesman, living in the ghetto district of Watts.
"I stayed out about eighty days," Alston reported, "and I
missed the Army something terrible. I'd become used to a certain kind of life. But in Los Angeles, everyone around us was
the same race, the same type, the same character. I felt lost.
Here I was in the middle of my own people, and I felt lost."
The final case was that of Sgt.-Major Robert L. Renfro, 44,
who held the rank of captain when he was discharged in the
Pentagon's big economy wave of 1957. In less than ninety days
Renfro was so disenchanted outside that he was willing to
come back as an enlisted man.

Once in service, many Negroes feel they must strive to be
better than white soldiers—because they feel they are more
harshly judged. One outward manifestation of this is that Negroes often have the neatest uniforms and the shiniest boots.
As Lt. Donald Holmes put it: "My boots are polished every
morning. I won't come in with a growth of beard; I don't care
if I've been out all night and have a hangover. I shave. This is
important. When a civilian sees a G.I. who's drunk or sloppily
dressed, he thinks all G.I.s are like that. One bad apple spoils
the whole cart. When you think about it, this applies to how
some Caucasions think about Negroes, too."

And looking ahead to the day when they leave the service—
as many of them will—the Negroes are determined to have a
better life outside. Over and over, those who had dropped out
of school before entering the military told *Newsweek* they
were heartily sorry they had ever done so. Many now vow to

continue their studies under the G.I. bill of rights when they get out. A great many already are preparing for civilian careers by attending service schools or taking correspondence courses—in everything from television repair to law.

In this kind of mood, not many Negro G.I.s are likely to be happy with second-class status when they get home. It is true that they are not too concerned with the civil-rights struggle now. But they have savored a freer life in the armed forces, and they may well be in the forefront of the Movement when they shed their uniforms. This is especially true of the Vietnam veterans, who have been asked to fight and risk their lives for their country. Said First Sgt. Ollie Henderson, a 22-year career man fighting his third war in Vietnam: "I feel right now I've qualified myself for anything anybody else has." Navy Chief Joe Jones declared: "I don't think I'm going to have as much patience as I did before when I go home. Why should I?" And M/Sgt. Frederick Robinson, at a Special Forces camp in the Mekong Delta, spat bluntly: "When I get back, I'm as good as any son of a bitch in the States."

Epilogue

OUT OF ALL THE TUMULTUOUS EVENTS that have occurred in the Negro-American revolution since 1954, the overriding development has been the changing face of the revolution itself. Whether or not black power survives as a war cry of the struggle, the Negroes today are engaged in a frank search for power on a broader scale than ever before. Many speak of "green power"—economic power—and are busily preparing themselves for better jobs and opening new businesses of their own. As the off-year election of 1966 made plain, the Negroes are sharpening the potent tool of political power, demonstrating a growing sophistication in their ability to vote as a bloc, to switch allegiance from traditional Democratic to Republican when that serves their best interest, and even to help elect the first Negro United States Senator (from Massachusetts) and the first Negro sheriff in the South (Alabama) since Reconstruction. There is also power of a sort in the sense of racial status that is slowly but surely developing among the Negroes. Not by any means have they abandoned their age-old effort to imitate white America, to adopt a kind of "cultural whiteness" (as the sociologists label it). But many have come to feel for the first time that they can stand up as Negroes, without humility, without shame.

At mid-passage in the revolution, however, the road from equality under the law to equality in fact remains as tortuous as ever. Negro leaders must somehow resolve their internal conflict, for their struggle is difficult enough without wasting their energy fighting among themselves. They must by confrontation and demonstration keep their plight constantly before white eyes, but do this without inviting a more ruinous backlash. They must fight the kind of white cynicism manifest in lip-service accommodation and the search for the "house Negro." They must also guard against any flagging of spirit in their own people, a flagging born of years of weary struggle and—in a curious way—the very victories achieved so far.

Particularly in the North, Negroes move now with a greater degree of freedom in the general society, and by some everyday yardsticks of American affluence they almost have it made; more than 90 per cent of them have television sets and nearly 60 per cent own automobiles. But as we have already seen, the fruits of the civil-rights struggle have not been distributed equally, and there is a widening gulf between the middle-class Negroes who have benefitted the most and the poorer Negroes who have benefitted hardly at all (in the Northern slums, only 14 per cent own cars). Worried Negro leaders have detected among middle-class Negroes a mounting malaise, a growing disposition to settle for what they have gained so far. It is almost as if these Negroes were saying, "I'm better off than I ever was and I may not get any more, so let's stop." In a revolution dedicated to nothing less than full equality, such a sentiment is—to say the very least—dismaying. But there is also malaise of another kind among many of the poorer Negroes, in the ghettos and in the rural South. For these Negroes the march of civil rights has not fully erased the futility born of centuries of subjugation and despair. Field workers in the Movement attest that their hardest job often is to rally their own people and show them the way. As one put it: "Tactics and goals sound academic alongside all the work it takes just to organize."

There is, perhaps, another task of Negro leaders that is not often discussed openly. Many Negroes regard it as the rankest sort of Uncle Tomism to suggest that the blacks might try to help themselves more than they have. They argue (and quite correctly) that the Negro has been denied equality through no fault of his own, and that this monumental injustice must be rectified before he can break out of the vicious circle of poverty and deprivation that rules his life. In their view, to suggest otherwise is simply to play into the hands of procrastinating whites. Yet there is also a growing feeling among Negroes themselves that there is much they can do to further their own cause. In many U.S. cities they have banded together to clean up their neighborhoods, to discourage crime and to take an active interest in their schools. In the summer of 1966 one of the most prominent figures in the civil-rights movement, Solicitor General Thurgood Marshall, delivered a speech in New York that did not please all of his associates, but stated the case for self-help very clearly. "We have not," said Marshall bluntly, "developed in our young Negroes the determination that just to get by is not enough. We have got to convince them that they can't rely on the crutch or excuse of racial segregation and discrimination."

For whites the choices obviously get harder as the Negro's revolution penetrates deeper into their world. A great many whites already feel that the Negroes have pressed too far. But they have missed the essential point that the revolution is one of ever-rising expectations. A victory here simply whets the Negro's appetite for a victory there, and his revolt will not stop on some convenient plateau of half-accommodation or half-integration. As we have seen, the white world also is split along class lines; tolerance for the Negro is a great deal less among lower-class urban whites who want to protect their homes from his incursion than it is among middle- and upper-class whites who dwell far away in the peaceful suburbs. But no class of whites has yet resolved the dilemma of race in the only meaningful way possible—which is simply to welcome the Negro at every level of white society. However grudgingly, the white welcome mat has been extended to the Negro in the areas where it has caused the least anguish to whites, but it has hardly been extended at all in the area that matters most: housing.

There can be no doubt that housing is now the major sticking point of the Negro's revolution, the one over which the battles of the foreseeable future will be fought. There can be no doubt that the Negro needs and must have a Federal open housing law, as he has needed laws to help him reach toward equality in voting, public accommodations, education and jobs. Recognizing this, President Johnson early in 1967 submitted a new civil-rights bill to Congress—this one calling for gradual integration of housing over a period of three years. But there also is a growing conviction—among both blacks and whites —that the Negro will make very little further progress until the major blight on his life is eradicated. That is the ghetto. Almost everything bad about the Negro's plight is traceable to America's ugly, festering ghettos. The nearly ten million Negroes who live in them are the most poverty-stricken and the least employable. They have the highest crime rate and the lowest morals. They are the least contented and the most potentially explosive. Some years ago Dr. James Bryant Conant, the former president of Harvard, compared the manifold, proliferating evils of the ghetto with the piling up of inflammatory material in an empty building. At the time Conant warned that "potentialities for trouble—indeed possibilities of disaster—are surely there."* His words were prophetic, for as every American knows all too well, the ghetto building already has burst into fitful, sporadic fire. And one of the most certain convictions of the Negroes now is that it will continue to burn unless the inflammatory stuffing is removed.

In a nation dedicated since its inception to the rule of law

* *Slums and Suburbs,* McGraw-Hill Book Co., New York, 1961.

and justice, such a course is surely intolerable to both whites and blacks. It is sometimes easy to forget that, as Gunnar Myrdal noted decades ago in his classic *An American Dilemma,** Negroes share equally with whites the constitutional heritage of their country. When they were torn from their birthplace in Africa they brought with them no great cultural tradition; instead they simply adopted the democratic ideals of their homeland. Thus the majority of Negroes, no less than whites, would rather see a peaceful solution to their problem than one forged with bricks and bottles in the streets.

Yet the agonizing question remains: What can be done about the ghettos?

Martin Luther King believes he has an answer in his plan to organize ghetto Negroes throughout the United States to agitate for a better life. But not even King supposes that the battle can be won without many billions of dollars in support from the government. One encouraging sign is that the problem itself has been recognized at the very highest levels of authority. Such government projects as Demonstration Cities to rebuild the slums and Head Start to help disadvantaged children—indeed, many of Lyndon Johnson's Great Society programs—are examples of new attempts to get at the root causes of minority troubles in the United States. They are, of course, pitifully small as yet compared with the immensity of the problem. But that very immensity is now also becoming recognized. Looking back, it was the Urban League's perceptive Whitney Young, Jr., who in 1963 first proposed what he called a "Marshall Plan" of assistance for the Negro—a conscious effort to *include* the Negro in American society that would be commensurate with all the effort to *exclude* him. Young's proposal went largely unheeded at the time, but a good deal of current thinking has been in the direction of massive, crash programs to eradicate the evils afflicting the Negro—and most of these are in the ghetto.

For all its superficiality and failure to come to grips with the

* Harper & Row, New York, 1944, 1962.

critical question of police brutality, the 1965 McCone* study of the riot in Watts recognized the need for intensive, all-out programs in at least two areas—jobs and education. Even before the McCone report appeared, the Federal government had dispatched a task force to Watts to launch a broad-scale rehabilitation program that included make-work projects, youth training, help for small businesses, distribution of surplus food and clothing, more recreational facilities, and accelerated housing construction.

Similarly the White House Conference on Civil Rights of 1966, hopefully (and perhaps euphorically) subtitled "To Fulfill These Rights," set forth a multi-billion dollar plan to wipe out slum housing, equalize education and either put everybody to work or else provide a guaranteed income to those still unable to hold a job. In the fall of 1966, A. Philip Randolph announced the formal outlines of the so-called Freedom Budget that he had conceived and Negro leaders had long been talking about. As drafted by a biracial coalition of civil-rights, religious and labor leaders, it called upon Congress to enact a ten-year program, at a staggering cost of $185 billion, to improve the lot of all disadvantaged Americans—not just the Negroes. The Freedom Budget also included the guaranteed annual income, as well as proposals for increased Social Security and welfare payments.

To many troubled Negro leaders, the need for massive programs such as these has become self-evident; the problem is so vast that only the most daring and radical departures from accepted thinking will suffice to cope with it. As the NAACP's Roy Wilkins told *Newsweek,* the problem cannot be attacked "with a business-as-usual attitude or in 1988 we'll get to this —we need drastic steps." But it has also seemed to the Negro leaders that too much precious time can be wasted in study and proposal. In their view, there is a real danger that the

---

* Named for John A. McCone, former director of the CIA who headed the $250,000 investigation authorized by the state of California.

Negro problem can simply become a subject for conscience-salving diagnosis, to be dissected like a specimen in a laboratory, clucked over and deplored, and then forgotten. Said Roy Wilkins: "If you have an explosion in midtown New York, it's an emergency—you don't put up $250,000 to do a survey on it."

There are hard practical realities as well. The sheer cost of some of the proposals presupposes a national commitment on a scale unprecedented in U.S. history, save for the waging of war. A common remark among militant blacks and liberal whites is that the ghettos could be wiped out in no time if the nation earmarked the same amount of effort, brainpower and money to them that it has to the conquest of space or the war in Vietnam. Martin Luther King himself is fond of saying that a country with a Gross National Product in excess of $744 billion can easily afford the price. Undoubtedly there is a great deal of truth to all this. There is truth, too, to the assertion of Negro leaders that the attack on their problem *is* a war, to be waged on the same scale as an armed conflict. Yet such a commitment also presupposes a national will and purpose on the part of the great mass of American whites and their elected representatives in government. Unhappily for the Negro, the prospect of rallying that collective will any time soon seems quite remote (though, obviously, Negro leaders have every intention of trying). On the practical political level, the backlash vote of 1966 helped install sizable numbers of conservative congressmen who threaten even the modest goals of the Great Society. And there appears to be little disposition on the part of American whites to give the Negro any kind of special consideration. In the *Newsweek* survey, whites were asked if Negroes should not be given favored treatment in just one area of need: jobs. A thundering 90 per cent of them said "no."

As the Negro's revolution moved into 1967, there remained strong omens of hope in the Negro's enduring optimism, and the white's growing recognition of the injustice he has perpetrated far too long. But the immediate outlook is, unfortunately, bleak, for the alternatives to full equality are not very pleasant. Conceivably the civil-rights movement could bog down into an agonizing attrition in the streets—a circumstance that would only deepen the cleavage between the races and might even bring out those Negro extremists who have been stockpiling guns and plotting sabotage. Some civil-rights observers genuinely fear the evolvement of a sort of police state in which the whites would retire behind the barricades of prejudice and let law enforcement agencies contain the Negroes in their seething ghettos. For the white political power structure, the alternative is no less unpleasant. President Lyndon Johnson has committed himself too fully to racial equality to back down, but he also cannot tolerate continued uprisings in the streets. Responsive as they must be to the majority will of America, and dependent also upon the majority for election, political candidates may well be left to wonder which voice to heed—black or white. It would be a sorry day for America if any great number of those who govern should forsake the black, for as one Negro leader has put it: "If whites will never help Negroes, and cannot be forced to in terms of their own interests, then the cause of Negroes is hopeless."

Negro leaders, of course, do not view the cause as hopeless, nor do they intend to slacken their drive for freedom. Thoughtful Americans can only hope that it will be a peaceful quest, directed by a man like Martin Luther King, who more than any other Negro has the confidence and the trust of his people, and whose tactics and goals are closest to their wishes. Yet not even King believes that deliverance for the Negro is near at hand. He has estimated that his organizing drive among the ghetto Negroes will take at least five years; after that, he can't even guess how long it will take whites to respond to the demands of his organized legions. With dark undercurrents of distrust and tragedy still running strong on both sides of the color line, the inescapable conclusion is that race will remain an overriding issue in America for decades to come.

The Negro Questionnaire

Here are the questions as actually asked in the survey of Negro people on which this book is based:

1(a) I want to ask about how you feel you and your family are personally doing compared to three years ago. As far as your (work situation, etc.) goes, do you feel you are better off today than you were three years ago, worse off, or about the same as you were then?

(b) Now thinking ahead to five years from now, if you had to say right now, do you feel in your (work situation, etc.) you will be better off, worse off, or about the same as you are right now?

	(a) Today				(b) In Five Years			
	Better off	Worse off	About same	Not sure	Better off	Worse off	About same	Not sure
(1) Your work situation	—	—	—	—	—	—	—	—
(2) Your housing accommodations	—	—	—	—	—	—	—	—
(3) Your pay	—	—	—	—	—	—	—	—
(4) Being able to register and vote	—	—	—	—	—	—	—	—
(5) Being able to eat in any restaurant	—	—	—	—	—	—	—	—
(6) Being able to get your children educated with white children	—	—	—	—	—	—	—	—
(7) Being able to live in neighborhoods with whites if you want to	—	—	—	—	—	—	—	—
(8) Transportation to and from work	—	—	—	—	—	—	—	—

(c) All in all, compared with three years ago, do you think things for people such as yourself and your family are better, worse or about the same?

Better_____ Worse_____ Same_____ Not sure_____

(d) Why do you feel this way? Any other reason?

(e) As far as you personally are concerned, what do you feel are the two or three biggest problems facing Negro people that you feel something should be done about?

(f) What do you think ought to be done about it? (for each)

(g) Where is it most important to work on it—in Washington, here in the state, or right here in town? (for each)

2(a) In what trades or fields do you think Negroes are getting a better break these days as far as jobs go? Any others?

(b) What trades or fields do you feel are the worse as far as giving Negroes jobs? Any others?

(c) Do you feel that if you do the same work as a white man you will be paid the same as he will get for that work or will you probably get paid less?

Same pay_____ Less pay_____ Not sure_____

(d) Would you rather work for a company run by a white man or by a Negro, or doesn't it make any difference to you?

White_____ Negro_____ No difference_____ Not sure_____

(e) At work, would you rather work alongside mostly other Negroes, or would you rather work with a mixed group of whites and Negroes?

Mostly other Negroes_____ Mixed group_____ Not sure_____

(f) Have you or has anyone in your family been discriminated against in trying to get ahead on the job or in trying to get a job or not?

Discriminated against_____ Not discriminated against_____
Not sure_____

(g) What happened then? What was that? Anything else?

3 In general, if you were to get a house, or apartment (flat), the same as a white person, do you feel you would pay more rent or the same as the white person would pay?

Same_____ More_____ Not sure_____

4 Would you like to live in a private house, a housing project, or an apartment (flat)?

Private house_____   Housing project_____   Apartment (flat)_____
Not sure_____

5(a) In living in a neighborhood, if you could find the housing you want and like, would you rather live in a neighborhood with Negro families, or in a neighborhood that had both whites and Negroes?

Negroes_____   Whites and Negroes_____   Not sure_____

(b) Why do you feel this way? Anything else?

6(a) Do you feel that Negro children would do better or worse if they all went to a school along with white children today?

Better_____   Worse_____   About the same_____   Not sure_____

(b) Would you like to see all Negro children in your family go to school with white children or not?

Go with whites_____   Not go with whites_____   Not sure_____

(c) Of course, because of where they live today, many Negro children go to all-Negro schools and whites to white schools. Would you like to see children in your family be picked up in buses every day so they could go to another part of town to go to school with white children or would that be too hard on the children?

Picked up by bus_____   Too hard on children_____   Not sure_____

(d) Have any young boys or girls in your family dropped out of high school?

Yes_____   No_____

(e) Well, do you think they ought to drop out of school like that if they want to, or do you think they ought to stay in school?

Ought to drop out if want to____   Ought to stay in____   Not sure____

(f) All in all, do you feel your children (children in your family) are receiving as good an education as white children around here get, or are they getting not as good an education?

As good as whites_____   Inferior education_____   Not sure_____

(g) Why do you feel this way? Any other reason?

7(a) Did you vote in the election for President in 1964 when Johnson and Goldwater ran?

Voted_____   Didn't vote_____   Not sure_____

(b) Did you vote in the election for President in 1960 when Nixon and Kennedy ran?

Voted_____ Didn't vote_____ Not sure_____

8 Regardless of how you may vote, what do you usually consider yourself—a Republican, a Democrat, or what)

Republican_____ Democrat_____Independent_____

Other (specify)_____ Not sure_____

9(a) In 1964 for President, did you vote for Johnson, the Democrat, or Goldwater, the Republican?

Johnson_____ Goldwater_____ Can't recall_____

(b) In 1960 for President, did you vote for Nixon, the Republican, or Kennedy, the Democrat?

Nixon_____ Kennedy_____ Can't recall_____

10(a) Are you registered to vote now?

Yes_____ No_____ Not sure_____

(b) What are you registered as—a Democrat, a Republican, or what?

Democrat_____ Republican_____ Independent_____

Other (specify)_____ Not sure_____

(c) When did you first register to vote?

In past year_____

1–2 years ago_____

2–5 years ago_____

Over 5 years ago_____

Not sure_____

(d) How did you happen to register to vote? Who urged you to vote? Who helped you register? Why did you do it at this time?

(e) Are any (other) members of your family registered to vote?

Yes_____ No_____ Not sure_____

(f) Have you ever tried to vote?

Tried_____ Not tried_____ Not sure_____

(g) What's the main reason you haven't tried to register to vote? Any other reason?

11(a) In politics, do you feel Negroes should work mainly together as a separate group outside the two political parties or as individuals within one or the other party?

Mainly as a separate group_____ Mainly within parties_____

Both_____ Not sure_____

(b) What's the main reason you feel that way?

12 Have you ever:

	Did	Did not	Not sure
(1) Belonged to a political club or group	_____	_____	_____
(2) Worked for a political candidate for office	_____	_____	_____
(3) Asked people to register to vote	_____	_____	_____
(4) Asked people to vote for one candidate over another	_____	_____	_____
(5) Gone to a political meeting	_____	_____	_____
(6) Written or spoken to your congressman	_____	_____	_____
(7) Given money to a candidate or a political party	_____	_____	_____

13(a) Which party—the Republican or the Democratic—do you feel will do more to help Negroes in the next few years, or do you think there isn't much difference between the two?

Republican_____ Democratic_____ Other_____

No difference_____ Not sure_____

(b) What are the two or three main reasons why you feel this way? Any others?

14(a) What is your religion? What church do you attend?

Baptist_____ Methodist_____ Fundamentalist_____

Catholic_____ Other_____ No religion_____

(b) How often do you go to church?

More than once a week_____ Once a week_____

Two or three times a month_____ Once a month_____

Less often_____ Not sure_____

(c) Do you feel Negro ministers and preachers have been outstanding in their work for civil rights for Negroes, pretty good, only fair, or poor?

Outstanding_____ Pretty good_____Only fair_____ Poor_____

Not sure_____

(d) Why do you say this? Any other reason?

(e) Do you feel deeply about religion, or isn't it that important to you?

Deeply religious_____ Isn't that important_____Not sure_____

15(a) Some people are saying that Negroes have tried to work out their problems with white people and there's been a lot of talk but not much action. Now, they say Negroes should give up working together with whites and just depend on their own people. Do you tend to agree or disagree with people who say this?

Agree_____ Disagree_____ Not sure_____

(b) On the whole, do you approve or disapprove of Black Nationalism?

Approve_____ Disapprove_____ Not sure_____

(c) On the whole, do you approve or disapprove of the Black Muslim movement?

Approve_____ Disapprove_____ Not sure_____

(d) Why do you feel that way? Any other reason?

(e) Have you ever been talked to by or asked to join the Black Nationalists or the Black Muslims?

Talked to or asked____ Not talked to or asked____ Not sure_____

16(a) Have you stopped buying certain companies' products because you have heard they discriminate against Negroes?

Yes_____ No_____ Not sure_____

(b) What companies and products are these?

Products_____

Companies_____

(c) For most things you buy, do you feel you pay more than white people do for the same thing, less, or the same as whites?

Pay more_____ Pay less_____ Pay same_____ Not sure_____

(d) Has this situation gotten better or worse in the past five years or hasn't it changed much?

Better_____ Worse_____ Not changed_____Not sure_____

(e) If you had $20 more a week to spend, what would be the first things you would do with the money? Anything else?

(f) If you had $300 cash to spend right now, what would you do with the money? Anything else?

(g) Do you think as far as the things you want to buy, you want what most white people have or do you think Negroes like yourself want different things than most white people?

Want what most whites want_____ Want different things_____

Not sure_____

17(a) In the cause of Negro rights, have you personally or has any member of your family:

(b) If you were asked would you:

	(a)		(b)		
	Done	Not done	Would	Would not	Not sure
(1) Take(n) part in a sit-in	_____	_____	_____	_____	_____
(2) March(ed) in a demonstration	_____	_____	_____	_____	_____
(3) Picket(ed) a store	_____	_____	_____	_____	_____
(4) Stop(ped) buying at a store	_____	_____	_____	_____	_____
(5) Go(ne) to jail	_____	_____	_____	_____	_____

(c) What effect do you feel the demonstrations of Negroes all over the country have had up to now?

18(a) Some Negro leaders have said that Negroes can only succeed in winning rights if they use nonviolent means to demonstrate. Others disagree. Do you personally feel Negroes today can win their rights without resorting to violence or do you think it will have to be an eye for an eye and a tooth for a tooth?

Can win without violence_____ Will have to use violence_____

Not sure_____

(b) Why do you believe this? Any other reason?

(c) Some people have said that since there are 10 whites for every Negro in America, if it came to white against Negro, the Negroes would lose. Do you agree with this or disagree with it?

Agree_____ Disagree_____ Not sure_____

(d) Why do you feel this way?

(e) What do you think are the two or three main reasons riots have broken out in Los Angeles and other cities in Negro areas? Any other reasons?

(f) Do you think the riots that have taken place in Los Angeles and other cities have helped or hurt the cause of Negro rights or don't you think it makes much difference?

Helped___ Hurt___ Not much difference___ Not sure___

(g) Why do you say that? Any other reason?

(h) Do you think there will be more riots in other cities in the months ahead or not?

Will be_____ Will not be_____ Not sure_____

(i) Would you join in something like that or not?

Would join_____ Would not join_____ Not sure_____

19(a) If you had to say how you feel, what would you personally like most to see changed in America today? What is it that you'd most like to see done? Anything else?

(b) As far as all the things that have been going on lately with Negro rights, do you think things are moving about right these days, too fast, or too slow?

About right_____ Too fast_____ Too slow_____ Not sure_____

(c) Why do you say that?

(d) If the present demonstrations are successful, do you think in the next five years it will lead to a good deal of mixing of the races, some but not a lot, or only a little mixing of the races?

A lot_____ Some but not a lot_____ Only a little_____

Not sure_____

(e) Would you actually personally like to see a lot of integration or would you just prefer that Negroes be treated like other people, even though there might not be much integration?

Like lot of integration_____ Just treated like others_____

Not sure_____

(f) Some Negro leaders have proposed that whites and Negroes won't live well together so the only situation is to set up a separate Negro state or states in this country or in Africa. Do you favor or oppose this?

Favor_____ Oppose_____ Not sure_____

(g) Do you feel Negroes in the South are acting different from Negroes in the North these days?

Southern and Northern Negroes acting different_____

Nearly all the same_____ Not sure_____

20(a) The Communists say under their system there's no discrimination. Do you believe that or not?

Believe_____ Don't believe_____ Not sure_____

(b) What country of the world today do you feel is giving Negroes and other minorities the fairest break?

(c) If the United States got into a big world war today would you personally feel this country was worth fighting for?

Worth fighting for_____ Not worth it_____ Not sure_____

(d) Why do you feel this way about fighting for this country? Any other reason?

(e) Do you think the present draft laws are fair or unfair to Negroes?

Fair_____ Unfair_____ Not sure_____

(f) Why do you feel this way? Any other reason?

(g) How would you rate the (Army, etc.) as a place for a young man to serve—excellent, pretty good, only fair, or poor?

	Excellent	Pretty good	Only fair	Poor	Not sure
Army	_____	_____	_____	_____	_____
Navy	_____	_____	_____	_____	_____
Marine Corps	_____	_____	_____	_____	_____
Air Force	_____	_____	_____	_____	_____

(h) Now where do you think a young Negro just starting out will have a better chance to get a break: in the armed forces or in civilian life?

Armed forces_____ Civilian life_____ Not sure_____

(i) Why do you feel this way? Any other reason?

(j) How would you rate the job President Johnson is doing in handling the war in Vietnam—excellent, pretty good, only fair or poor?

Excellent_____ Pretty good_____ Only fair_____ Poor_____

Not sure_____

(k) All in all, what do you think we should do about Vietnam? We can follow one of three courses: carry the ground fighting into North Vietnam at the risk of bringing Red China into the fighting; withdraw our support and troops from Vietnam, or continue to fight there until the Communists are defeated or sit down to negotiate?

Carry ground fighting into North Vietnam_____ Withdraw_____

Continue to fight_____ Not sure_____

(l) Why do you feel this way? Any other reason?

(m) Do you think that Negroes are sending a higher percentage (number) of young men to Vietnam than any other group in the population, about the same, or less?

Higher_____ About the same_____ Less_____ Not sure_____

(n) (If answer is higher) Do you think this is right or wrong?

Right_____ Wrong_____ Not sure_____

(o) I want to read you some statements about the war in Vietnam. Tell me for each if you tend to agree or disagree:

	Agree	Disagree	Not sure
(1) Money spent in Vietnam means less money for civil rights and poverty programs here at home	____	____	____
(2) Negroes should be against the war in Vietnam because they have less freedom to fight for	____	____	____
(3) When Negroes fight in Vietnam, they prove they are as good as any other people	____	____	____
(4) Negroes make better soldiers in combat than whites	____	____	____

21(a) Do you think a Negro who gets to college and is qualified can get as good a job, a better job, or not as good a job as a white man with the same qualifications in:

	As good	Better	Not as good	Not sure
(1) Government	___	___	___	___
(2) Science	___	___	___	___
(3) Industry	___	___	___	___
(4) Retail business	___	___	___	___
(5) Teaching	___	___	___	___
(6) Social work	___	___	___	___

(b) Do you think a Negro high-school student with good grades has as good a chance, not as good a chance or a better chance of getting into a top college than a white student with the same grades?

As good a chance_____ Not as good_____ Better_____

Not sure_____

(c) Do you think a Negro college graduate with good grades has as good a chance, not as good a chance or a better chance of getting into:

	As good a chance	Not as good	Better chance	Not sure
(1) A top law school	___	___	___	___
(2) A top medical school	___	___	___	___
(3) A top engineering school	___	___	___	___
(4) A top scientific school	___	___	___	___

(d) All in all, do you think the opportunities for Negroes to get ahead in the professions has improved a lot in the past three years, gotten worse, or remains about what it was then?

Improved a lot_____ Gotten worse_____

About what it was_____ Not sure_____

(e) Why do you feel this way? Any other reason?

22(a) As far as you are concerned, what is the most important single event or happening that has meant most to you in the fight for Negro civil rights? Why do you feel that?

(b) Now I want to read you a list of things that have happened in the civil rights fight. Do you remember:

(c) (for each remembered) Would you say this meant a lot to you personally or not?

(d) (for each remembered) Do you think this really helped the civil-rights cause or didn't it count too much?

	(b)	(c)		(d)		
	Recall	Meant a lot	Didn't mean a lot	Helped cause	Didn't count	Not sure
Scottsboro Boys trial	_____	_____	_____	_____	_____	_____
Emmett Till lynching	_____	_____	_____	_____	_____	_____
Montgomery bus boycott	_____	_____	_____	_____	_____	_____
Medgar Evers murder	_____	_____	_____	_____	_____	_____
Supreme Court education decision	_____	_____	_____	_____	_____	_____
March on Washington in 1963	_____	_____	_____	_____	_____	_____
Viola Liuzzo murder	_____	_____	_____	_____	_____	_____
Selma march in 1965	_____	_____	_____	_____	_____	_____
The Mississippi murder of three civil-rights workers	_____	_____	_____	_____	_____	_____
Federal law desegregating eating places	_____	_____	_____	_____	_____	_____
Federal Civil Rights Voting Act	_____	_____	_____	_____	_____	_____
The shooting of James Meredith	_____	_____	_____	_____	_____	_____

23(a) Now I want to read off to you a list of groups and people who have been prominent in the fight for Negro rights. For each I wish you would tell me how you would rate the job that person or group has done—excellent, pretty good, only fair, or poor?

	Excellent	Pretty good	Only fair	Poor	Not sure
A. Philip Randolph	_____	_____	_____	_____	_____
Stokely Carmichael	_____	_____	_____	_____	_____
Floyd McKissick	_____	_____	_____	_____	_____
NAACP	_____	_____	_____	_____	_____
Martin Luther King	_____	_____	_____	_____	_____
CORE	_____	_____	_____	_____	_____
Adam Clayton Powell	_____	_____	_____	_____	_____
Elijah Muhammad	_____	_____	_____	_____	_____
James Meredith	_____	_____	_____	_____	_____
James Farmer	_____	_____	_____	_____	_____
Urban League	_____	_____	_____	_____	_____
SNCC	_____	_____	_____	_____	_____

	Excellent	Pretty good	Only fair	poor	Not sure
Southern Christian Leadership Conference	___	___	___	___	___
Roy Wilkins	___	___	___	___	___
Ralph Bunche	___	___	___	___	___
Jackie Robinson	___	___	___	___	___
Bayard Rustin	___	___	___	___	___
Thurgood Marshall	___	___	___	___	___
Charles Evers	___	___	___	___	___
Black Muslims	___	___	___	___	___
Dick Gregory	___	___	___	___	___
Julian Bond	___	___	___	___	___
Whitney Young	___	___	___	___	___

(b) What do you think are the main aims these days of the leaders of the civil rights movement? What are they trying to get done? Anything else?

(c) Do you think the methods the civil rights leaders use, like marches, picketing, and demonstrations, are helping or hurting the civil rights cause?

Helping____Hurting____ Makes no difference (value)____

Not sure____

(d) Do you think the leaders of the civil rights movement have gotten involved too much in the Vietnam war question, too little, or about the right amount?

Too much____ Too little____ About the right amount____

Not sure____

(e) Do you think civil rights leaders are ahead of their people, behind their people, or right with them?

Ahead__ Behind__ Right with them__ Not sure__

(f) Why do you say that? Any other reason?

(g) Now I want to ask about Cassius Clay (Muhammad Ali). Tell me if as a person you admire him. Or do you dislike him? Or don't you have strong feelings either way?

Admire him____ Dislike him____

Don't have strong feelings either way____ Not sure____

(h) Why do you feel that way? Any other reason?

24(a) If the election for President were being held today and if it were between Governor George Romney, the Republican, and President Lyndon Johnson, the Democrat, and if you had to choose right now—would you vote for Romney or for Johnson?

Romney_____   Johnson_____   Not sure_____

(b) Suppose for President it were between Richard Nixon, the Republican, and President Lyndon Johnson, the Democrat, who would you be for?

Nixon_____   Johnson_____   Not sure_____

(c) And if it were between Mayor John Lindsay, of New York City, the Republican, and President Lyndon Johnson, the Democrat, who would you be for?

Lindsay_____   Johnson_____   Not sure_____

(d) Which of the last five Presidents—Roosevelt, Truman, Eisenhower, Kennedy, or Johnson—do you feel did most for Negro rights in this country?

Roosevelt_____   Truman_____   Eisenhower_____

Kennedy_____   Johnson_____   Not sure_____

25(a) Now I want to give you a list of different people and groups that are run by white people. Do you think (white churches, etc.) have been more helpful or more harmful to Negro rights?

(b) Now which *one* of all these groups run by white people do you think has been most helpful to Negro rights?

(c) And which *one* has been most harmful to Negro rights?

	(a)			*(b)*	*(c)*
	More helpful	*More harmful*	*Not sure*	*Most helpful*	*Most harmful*
White churches	_____	_____	_____	_____	_____
Local police	_____	_____	_____	_____	_____
Labor unions	_____	_____	_____	_____	_____
White businesses	_____	_____	_____	_____	_____
Catholic priests	_____	_____	_____	_____	_____
Jews	_____	_____	_____	_____	_____
Bus companies	_____	_____	_____	_____	_____
Hotels and motels	_____	_____	_____	_____	_____

	(a)			(b)	(c)
	More helpful	More harmful	Not sure	Most helpful	Most harmful
Movie theaters	___	___	___	___	___
Real estate companies	___	___	___	___	___
Newspapers	___	___	___	___	___
Federal government under Johnson	___	___	___	___	___
Television	___	___	___	___	___
Congress	___	___	___	___	___
U.S. Supreme Court	___	___	___	___	___
Local authorities	___	___	___	___	___
State government	___	___	___	___	___
Puerto Ricans	___	___	___	___	___
The Federal Anti-Poverty program	___	___	___	___	___
White college students	___	___	___	___	___

26(a) On the whole, do you think most white people want to see Negroes get a better break, or do they want to keep Negroes down, or do you think they don't care one way or the other?

Better break_____ Keep down_____

Don't care one way or the other_____ Not sure_____

(b) Why do you say that? Anything else?

27(a) Do you think whites in the North care more about giving Negroes a better break than do whites in the South, or don't you think there is much difference?

North better than South_____ Not much difference_____

Not sure_____

(b) What do you think is the main reason why some white people want to keep Negroes down? Any other reasons? What kind of people are they?

(c) Compared to five years ago, do you think white people have changed their attitude about Negro rights for the better, for worse, or has there not been much change?

Better_____ Worse_____ Not much change_____

Not sure_____

(d) Why do you feel this way? What's made it that way?

(e) In the next five years, do you think the attitude of white people about Negro rights will get better, worse, or stay about the same?

Better_____ Worse_____ Stay the same_____ Not sure_____

(f) Why do you think it will go that way?

(g) In the end, do you think white people will take a better attitude toward Negroes mainly because they will be forced to by Negro action, or mainly because they can be persuaded that this is the only right thing to do?

Mainly force_____ Mainly persuasion_____ Not sure_____

(h) Why do you feel that way?

(i) In both the South and North, there are some whites who are against the KKK and who want to see Negroes get a better break. But they also think that progress on Negro rights will not be as fast as Negro groups want. They are known as white moderates. On the whole, do you think these white moderates are more helpful or more harmful to Negro rights?

More helpful_____ More harmful_____ Not sure_____

(j) Why do you feel this way?

28(a) How would you rate the job Lyndon B. Johnson has done as President—excellent, pretty good, only fair or poor?

Excellent_____ Pretty good_____ Only fair_____ Poor_____

Not sure_____

(b) What are the two or three main reasons you feel this way? Any other reasons?

(c) What two or three white leaders and organizations do you respect and trust the most? Any others?

(d) What two or three white leaders and organizations do you dislike and trust the least? Any others?

29 Now I want to ask you some questions about different types of people and situations.

(a) Do you know anyone who:

(b) Is that someone close to you?

	(a)		(b)	
	Know someone	Don't know someone	Close to me	Not close to me
(1) Is an unwed mother	_____	_____		
(2) Is a teenager on dope	_____	_____	_____	_____
(3) Is a high school drop-out	_____	_____	_____	_____
(4) Has taken part in a riot	_____	_____	_____	_____
(5) Has been sent to jail	_____	_____	_____	_____
(6) Is a mother in a family where the father has left home	_____	_____	_____	_____

(c) (if know someone with "fatherless family") What's the hardest part of not having a husband around the house? Anything else?

(d) In most Negro families, do you think the mother or the father is usually the one who teaches the children to behave right?

Mother_____   Father_____   Both (volunteered)_____

Neither_____   Not sure_____

(e) Why is that? Anything else?

30(a) What does the phrase "Black Power" mean to you?

(b) Do you favor the idea of Black Power or not?

Favor_____   Don't favor_____   Not sure_____

31(a) Do you agree or disagree that Negroes can get what they want only by banding together as black people against the whites, because the whites will never help Negroes?

Agree_____   Disagree_____   Not sure_____

(b) Why do you feel that way?

32(a) Do you agree or disagree that if Negroes try to operate against all white people that Negroes will lose because they are outnumbered nine to one?

Agree_____   Disagree_____   Not sure_____

(b) Why do you feel this way?

33(a) Do you think Negroes have more to gain or more to lose by resorting to violence in the civil rights movement?

More to gain_____   More to lose_____   Not sure_____

(b) Why do you feel this way?

34 Who would you prefer to see run for President in 1968, Lyndon Johnson or Robert Kennedy?

Johnson_____ Kennedy_____

FACTUAL

35(a) How old are you?

	Male	Female
18–20	____	____
21–34	____	____
35–49	____	____
50–64	____	____
65 and over	____	____

(b) How many people, counting both adults and children, live here?

One_____ Two–three_____ Four–five_____

Six–seven_____ Eight and over_____

(c) Are you married, divorced, widowed or single?

Married_____ Divorced_____ Widowed_____ Single_____

(d) How many children under 18 years of age live at home?

One_____ Two_____ Three_____ Four_____

Five or more_____ None_____

(e) How many are:

Under 2_____ 2-5_____ 6-10_____ 11-15_____ 16-17_____

36(a) What is the last grade of school you completed? Also what was the last grade of school your father completed?

	Respondent	Father
Did not attend school	____	____
1st–2nd grade	____	____
3rd–4th grade	____	____
5th–8th grade	____	____
Some high school	____	____
Completed high school	____	____
Some college	____	____
Completed college	____	____
Graduate school	____	____
Not sure	____	____

(b) (if respondent attended college) Which college did you attend? In what state is that?

College_____   State_____

37(a) Is the head of the household an hourly wage worker, salaried or self-employed?

Hourly wages_____   Salaried_____   Self-employed_____

If none of the above:

Retired_____   Student_____   Military service_____

Housewife_____   Unemployed_____   Other (specify)_____

(b) What type of work does the head of the household do?

Professional, technical (Engineers, doctors, teachers, editorial, clergy, etc.) _____

Managers, officials and proprietors (with the exception of farm managers), buyers, postmasters, railroad conductors, etc. _____

Clerical (secretaries, bank tellers, telephone operators, etc.) _____

Sales workers (retail, insurance, stocks and bonds, etc.) _____

Craftsmen, foremen (carpenters, mechanics, bakers, printers, tailors, etc.) _____

Operative workers (bus drivers, deliverymen, conductors, painters, laundry and dry cleaning, etc.) _____

Private household workers _____

Service workers [except private household workers] (policemen, watchmen, waiters, bargers, janitors, porters, etc.) _____

Farm laborers and foremen _____

Laborers [except farm and mine] (garage laborers, lumbermen, stevedores, gardeners, etc.) _____

Occupation not reported _____

(c) How many people in the family work?

1_____   2_____   3_____   4_____   5 or more_____

None_____

(d) Altogether, how much do the people in your family who live here earn a week?

(e) (if head of household employed) How much does the head of the household earn a week?

	(d)	(e)
$20 or less	———	———
$21–39	———	———
$40–49	———	———
$50–59	———	———
$60–74	———	———
$75–89	———	———
$90–100	———	———
$125–149	———	———
$150–199	———	———
$200 and over	———	———
Not sure	———	———

38(a) Do you receive any welfare or relief money?

Receive——— Don't receive——— Not sure———

(b) How much a week do you get in welfare or relief?

39(a) Are you a member of a labor union?

Yes——— No———

(b) Is any member of your family a member of a labor union?

Yes——— No———

(c) What union is that?

AFL–CIO——— Teamsters——— Other (specify)———

Don't know———

40(a) (if male) Have you ever served in the armed forces?

Yes——— No———

(b) What branch?

Army——— Navy——— Air Force——— Marines———

(c) Where were you stationed?

North——— Midwest——— South——— West———

Overseas———

(d) Is there anyone in your family who has been drafted and is currently serving in the armed forces?

Someone in family——— No one in family——— Not sure———

(e) Is there anyone in your family who is currently eligible for the draft?

Someone eligible_____   No one is eligible_____   Not sure_____

41(a) How long have you lived in this state?

    Less than a year_____   1–5 years_____   6–10 years_____

    11–15 years_____   16–19 years_____   20 or more years_____

(b) In what part of the country were you born and raised?

    North_____   South_____   Midwest_____   West_____

42(a) What organizations are you a member of or active in?

(b) Are you an officer in any organization(s)? Which one(s)?

43(a) Do you (and your family) own a car?

                Yes_____   No_____

(b) Do you (and your family) own a television set?

                Yes_____   No_____

(c) Do you (and your family) own a radio?

                Yes_____   No_____

(d) (whether owner or not) How much time did you spend yesterday watching TV or listening to the radio?

	Television	Radio
None	_____	_____
1–30 minutes	_____	_____
31–59 minutes	_____	_____
1–2 hours	_____	_____
2–4 hours	_____	_____
4 hours or more	_____	_____
Not sure	_____	_____

44(a) Do you carry a life insurance policy?

                Yes_____   No_____

(b) Does anyone have a life insurance policy in your immediate family living here?

                Yes_____   No_____

(c) Do you have a bank savings account or a checking account?

	Yes	No
Savings	——	——
Checking	——	——

(d) Have you bought anything on the installment or credit plan in the last year?

Yes_____ No_____

45(a) (record if apartment, private house or co-op)

Apartment_____ Private house_____ Co-op_____

(b) (if private house or co-op) Do you own or rent this house?

Own_____ Rent_____ Other (specify)_____

(c) How many rooms do you have?

One_____ Two_____ Three_____ Four_____

Five_____ Six plus_____

APPENDIX **B**

The White Questionnaire

Here are the questions as actually asked in the survey of white people on which this book is based:

1(a) Do you feel that our racial problems here at home have hurt this country abroad or not?

Hurt_____ Not hurt_____ Not sure_____

(b) Do you feel Negroes have tried to move too fast, too slow, or at about the right pace?

Too fast_____ Too slow_____ About right_____ Not sure_____

(c) Why do you feel this way? Any other reason?

(d) Do you feel Negroes are discriminated against in this country or not?

Discriminated against_____ Not discriminated against_____

Not sure_____

(e) What are the main ways and areas of life in which you feel Negroes are discriminated against? Any others?

(f) Why do you feel (aren't you sure) Negroes are not discriminated against? Any other reason?

(g) As an individual, what do you think it feels like to be discriminated against as a Negro? What do you feel it does to Negroes as individuals? Anything else?

2(a) Over the past few years, Congress has passed several laws guaranteeing rights of Negroes. Do you personally favor or oppose the laws Congress has passed?

	Favor	Oppose	Not sure
Giving Negroes equal voting rights	———	———	———
Outlawing segregation in education	———	———	———
Outlawing discrimination in housing	———	———	———
Guaranteeing Negroes equal use of buses and trains	———	———	———
Guaranteeing Negroes equal use of restaurants and restrooms	———	———	———

(b) It has now been proposed that Congress pass a new law which would guarantee fair jury trials for Negroes. Do you favor or oppose such a law?

(c) It has also been proposed that any attack of violence against a civil rights worker be a federal offense. Do you favor or oppose such a law?

(d) It has been suggested that a law be passed outlawing discrimination in housing. Do you favor or oppose such a law?

	Favor	Oppose	Not sure
Guaranteeing jury trials	———	———	———
Making attacks on civil rights workers	———	———	———
Outlawing discrimination in housing	———	———	———

3 Now I want to give you a list of groups and institutions. Do you think (U.S. Supreme Court, etc.) has tended more to help Negroes or has tended more to keep Negroes down?

	Help more	Keep down more	Not sure
U.S. Supreme Court	———	———	———
Johnson administration	———	———	———
Business corporations	———	———	———
Real estate companies	———	———	———
Congress	———	———	———
White Protestant churches	———	———	———
Professions (law, medicine, etc.)	———	———	———
Retail stores	———	———	———
Labor unions	———	———	———
Catholic Church	———	———	———
Local government here	———	———	———
State government here	———	———	———
Restaurants, hotels, motels	———	———	———
Railroads, bus companies	———	———	———
Local police	———	———	———

4(a) Some people have said that jobs are hard enough to find these days, and that if Negroes are to be given jobs, it will mean taking jobs away from white people. Do you feel that will happen if better job opportunities are given to Negroes, or don't you think that would happen?

Would happen_____   Wouldn't happen_____   Not sure_____

(b) Do you feel this could happen with your (your husband's) job or not?

Could happen_____   Couldn't happen_____   Not sure_____

(c) Some people have suggested that Negroes, who are 10 per cent of the population, should be guaranteed 10 per cent of the jobs that are available. Would you favor or oppose such a quota system?

Favor_____   Oppose_____   Not sure_____

(d) Some Negroes have suggested that since Negroes have been discriminated against for 100 years, they should be given special consideration in jobs, that they should actually be given a preference for a job opening, such as a veteran gets today in a government job. Do you agree or disagree with the idea of job preference for Negroes?

Agree_____   Disagree_____   Not sure_____

(e) Compared with five years ago, do you feel Negroes are getting a better break in jobs now, a worse break, or about the same now as five years ago?

Better break_____   Worse break_____   About same_____

Not sure_____

(f) As far as education goes, do you feel that Negroes have been receiving as good an education in this country as white people, or not as good an education?

As good as whites_____   Not as good_____   Not sure_____

(g) If Negro children attended the same school as white children, do you feel they would receive a better education than they do now or wouldn't it make much difference?

Better education_____   Not much difference_____   Not sure_____

(h) It's been said that if Negro children all went to school with white children, the education of white children would suffer. The reason given is that the Negro children would hold back the white children. Do you believe that or not?

Believe_____ Don't believe_____ Not sure_____

(i) Why do you feel this way? Any other reason?

(j) Five years from now, do you think right around here most Negro and white children will be going to a school together, some but not a lot, or only a few will be going to school together?

Most_____ Some, not a lot_____ Only a few_____Not sure_____

5 As far as your own personal feelings go, would you be personally concerned or not if:

	Concerned	Not concerned	Not sure
(1) A Negro sat down next to you at a lunch counter	_____	_____	_____
(2) A Negro sat next to you in a movie theater	_____	_____	_____
(3) A Negro used the same public restroom as you	_____	_____	_____
(4) A Negro sat next to you on a bus	_____	_____	_____
(5) A Negro tried on a suit of clothes (a dress) before you did in a clothing store	_____	_____	_____
(6) Your child brought a Negro child home for supper	_____	_____	_____
(7) Your teenage child dated a Negro	_____	_____	_____
(8) A Negro family moved in next door to you	_____	_____	_____
(9) A close friend or relative married a Negro	_____	_____	_____

6(a) Do you feel that Negroes live in as good housing as white people or is their housing not as good?

As good housing_____ Not as good_____ Not sure_____

(b) Would it upset you a lot, some but not a lot, only a little, or not at all if Negroes moved into this neighborhood?

A lot_____ Some, not a lot_____ Only a little_____

Not at all_____ Not sure_____

(c) Why do you say that? Any other reason?

(d) Five years from now, do you think a lot more Negroes will be living in white neighborhoods, some but not a lot more, only a few more, or no more than do now?

A lot more_____   Some but not a lot_____

No more than now_____   Not sure_____

7 Now let me ask you some questions about Negroes as people. Leaving aside the whole question of laws or civil rights, I'd like to know how you feel as an individual. Do you personally tend to agree more or disagree more with these statements?

	Agree more	Disagree more	Not sure
(1) Negroes tend to have less ambition than white people	_____	_____	_____
(2) Negroes care less for the family than whites do	_____	_____	_____
(3) Negroes keep untidy homes	_____	_____	_____
(4) Negroes have looser morals than white people	_____	_____	_____
(5) Negroes smell different	_____	_____	_____
(6) Negroes breed crime	_____	_____	_____
(7) Negroes laugh a lot	_____	_____	_____
(8) Negroes have less native intelligence than white people	_____	_____	_____
(9) Negroes want to live off the handout	_____	_____	_____
(10) Negroes are inferior to white people	_____	_____	_____

8(a) It has been claimed that white policemen often engage in police brutality against Negroes. Do you tend to believe that is true or not true?

True_____   Not true_____   Not sure_____

(b) Why do you say that? Any other reason?

(c) Why do you think Negroes have taken to direct action all over the country? Any other reason?

(d) All in all, do you feel the demonstrations by Negroes have helped more or hurt more the advancement of Negro rights?

Helped more_____   Hurt more_____   Not sure_____

(e) Why do you feel that way? Any other reason?

(f) What do you feel Negroes want in their demonstrations? Anything else?

(g) What do you think are the two or three main reasons riots have broken out in Los Angeles and other cities in Negro areas? Any other reasons?

(h) Do you think the riots that have taken place in Los Angeles and other cities have helped or hurt the cause of Negro rights or don't you think it makes much difference?

Helped_____ Hurt_____ Not much difference_____

Not sure_____

(i) On the whole, do you feel Negroes are asking for more than they are ready for or not?

Asking for more than ready for_____

Not asking for more than ready for_____ Not sure_____

(j) Now on each of the following, I'd like to ask you if you were in the same position as Negroes, if you think it would be justified or not:

	Justified	Not justified	Not sure
(1) To march and protest in demonstrations	_____	_____	_____
(2) To protest against discrimination in jobs	_____	_____	_____
(3) To protest against discrimination in education	_____	_____	_____
(4) To protest against discrimination in housing	_____	_____	_____

9(a) Compared to a year ago, are you personally more worried about violence and safety on the streets, less worried, or do you feel the same as you did then?

More worried_____ Less worried_____ Feel the same_____

Not sure_____

(b) Does the fear of racial violence make you feel personally more uneasy on the streets or not?

Makes feel uneasy_____ Doesn't make feel uneasy_____

Not sure_____

FACTUAL

10(a) Were all four of your grandparents born in the United States?

Yes_____ No_____

(b) In what country or countries were your grandparents born?

America:

United States_____   French Canadian_____

Other Canadian_____   Puerto Rico_____

Other Latin America_____

Europe:

Ireland_____   England or Scotland_____   Scandinavia_____

Germany_____   France_____   Italy_____   Portugal_____

Other Western Europe (specify)_____   Austria or Hungary_____

Poland_____   Russia_____   Other Eastern Europe_____

Other_____

11(a) Is the head of the household an hourly wage worker, salaried or self-employed?

Hourly wages_____   Salaried_____   Self-employed_____

None of the above:

Retired_____   Student_____   Military service_____

Housewife_____   Unemployed_____   Other (specify)_____

(b) What type of work does the head of the household do?

Professional, technical (Engineers, doctors, teachers, editorial, clergy, etc.)   _____
Farmers and farm managers   _____
Managers, officials and proprietors (with the exception of farm managers), buyers, postmasters, railroad conductors, etc.   _____
Clerical (secretaries, bank tellers, telephone operators, etc.)   _____
Sales workers (retail, insurance, stocks and bonds, etc.)   _____
Craftsmen, foremen (carpenters, mechanics, makers, printers, tailors, etc.)   _____
Operative workers (bus drivers, deliverymen, conductors, painters, laundry and dry cleaning, etc.)   _____

Private household workers _____

Service workers [except private household workers] (policemen, watchmen, waiters, bargers, janitors, porters, etc.) _____

Farm laborers and foremen _____

Laborers [except farm and mine] (garage laborers, lumbermen, stevedores, gardeners, etc.) _____

Other (specify) _____

12 How old are you?

	Male	Female
21–34	_____	_____
35–49	_____	_____
50–64	_____	_____
65 and over	_____	_____

13(a) How many people, counting both adults and children, live here?

One_____   Two–three_____   Four–five_____   Six–seven_____

Eight and over_____

(b) Are you married, single, divorced or widowed?

Married_____   Divorced_____   Widowed_____   Single_____

(c) How many children under 18 years of age live at home?

One_____   Two_____   Three_____   Four_____

Five or more_____   None_____

(d) How many are:

Under 2_____   2-5_____   6-10_____   11-15_____   16-17_____

14 What is the last grade of school you completed? Also, what was the last grade of school your father completed?

	Respondent	Father
Did not attend school	_____	_____
1st–2nd grade	_____	_____
3rd–4th grade	_____	_____
5th–8th grade	_____	_____
Some high school	_____	_____
Completed high school	_____	_____
Some college	_____	_____
Completed college	_____	_____
Graduate school	_____	_____
Not sure	_____	_____

15(a) How many people in the family work?

1_____   2_____   3_____   4_____   5 or more_____   None_____

(b) For statistical purposes only, we need to know your total family income for 1965. Will you take this card and tell me which best represents all the money the members of this household either earned or received from salary or wages or other sources such as pension, stocks and bonds, real estate and other investments in 1965 before taxes?

Under $3,000_____	$10,000–14,999_____
$3,000–4,999_____	$15,000–19,999_____
$5,000–6,999_____	$20,000–24,999_____
$7,000–9,999_____	$25,000 and over_____

Don't know_____

16 How long have you lived in this state?

Less than a year_____   1–5 years_____   6–10 years_____

11–15 years_____   16–19 years_____   20 or more years_____

17 What is your religion?

Catholic_____   Protestant_____   Jewish_____

Other (specify)_____   None_____   Refused_____

Negro Leadership Sample

BELOW IS A LIST OF THE LEADING American Negroes who were interviewed in 1966 in the *Newsweek* survey. The list includes persons nationally known for their role in the civil-rights movement as well as individuals outstanding in their community or profession. In selecting them, *Newsweek* consulted Negroes themselves among other advisers.

Rev. William Ardrey, *minister, Detroit, Mich.*
Warren Bacon, *businessman, Chicago, Ill.*
James Baldwin, *author*
Marion Barry, *SNCC director, Washington, D.C.*
L. C. Bates, *NAACP, Little Rock, Ark.*
Mrs. Ruth M. Batson, *community leader, Boston, Mass.*
Edwin C. Berry, *National Urban League, Chicago, Ill.*
Weldon H. Berry, *attorney, Houston, Tex.*
Rev. James L. Bevel, *SCLC, Chicago, Ill.*
Mrs. Lena Bivens, *Anti-Poverty War advisor, Detroit, Mich.*
Julian Bond, *SNCC, Atlanta, Ga.*
William H. Booth, *Commission on Human Rights, New York, N.Y.*

Thomas Bradley, *city council, Los Angeles, Calif.*
Arthur M. Brazier, *civic leader, Chicago, Ill.*
Dr. H. H. Brookins, *United Civil Rights Committee, Los Angeles, Calif.*
Deton J. Brooks, *Anti-Poverty War director, Chicago, Ill.*
Willie L. Brown, Jr., *state assemblyman, California*
Dr. Thomas N. Burbridge, *educator, San Francisco, Calif.*
Herb Callender, *CORE, New York, N.Y.*
Kenneth Campbell, *alderman, Chicago, Ill.*
Julius Carter, *editor, Houston, Tex.*
Rev. James C. Chambers, *minister, Detroit, Mich.*
Dr. Kenneth Clark, *educator, New York, N.Y.*
William L. Clay, *alderman, St. Louis, Mo.*
Rev. Albert Cleage, *minister, Detroit, Mich.*
John Conyers, Jr., *state representative, Michigan*
George Crockett, *attorney, Detroit, Mich.*
Sammy Davis, Jr., *entertainer*
Ivanhoe Donaldson, *SNCC, New York, N.Y.*
Mervyn M. Dymally, *state assemblyman, California*
Nelson Jack Edwards, *union official, Detroit, Mich.*
Charles Evers, *NAACP, Mississippi*
James Farmer, *former CORE head, New York, N.Y.*
Rev. Walter Fauntroy, *SCLC, Washington, D.C.*
Terry A. Francois, *alderman, San Francisco, Calif.*
Dr. Carlton B. Goodlet, *publisher, San Francisco, Calif.*
Rev. Arthur D. Griffen, *minister, Chicago, Ill.*
Booker Griffin, *Westminster Neighborhood Association, Los Angeles, Calif.*
Robert Lee Hall, *Operation Bootstrap, Los Angeles, Calif.*
Augustus F. Hawkins, *congressman, California*
Julius Hobson, *ACT, Washington, D.C.*
Nick Hood, *councilman, Detroit, Mich.*
Norman Houston, Jr., *businessman, Los Angeles, Calif.*
Mrs. Ellen M. Jackson, *Operation Exodus, Boston, Mass.*
Rev. Joseph Jackson, *National Baptist Convention*
Tommy Ray Jacquette, *SLANT, Los Angeles, Calif.*
Leroy Johnson, *state senator, Georgia*
Rev. James Edward Jones, *minister, Los Angeles, Calif.*
Miss Barbara Jordan, *attorney, Houston, Tex.*

Vernon E. Jordan, Jr., *Voter Education Project, SRC, Atlanta, Ga.*
Ron Karenga, *chairman US, Los Angeles, Calif.*
Damon J. Keith, *Civil Rights Commission, Michigan.*
J. Harvey Kerns, *Urban League, New Orleans, La.*
Dr. Martin Luther King, Jr., *president SCLC, Atlanta, Ga.*
Melvin H. King, *social worker, Boston, Mass.*
Dr. John S. Lash, *educator, Houston, Tex.*
Rev. William Lawson, *Operation Upward Bound, Houston, Tex.*
Louis E. Lomax, *TV moderator, Los Angeles, Calif.*
Lincoln Lynch, *CORE, New York, N.Y.*
Stanley R. Malone, Jr., *attorney, Los Angeles, Calif.*
Thurgood Marshall, *U.S. Solicitor General*
Dr. Benjamin E. Mays, *educator, Atlanta, Ga.*
James Meredith, *law student, New York, N.Y.*
Loren Miller, *judge, Los Angeles, Calif.*
Cecil B. Moore, *NAACP, Philadelphia, Pa.*
Richard Newhouse, Jr., *lawyer, Chicago, Ill.*
Rev. I. Dequincy Newman, *NAACP, South Carolina*
Dr. Benjamin Payton, *National Council of Churches, New York, N.Y.*
Rev. Channing Phillips, *minister, Washington, D.C.*
Cecil F. Poole, *U.S. attorney, Northern California*
Albert Raby, *civil-rights leader, Chicago, Ill.*
A. Philip Randolph, *union president, New York, N.Y.*
John Laurence Rayon, *editor, San Francisco, Calif.*
Chester Robinson, *community leader, Chicago, Ill.*
Jackie Robinson, *businessman, New York, N.Y.*
Rev. T. Y. Rogers, Jr., *minister, Tuscaloosa, Ala.*
Carl T. Rowan, *columnist, Washington, D.C.*
W. Byron Rumford, *assemblyman, California*
Bayard Rustin, *A. Philip Randolph Institute, New York, N.Y.*
Cornelius A. Scott, *editor, Atlanta, Ga.*
John Shabazz, *minister, Los Angeles, Calif.*
Horace Sheffield, *union official, Detroit, Mich.*
Lou Smith, *CORE, Los Angeles, Calif.*
Muriel Snowden, *Freedom House, Boston, Mass.*
Rev. Lynward Stevenson, *minister, Chicago, Ill.*
Carl Stokes, *state representative, Ohio*
Herbert E. Tucker, Jr., *Assistant Attorney General, Massachusetts*

Rev. James Wadsworth, *NAACP, Detroit, Mich.*

James A. Washington, Jr., *Public Utilities Commission, Washington, D.C.*

Walter E. Washington, *National Capitol Housing Authority, Washington, D.C.*

Robert C. Weaver, *Cabinet member, Washington, D.C.*

John Wheeler, *banker, Durham, N.C.*

Clinton W. White, *NAACP, Oakland, Calif.*

Roy Wilkins, *NAACP, New York, N.Y.*

Hosea Williams, *SCLC, Atlanta, Ga.*

Bishop Smallwood Williams, *minister, Washington, D.C.*

Miss Marian Wright, *attorney, Jackson, Miss.*

Rev. Virgil A. Wood, *minister, Boston, Mass.*

A. Z. Young, *Voters' League, Bogalusa, La.*

Whitney Young, Jr., *National Urban League*

Supplementary Statistical Tables

NOTE: This appendix contains tables not included in the text, as well as more detailed versions of tables summarized in the text. Not every question from the questionnaires is represented by a table in this appendix (or in the text). Those questions that are included here are presented in the order of the chapters to which they relate, and within each chapter, according to the order of their discussion. For convenience of reference, they carry the same numbers that they have in the text.

CHAPTER I

Questions from White Questionnaire

9(a) Compared to a year ago, are you personally more worried about violence and safety on the streets, less worried, or do you feel the same as you did then?

	Total 1966	Total 1963	East	Midwest
	%	%	%	%
More worried	49	—	47	46
Less worried	3	—	6	2
Feel the same	44	—	44	46
Not sure	4	—	3	6

9(b) Does the fear of racial violence make you feel personally more uneasy on the streets or not?

	Total 1966	Total 1963	East	Midwest
	%	%	%	%
Makes feel uneasy	43	—	45	36
Doesn't make feel uneasy	50	—	48	56
Not sure	7	—	7	8

1(b) Do you feel Negroes have tried to move too fast, too slow, or at about the right pace?

	Total 1966	Total 1963	East	Midwest
	%	%	%	%
Too fast	70	64	64	69
Too slow	4	6	4	4
About right	14	17	17	16
Not sure	12	13	15	11

South	West	Metropolitan city	Urban town	Suburban town	Rural area	Men	Women
%	%	%	%	%	%	%	%
52	54	62	39	57	40	48	50
1	2	4	3	3	2	3	3
44	40	32	57	36	50	45	43
3	4	2	1	4	8	4	4

South	West	Metropolitan city	Urban town	Suburban town	Rural area	Men	Women
%	%	%	%	%	%	%	%
44	49	59	34	45	32	41	45
48	46	38	62	47	56	52	48
8	5	3	4	8	12	7	7

South	West	Metropolitan city	Urban town	Suburban town	Rural area	Goldwater 1964	Johnson 1964
%	%	%	%	%	%	%	%
81	75	68	81	64	72	78	67
1	5	4	3	8	*	1	6
8	12	15	11	16	13	10	16
10	8	13	5	12	15	11	11

*—Less than 1 percent.

8(j) Now on each of the following I'd like to ask you, if you were in the same position as Negroes, if you think it would be justified or not:

	Total 1966 %	Total 1963 %
To march and protest in demonstrations		
Justified	35	53
Not justified	50	37
Not sure	15	10
To protest against discrimination in jobs		
Justified	59	—
Not justified	30	—
Not sure	11	—
To protest against discrimination in education		
Justified	60	—
Not justified	30	—
Not sure	10	—
To protest against discrimination in housing		
Justified	49	—
Not justified	36	—
Not sure	15	—

CHAPTER II

Questions from Negro Questionnaire

1(a) I want to ask about how you feel you and your family are personally doing compared to three years ago. As far as your "work situation" goes, do you feel you are better off today than you were three years ago, worse off, or about the same as you were then?

	Total all inter-views		Total non-South		Non-South Low income		Lower middle income		Middle and upper income	
	1966 %	1963 %	1966 %	1963 %	1966 %	1963 %	1966 %	1963 %	1966 %	1963 %
Better off	54	45	51	44	24	31	52	41	59	72
Worse off	9	15	9	15	18	25	5	16	5	5
About the same	32	33	36	34	52	38	41	36	34	21
Not sure	5	7	4	7	6	6	2	7	2	2

East %	Midwest %	South %	West %	Metropolitan city %	Urban town %	Suburban town %	Rural area %
41	42	15	37	38	34	46	25
43	46	68	49	54	52	41	54
16	12	17	14	8	14	13	21
64	70	43	51	57	62	63	54
26	21	42	38	36	30	25	30
10	9	15	11	7	8	12	16
65	70	45	53	58	64	65	56
25	22	40	40	35	28	26	30
10	8	15	7	7	8	9	14
57	59	25	48	45	54	56	43
30	28	53	41	45	33	28	38
13	13	22	11	10	13	16	19

		South						Age			Civil rights pace too slow	Negro community leaders
Total South		Urban		Non-urban		Middle and upper income		Under 35	35–49	50 and over		
1966	1963	1966	1963	1966	1963	1966	1963	1966	1966	1966	1966	1966
%	%	%	%	%	%	%	%	%	%	%	%	%
58	46	58	44	58	44	71	73	58	56	50	55	50
9	14	8	17	10	13	5	4	7	9	11	10	8
27	33	30	32	25	35	21	23	31	31	33	32	34
6	7	4	7	7	8	3	—	4	4	6	3	8

1(a) As far as your "housing accommodations" go, do you feel you are better off today than you were three years ago, worse off, or about the same as you were then?

	Total all inter-views		Total non-South		Non-South					
					Low income		Lower middle income		Middle and upper income	
	1966	1963	1966	1963	1966	1963	1966	1963	1966	1963
	%	%	%	%	%	%	%	%	%	%
Better off	43	43	39	41	27	25	33	40	39	61
Worse off	8	11	9	11	3	31	11	12	7	—
About the same	44	42	47	44	67	44	51	44	49	37
Not sure	5	4	5	4	3	—	5	4	5	2

1(a) As far as your "pay" goes, do you feel you are better off today than you were three years ago, worse off, or about the same as you were then?

	Total all inter-views		Total non-South		Non-South					
					Low income		Lower middle income		Middle and upper income	
	1966	1963	1966	1963	1966	1963	1966	1963	1966	1963
	%	%	%	%	%	%	%	%	%	%
Better off	55	54	55	55	21	13	54	54	66	75
Worse off	9	13	11	15	28	31	9	15	7	9
About the same	29	28	28	25	47	56	30	25	23	16
Not sure	7	5	6	5	4	—	7	6	4	—

	South							Age			Civil rights pace too slow	Negro community leaders
Total South		Urban		Non-urban		Middle and upper income		Under 35	35–49	50 and over		
1966 %	1963 %	1966 %	1963 %	1966 %	1963 %	1966 %	1963 %	1966 %	1966 %	1966 %	1966 %	1966 %
45	45	43	43	48	46	47	55	44	40	45	44	29
8	11	9	14	7	6	2	6	8	9	6	9	3
41	41	41	39	40	45	46	39	43	47	44	42	59
6	3	7	4	5	3	5	—	5	4	5	5	9

	South							Age			Civil rights pace too slow	Negro community leaders
Total South		Urban		Non-urban		Middle and upper income		Under 35	35–49	50 and over		
1966 %	1963 %	1966 %	1963 %	1966 %	1963 %	1966 %	1963 %	1966 %	1966 %	1966 %	1966 %	1966 %
55	54	55	52	54	52	73	81	58	56	50	54	53
7	12	5	14	9	11	5	2	9	7	10	11	7
30	29	34	27	27	33	18	17	27	30	32	30	31
8	5	6	7	10	4	4	—	6	7	8	5	9

1(a) As far as your "being able to register and vote," do you feel you are better off today than you were three years ago, worse off, or about the same as you were then?

	Total all inter-views		Total non-South		Non-South					
					Low income		Lower middle income		Middle and upper income	
	1966 %	1963 %	1966 %	1963 %	1966 %	1963 %	1966 %	1963 %	1966 %	1963 %
Better off	53	31	38	16	21	13	43	16	32	7
Worse off	1	2	2	*	3	—	1	*	1	—
About the same	38	58	53	79	66	81	45	79	62	93
Not sure	8	9	7	5	10	6	11	5	5	—

*—Less than one percent.

1(a) As far as your "being able to eat in any restaurant," do you feel you are better off today than you were three years ago, worse off, or about the same as you were then?

	Total all inter-views		Total non-South		Non-South					
					Low income		Lower middle income		Middle and upper income	
	1966 %	1963 %	1966 %	1963 %	1966 %	1963 %	1966 %	1963 %	1966 %	1963 %
Better off	55	36	49	24	34	19	46	23	48	36
Worse off	2	4	1	3	3	13	—	3	1	—
About the same	27	44	36	59	43	56	34	59	41	59
Not sure	16	16	14	14	20	12	20	15	10	5

*—Less than 1 percent.

Total South			South						Age			Civil rights pace too slow	Negro community leaders
		Urban		Non-urban		Middle and upper income		Under 35	35-49	50 and over		
1966	1963	1966	1963	1966	1963	1966	1963	1966	1966	1966	1966	1966
%	%	%	%	%	%	%	%	%	%	%	%	%
67	42	69	44	65	43	69	21	49	55	56	48	13
1	4	–	4	2	3	–	6	2	1	1	2	1
23	42	23	40	23	39	25	73	39	38	37	44	78
9	12	8	12	10	15	6	–	10	6	6	6	8

Total South			South						Age			Civil rights pace too slow	Negro community leaders
		Urban		Non-urban		Middle and upper income		Under 35	35-49	50 and over		
1966	1963	1966	1963	1966	1963	1966	1963	1966	1966	1966	1966	1966
%	%	%	%	%	%	%	%	%	%	%	%	%
61	45	73	50	50	30	74	90	50	59	57	55	35
3	4	*	3	6	6	1	2	2	3	2	2	1
19	33	11	28	25	44	16	6	33	27	21	31	51
17	18	16	19	19	20	9	2	15	11	20	12	13

1(a) As far as your "being able to get your children educated with white children," do you feel you are better off today than you were three years ago, worse off, or about the same as you were then?

	Total all interviews		Total non-South		Non-South Low income		Non-South Lower middle income		Non-South Middle and upper income	
	1966	1963	1966	1963	1966	1963	1966	1963	1966	1963
	%	%	%	%	%	%	%	%	%	%
Better off	58	39	47	28	39	31	42	28	45	27
Worse off	3	5	3	6	3	13	3	6	3	5
About the same	23	35	34	45	43	50	40	44	36	46
Not sure	16	21	16	21	15	6	15	22	16	22

1(a) As far as your "being able to live in neighborhoods with whites, if you want to," do you feel you are better off today than you were three years ago, worse off, or about the same as you were then?

	Total all interviews		Total non-South		Non-South Low income		Non-South Lower middle income		Non-South Middle and upper income	
	1966	1963	1966	1963	1966	1963	1966	1963	1966	1963
	%	%	%	%	%	%	%	%	%	%
Better off	50	X	44	X	41	X	41	X	43	X
Worse off	4	X	5	X	—	X	3	X	6	X
About the same	32	X	40	X	44	X	42	X	44	X
Not sure	14	X	11	X	15	X	14	X	7	X

X—Question not asked in 1963.

	South							Age			Civil rights pace too slow	Negro community leaders
Total South		Urban		Non-urban		Middle and upper income		Under 35	35–49	50 and over		
1966	1963	1966	1963	1966	1963	1966	1963	1966	1966	1966	1966	1966
%	%	%	%	%	%	%	%	%	%	%	%	%
68	48	74	58	64	31	78	59	57	55	62	55	22
3	4	1	4	4	4	–	2	3	4	2	4	10
13	28	12	19	13	40	9	33	25	28	17	27	52
16	20	13	19	19	25	13	6	15	13	19	14	16

	South							Age			Civil rights pace too slow	Negro community leaders
Total South		Urban		Non-urban		Middle and upper income		Under 35	35–49	50 and over		
1966	1963	1966	1963	1966	1963	1966	1963	1966	1966	1966	1966	1966
%	%	%	%	%	%	%	%	%	%	%	%	%
54	X	63	X	45	X	53	X	44	49	56	49	31
4	X	3	X	5	X	5	X	6	4	3	5	8
25	X	19	X	31	X	33	X	36	33	28	37	50
17	X	15	X	19	X	9	X	14	14	13	9	11

1(a) As far as your "transportation to and from work," do you feel you are better off today than you were three years ago, worse off, or about the same as you were then?

	Total all inter-views		Total non-South		Low income		Lower middle income		Middle and upper income	
					Non-South					
	1966	1963	1966	1963	1966	1963	1966	1963	1966	1963
	%	%	%	%	%	%	%	%	%	%
Better off	39	X	29	X	17	X	25	X	28	X
Worse off	7	X	7	X	6	X	8	X	6	X
About the same	42	X	51	X	59	X	57	X	57	X
Not sure	12	X	13	X	18	X	10	X	9	X

X—*Question not asked in 1963.*

1(c) All in all, compared with three years ago, do you think things for people such as yourself and your family are better, worse, or about the same?

	Total all inter-views		Total non-South		Low income		Lower middle income		Middle and upper income	
					Non-South					
	1966	1963	1966	1963	1966	1963	1966	1963	1966	1963
	%	%	%	%	%	%	%	%	%	%
Better	67	X	63	X	29	X	60	X	66	X
Worse	5	X	5	X	20	X	7	X	3	X
About the same	23	X	28	X	37	X	30	X	29	X
Not sure	5	X	4	X	14	X	3	X	2	X

X—*Question not asked in 1963.*

		South						Age			Civil rights pace too slow	Negro community leaders
Total South		Urban		Non-urban		Middle and upper income		Under 35	35–49	50 and over		
1966 %	1963 %	1966 %	1963 %	1966 %	1963 %	1966 %	1963 %	1966 %	1966 %	1966 %	1966 %	1966 %
47	X	51	X	43	X	46	X	39	38	40	37	13
7	X	4	X	9	X	3	X	5	9	6	7	4
35	X	34	X	36	X	42	X	45	43	41	48	68
11	X	11	X	12	X	9	X	11	10	13	8	15

		South						Age			Civil rights pace too slow	Negro community leaders
Total South		Urban		Non-urban		Middle and upper income		Under 35	35–49	50 and over		
1966 %	1963 %	1966 %	1963 %	1966 %	1963 %	1966 %	1963 %	1966 %	1966 %	1966 %	1966 %	1966 %
72	X	73	X	71	X	75	X	70	68	65	67	52
4	X	3	X	5	X	2	X	2	4	8	5	9
18	X	19	X	17	X	17	X	24	25	20	25	22
6	X	5	X	7	X	6	X	4	3	7	3	17

2(e) At work, would you rather work alongside mostly other Negroes, or would you rather work with a mixed group of whites and Negroes?

	Total all inter-views		Total non-South		Non-South					
					Low income		Lower middle income		Middle and upper income	
	1966 %	1963 %	1966 %	1963 %	1966 %	1963 %	1966 %	1963 %	1966 %	1963 %
Mostly other Negroes	10	11	6	6	4	20	6	6	6	—
Mixed group	80	76	86	84	93	74	89	84	85	88
Not sure	10	13	8	10	3	6	5	10	9	12

5(a) In living in a neighborhood, if you could find the housing you want and like, would you rather live in a neighborhood with Negro families, or in a neighborhood that had both whites and Negroes?

	Total all inter-views		Total non-South		Non-South					
					Low income		Lower middle income		Middle and upper income	
	1966 %	1963 %	1966 %	1963 %	1966 %	1963 %	1966 %	1963 %	1966 %	1963 %
Negroes	17	20	8	11	10	19	7	11	6	12
Whites and Negroes	68	64	79	75	79	75	78	75	80	69
Not sure	15	16	13	14	11	6	15	14	14	19

		South						Age			Civil rights pace too slow	Negro community leaders
Total South		Urban		Non-urban		Middle and upper income		Under 35	35–49	50 and over		
1966 %	1963 %	1966 %	1963 %	1966 %	1963 %	1966 %	1963 %	1966 %	1966 %	1966 %	1966 %	1966 %
13	17	8	14	18	22	3	2	11	9	10	8	6
75	68	81	72	69	63	86	75	80	80	81	84	51
12	15	11	14	13	15	11	23	9	11	9	8	43

		South						Age			Civil rights pace too slow	Negro community leaders
Total South		Urban		Non-urban		Middle and upper income		Under 35	35–49	50 and over		
1966 %	1963 %	1966 %	1963 %	1966 %	1963 %	1966 %	1963 %	1966 %	1966 %	1966 %	1966 %	1966 %
26	27	22	26	29	33	17	6	12	17	21	13	10
57	55	58	57	56	50	70	69	75	67	63	75	59
17	18	20	17	15	17	13	25	13	16	16	12	31

6(b) Would you like to see all Negro children in your family go to school with white children or not?

	Total all inter-views		Total non-South		Non-South					
					Low income		Lower middle income		Middle and upper income	
	1966	1963	1966	1963	1966	1963	1966	1963	1966	1963
	%	%	%	%	%	%	%	%	%	%
Go with whites	70	70	82	79	78	77	86	79	83	77
Not go with whites	11	10	5	7	6	6	4	9	5	—
Not sure	19	20	13	14	16	17	10	12	12	23

25(a) Now I want to give you a list of different people and groups that are run by white people. Do you think _____ have been more helpful or more harmful to Negro rights?

	Total all inter-views		Total non-South		Non-South					
					Low income		Lower middle income		Middle and upper income	
	1966	1963	1966	1963	1966	1963	1966	1963	1966	1963
	%	%	%	%	%	%	%	%	%	%
White Churches										
More helpful	30	23	36	29	45	38	43	27	40	36
More harmful	16	23	14	25	3	25	12	23	15	35
Not sure	54	54	50	46	52	37	45	50	45	29
Local Police										
More helpful	26	X	20	X	25	X	19	X	17	X
More harmful	33	X	41	X	38	X	48	X	50	X
Not sure	41	X	39	X	37	X	33	X	33	X
Labor Unions										
More helpful	43	38	45	41	42	31	47	41	54	40
More harmful	13	25	17	31	5	50	19	29	17	42
Not sure	44	37	38	28	53	19	34	30	29	18
White Businesses										
More helpful	31	18	31	20	24	19	34	20	35	21
More harmful	19	38	23	39	18	44	25	39	28	40
Not sure	50	44	46	41	58	37	41	41	37	39

| Total South | | | South | | | | | Age | | | Civil rights pace too slow | Negro community leaders |
| | | Urban | | Non-urban | | Middle and upper income | | Under 35 | 35–49 | 50 and over | | |
1966 %	1963 %	1966 %	1963 %	1966 %	1963 %	1966 %	1963 %	1966 %	1966 %	1966 %	1966 %	1966 %
60	63	70	66	51	58	63	69	72	69	70	77	69
16	12	13	10	19	16	9	4	10	12	12	8	4
24	25	17	24	30	26	28	27	18	19	18	15	27

| Total South | | | South | | | | | Age | | | Civil rights pace too slow | Negro community leaders |
| | | Urban | | Non-urban | | Middle and upper income | | Under 35 | 35–49 | 50 and over | | |
1966 %	1963 %	1966 %	1963 %	1966 %	1963 %	1966 %	1963 %	1966 %	1966 %	1966 %	1966 %	1966 %
24	19	24	22	23	13	31	36	27	31	33	30	34
19	21	21	19	17	22	18	32	18	16	15	19	38
57	60	55	59	60	65	51	32	55	53	52	51	28
31	X	30	X	32	X	35	X	22	26	30	21	2
26	X	32	X	21	X	25	X	41	33	28	43	84
43	X	38	X	47	X	40	X	37	41	42	36	14
41	36	49	39	35	29	56	49	41	45	46	48	43
8	20	10	18	6	20	5	38	15	13	11	17	31
51	44	41	43	59	51	39	13	44	42	43	35	26
32	17	35	19	28	12	35	26	25	31	40	28	18
15	36	17	33	14	40	17	45	27	18	13	28	54
53	47	48	48	58	48	48	29	48	51	47	44	28

25(a) Now I want to give you a list of different people and groups that are run by white people. Do you think _____ have been more helpful or more harmful to Negro rights?

	Total all inter-views		Total non-South		Non-South					
					Low income		Lower middle income		Middle and upper income	
	1966 %	1963 %	1966 %	1963 %	1966 %	1963 %	1966 %	1963 %	1966 %	1963 %
Catholic Priests										
More helpful	53	55	61	54	72	62	63	53	66	61
More harmful	3	5	4	8	—	13	4	7	4	7
Not sure	44	40	35	38	28	25	33	40	30	32
Jews										
More helpful	33	42	41	49	51	44	33	49	44	54
More harmful	5	9	6	10	3	13	5	10	8	12
Not sure	62	49	53	41	46	43	62	41	48	34
Bus Companies										
More helpful	45	37	47	34	30	25	46	35	54	23
More harmful	9	41	10	43	3	38	13	42	12	56
Not sure	46	22	43	23	67	37	41	23	34	21
Hotels and Motels										
More helpful	37	15	40	17	29	19	29	18	44	9
More harmful	14	41	16	43	12	38	18	42	18	56
Not sure	49	44	44	40	59	43	53	40	38	35

	South								Age			Civil rights pace too slow	Negro community leaders
Total South		Urban		Non-urban		Middle and upper income		Under 35	35–49	50 and over		
1966	1963	1966	1963	1966	1963	1966	1963	1966	1966	1966	1966	1966
%	%	%	%	%	%	%	%	%	%	%	%	%
46	57	54	67	39	40	64	75	51	57	55	61	53
2	3	3	1	2	6	—	—	4	2	3	5	14
52	40	43	32	59	54	36	25	45	41	42	34	33
26	37	35	40	17	28	34	60	26	36	38	37	59
4	7	7	6	2	9	2	9	8	4	4	7	8
70	56	58	54	81	63	64	31	66	60	58	56	33
43	39	50	41	37	36	49	38	45	43	47	48	19
9	40	11	37	7	41	11	51	12	7	10	14	37
48	21	39	22	56	23	40	11	43	50	43	38	44
34	13	45	14	24	9	45	28	36	36	40	37	27
12	40	11	37	13	41	11	52	19	10	13	19	40
54	47	44	49	63	50	44	20	45	54	47	44	33

25(a) Now I want to give you a list of different people and groups that are run by white people. Do you think _____ have been more helpful or more harmful to Negro rights?

	Total all inter-views		Total non-South		Non-South					
					Low income		Lower middle income		Middle and upper income	
	1966 %	1963 %	1966 %	1963 %	1966 %	1963 %	1966 %	1963 %	1966 %	1963 %
Movie Theaters										
More helpful	40	19	45	25	38	19	34	25	50	23
More harmful	10	36	9	33	—	25	14	32	12	37
Not sure	50	45	46	42	62	56	52	43	38	40
Real Estate Companies										
More helpful	22	15	20	14	18	13	19	15	24	2
More harmful	29	44	42	55	27	44	46	52	47	79
Not sure	49	41	38	31	55	43	35	33	29	19
Newspapers										
More helpful	48	X	50	X	62	X	48	X	52	X
More harmful	11	X	13	X	9	X	15	X	16	X
Not sure	41	X	37	X	29	X	37	X	32	X
Federal Government Under Johnson										
More helpful	74	83	77	82	82	81	80	81	86	84
More harmful	2	2	3	3	3	—	3	2	1	9
Not sure	24	15	20	15	15	19	17	17	13	7

*—Less than 1 percent.

		South						Age			Civil rights pace too slow	Negro community leaders
Total South		Urban		Non-urban		Middle and upper income		Under 35	35–49	50 and over		
1966 %	1963 %	1966 %	1963 %	1966 %	1963 %	1966 %	1963 %	1966 %	1966 %	1966 %	1966 %	1966 %
35	14	44	15	28	12	46	26	44	37	40	43	23
10	40	10	38	11	40	10	49	11	10	9	13	35
55	46	46	47	61	48	44	25	45	53	51	44	42
23	16	26	17	20	16	22	13	23	18	26	23	2
17	36	20	32	14	34	25	72	33	31	24	37	84
60	48	54	51	66	50	53	15	44	51	50	40	14
46	X	46	X	46	X	53	X	47	48	51	50	45
10	X	12	X	8	X	9	X	14	12	9	16	33
44	X	42	X	46	X	38	X	39	40	40	34	22
72	85	76	90	68	75	76	98	79	73	76	80	74
1	1	2	1	1	*	1	—	3	1	1	3	8
27	14	22	9	31	25	23	2	18	26	23	17	18

25(a) Now I want to give you a list of different people and groups that are run by white people. Do you think _____ have been more helpful or more harmful to Negro rights?

	Total all inter-views		Total non-South		Non-South					
					Low income		Lower middle income		Middle and upper income	
	1966 %	1963 %	1966 %	1963 %	1966 %	1963 %	1966 %	1963 %	1966 %	1963 %
Television										
More helpful	64	X	68	X	66	X	72	X	72	X
More harmful	5	X	6	X	6	X	4	X	10	X
Not sure	31	X	26	X	28	X	24	X	18	X
Congress										
More helpful	60	54	60	51	57	31	61	53	63	47
More harmful	3	9	5	13	3	13	8	11	4	28
Not sure	37	37	36	36	40	56	31	36	33	25
U.S. Supreme Court										
More helpful	65	80	70	79	79	62	70	78	77	93
More harmful	3	2	3	2	3	13	8	2	3	—
Not sure	32	18	27	19	18	25	22	20	20	7
Local Authorities										
More helpful	35	28	37	33	32	25	33	33	37	33
More harmful	18	39	21	32	18	31	25	31	28	41
Not sure	47	33	42	35	50	44	42	36	35	26

X—Not asked in 1963.

						South				Age			Civil rights pace too slow	Negro community leaders
Total South		Urban		Non-urban		Middle and upper income		Under 35	35–49	50 and over				
1966 %	1963 %	1966 %	1963 %	1966 %	1963 %	1966 %	1963 %	1966 %	1966 %	1966 %	1966 %	1966 %		
62	X	63	X	62	X	71	X	68	64	64	70	63		
3	X	6	X	*	X	1	X	6	5	4	6	18		
35	X	31	X	38	'X	28	X	26	31	32	24	19		
60	56	67	61	55	52	76	40	61	60	63	66	68		
2	7	3	6	1	5	2	23	5	3	2	5	9		
38	37	30	33	44	43	22	37	34	37	35	29	23		
62	81	65	85	59	73	72	98	68	65	67	70	82		
3	1	4	1	2	1	2	2	4	2	3	6	4		
35	18	31	14	39	26	26	—	28	33	30	24	14		
34	24	37	27	31	14	40	47	33	35	39	36	14		
16	44	18	41	15	50	20	38	22	18	16	27	57		
50	32	45	32	54	36	40	15	45	47	45	37	29		

*—Less than 1 percent.

25(a) Now I want to give you a list of different people and groups that are run by white people. Do you think _____ have been more helpful or more harmful to Negro rights?

	Total all inter- views		Total non- South		Non-South					
					Low income		Lower middle income		Middle and upper income	
	1966 %	1963 %	1966 %	1963 %	1966 %	1963 %	1966 %	1963 %	1966 %	1963 %
State Government										
More helpful	42	33	46	40	51	31	43	42	45	37
More harmful	16	35	13	29	6	25	16	27	17	44
Not sure	42	32	41	31	43	44	41	31	38	19
Puerto Ricans										
More helpful	9	10	11	14	3	19	12	14	12	9
More harmful	10	20	12	25	7	25	10	24	14	33
Not sure	81	70	77	61	90	56	78	62	74	58
The Federal Anti- Poverty Program										
More helpful	66	X	70	X	76	X	76	X	73	X
More harmful	3	X	4	X	3	X	5	X	3	X
Not sure	31	X	26	X	21	X	19	X	24	X
White College Students										
More helpful	47	X	53	X	53	X	54	X	55	X
More harmful	5	X	5	X	3	X	6	X	6	X
Not sure	48	X	42	X	44	X	40	X	39	X

X—Question not asked in 1963.

							Middle and upper income		Age			Civil rights pace too slow	Negro community leaders
		South											
Total South		Urban		Non-urban				Under 35	35–49	50 and over		
1966 %	1963 %	1966 %	1963 %	1966 %	1963 %	1966 %	1963 %	1966 %	1966 %	1966 %	1966 %	1966 %
38	27	40	29	36	19	49	45	41	42	45	44	19
19	40	19	37	19	44	21	42	19	14	16	22	45
43	33	41	34	45	37	30	13	40	44	39	34	36
7	6	9	6	5	5	11	17	9	10	8	10	23
7	17	8	13	6	20	6	19	12	7	11	13	2
86	77	83	81	89	75	83	64	79	83	81	77	75
62	X	60	X	63	X	75	X	64	68	69	69	55
2	X	4	X	1	X	2	X	4	2	2	5	15
36	X	36	X	36	X	23	X	32	30	29	26	30
41	X	51	X	33	X	57	X	47	49	47	52	73
5	X	4	X	5	X	6	X	7	4	4	9	2
54	X	45	X	62	X	37	X	46	47	49	39	25

CHAPTER III

23(a) Now I want to read off to you a list of groups and people who have been prominent in the fight for Negro rights. For each I wish you would tell me how you would rate the job that person or group has done—excellent, pretty good, only fair, or poor.

	Total all inter-views		Total non-South		Low income		Lower middle income		Middle and upper income	
	Non-South									
	1966 %	1963 %	1966 %	1963 %	1966 %	1963 %	1966 %	1963 %	1966 %	1963 %
A. Philip Randolph										
Excellent	16	X	17	X	14	X	12	X	22	X
Pretty good	19	X	22	X	25	X	20	X	24	X
Only fair	5	X	8	X	3	X	9	X	8	X
Poor	°	X	1	X	—	X	1	X	1	X
Not sure	60	X	52	X	58	X	58	X	45	X
Stokely Carmichael										
Excellent	7	X	6	X	3	X	6	X	7	X
Pretty good	12	X	14	X	15	X	12	X	12	X
Only fair	8	X	10	X	—	X	11	X	11	X
Poor	5	X	6	X	4	X	3	X	7	X
Not sure	68	X	64	X	78	X	68	X	63	X
Floyd McKissick										
Excellent	6	X	6	X	3	X	4	X	6	X
Pretty good	13	X	15	X	19	X	17	X	13	X
Only fair	7	X	8	X	—	X	8	X	7	X
Poor	3	X	3	X	3	X	3	X	4	X
Not sure	71	X	68	X	75	X	68	X	70	X

X—Question not asked in 1963.
°—Less than 1 percent.

		South						Age			Civil rights pace too slow	Negro community leaders
Total South		Urban		Non-urban		Middle and upper income		Under 35	35–49	50 and over		
1966 %	1963 %	1966 %	1963 %	1966 %	1963 %	1966 %	1963 %	1966 %	1966 %	1966 %	1966 %	1966 %
14	X	16	X	12	X	25	X	8	18	22	19	61
16	X	19	X	13	X	17	X	18	20	19	22	22
3	X	5	X	2	X	6	X	6	6	4	6	7
*	X	*	X	*	X	—	X	*	*	1	1	2
67	X	60	X	73	X	52	X	68	56	54	52	8
7	X	10	X	5	X	9	X	6	8	7	8	17
10	X	11	X	9	X	14	X	12	13	10	14	16
6	X	7	X	6	X	5	X	8	10	8	10	22
3	X	2	X	4	X	7	X	4	5	6	5	19
74	X	70	X	76	X	65	X	70	64	69	63	26
7	X	8	X	5	X	8	X	6	8	6	7	13
12	X	16	X	8	X	16	X	15	15	10	15	22
6	X	7	X	5	X	7	X	5	8	7	8	25
3	X	2	X	4	X	7	X	2	4	4	3	18
72	X	67	X	78	X	62	X	72	65	73	67	22

23(a) Now I want to read off to you a list of groups and people who have been prominent in the fight for Negro rights. For each I wish you would tell me how you would rate the job that person or group has done—excellent, pretty good, only fair, or poor.

NAACP (National Association for the Advancement of Colored People)

	Total all inter- views		Total non- South		Non-South					
					Low income		Lower middle income		Middle and upper income	
	1966	1963	1966	1963	1966	1963	1966	1963	1966	1963
	%	%	%	%	%	%	%	%	%	%
Excellent	58	75	58	72	56	57	56	72	58	79
Pretty good	23	16	29	21	32	25	32	21	31	16
Only fair	6	3	7	3	9	6	6	3	8	5
Poor	1	—	2	1	—	6	1	1	2	—
Not sure	12	6	4	3	3	6	5	3	1	—

Martin Luther King

	1966	1963	1966	1963	1966	1963	1966	1963	1966	1963
Excellent	75	78	77	82	80	59	75	81	83	93
Pretty good	13	10	16	11	14	23	17	11	15	7
Only fair	2	3	2	2	—	6	3	2	2	—
Poor	1	1	2	1	3	6	1	1	—	—
Not sure	9	8	3	4	3	6	4	5	—	—

CORE (Congress of Racial Equality)

	1966	1963	1966	1963	1966	1963	1966	1963	1966	1963
Excellent	34	38	36	37	35	19	39	36	35	50
Pretty good	26	21	33	24	29	19	34	23	36	36
Only fair	9	7	11	6	10	—	8	6	12	7
Poor	2	1	3	1	3	6	—	1	2	—
Not sure	29	33	17	32	23	56	19	34	15	7

						South		Age				
	Total South		Urban		Non-urban		Middle and upper income		Under 35	35–49	50 and over	Civil rights pace too slow	Negro community leaders
	1966 %	1963 %	1966 %	1963 %	1966 %	1963 %	1966 %	1963 %	1966 %	1966 %	1966 %	1966 %	1966 %
	57	77	63	81	53	68	64	89	52	57	64	59	49
	18	12	19	11	16	14	21	9	28	24	19	24	23
	4	2	3	1	5	5	1	2	7	6	5	8	14
	1	–	1	–	*	–	–	–	2	1	1	2	7
	20	9	14	7	26	13	14	–	11	12	11	7	7
	73	77	81	82	67	70	83	90	76	75	76	80	68
	11	9	7	6	13	12	6	6	16	13	10	13	19
	1	3	1	2	1	4	*	2	1	2	2	2	3
	*	1	*	1	1	–	1	2	1	1	1	1	4
	15	10	11	9	18	14	10	–	6	9	11	4	6
	31	39	39	40	25	37	43	44	32	37	33	40	24
	20	18	22	21	18	12	25	28	31	23	26	29	41
	7	8	6	8	8	8	5	13	10	10	8	9	16
	1	–	1	–	1	–	2	2	1	2	3	2	8
	41	35	32	31	48	43	25	13	26	28	30	20	11

*—Less than 1 percent.

23(a) Now I want to read off to you a list of groups and people who have been prominent in the fight for Negro rights. For each I wish you would tell me how you would rate the job that person or group has done—excellent, pretty good, only fair, or poor.

| | | | | | Non-South | | | | | |
| | Total all interviews | | Total non-South | | Low income | | Lower middle income | | Middle and upper income | |
	1966 %	1963 %	1966 %	1963 %	1966 %	1963 %	1966 %	1963 %	1966 %	1963 %
Adam Clayton Powell										
Excellent	20	27	21	26	23	6	20	29	20	9
Pretty good	24	24	28	27	29	20	26	25	26	36
Only fair	14	16	18	19	19	14	21	19	22	20
Poor	7	7	13	9	9	—	9	8	17	21
Not sure	35	26	20	19	20	60	24	19	15	14
Elijah Muhammad										
Excellent	4	5	4	7	3	6	6	7	2	2
Pretty good	8	10	9	13	15	19	13	13	8	13
Only fair	7	6	10	8	3	13	15	6	8	18
Poor	36	29	48	40	49	31	36	39	58	51
Not sure	45	50	29	32	30	31	30	35	24	16
James Meredith										
Excellent	42	59	40	60	48	38	42	63	40	43
Pretty good	29	20	36	24	37	25	33	22	38	43
Only fair	9	5	13	5	3	—	13	4	16	7
Poor	1	1	1	1	—	6	1	1	—	7
Not sure	19	15	10	10	12	31	11	10	6	—
James Farmer										
Excellent	25	X	26	X	34	X	23	X	25	X
Pretty good	22	X	28	X	15	X	25	X	31	X
Only fair	8	X	10	X	—	X	12	X	13	X
Poor	1	X	2	X	—	X	2	X	2	X
Not sure	45	X	34	X	51	X	38	X	29	X

X—Question not asked in 1963.

| | South | | | | | | | | Age | | | Civil rights pace too slow | Negro community leaders |
| | Total South | | Urban | | Non-urban | | Middle and upper income | | Under 35 | 35–49 | 50 and over | | |
	1966 %	1963 %	1966 %	1963 %	1966 %	1963 %	1966 %	1963 %	1966 %	1966 %	1966 %	1966 %	1966 %
	19	27	21	30	18	22	28	29	18	23	21	26	18
	20	23	22	22	18	21	26	33	26	22	25	27	31
	10	14	15	14	6	12	13	26	17	11	16	17	23
	2	4	4	3	1	5	2	6	9	8	5	7	14
	49	32	38	31	57	40	31	6	30	36	33	23	14
	4	4	5	4	3	2	4	9	5	5	4	7	6
	7	6	8	7	6	5	3	9	11	9	5	10	9
	5	5	6	4	4	5	9	12	9	8	5	9	18
	26	22	34	21	19	17	43	46	39	35	37	41	47
	58	63	47	64	68	71	41	24	36	43	49	33	20
	44	58	48	66	41	47	56	62	42	40	48	50	15
	23	17	27	14	19	18	24	26	35	30	23	29	20
	5	5	6	3	5	8	6	4	11	9	7	11	41
	*	1	—	1	*	—	—	4	*	1	1	*	6
	28	19	19	16	35	27	14	4	12	20	21	10	18
	23	X	24	X	22	X	30	X	21	26	27	30	28
	16	X	21	X	11	X	21	X	26	22	19	24	42
	6	X	7	X	5	X	8	X	7	10	7	9	18
	*	X	1	X	—	X	—	X	1	2	1	1	4
	55	X	47	X	62	X	41	X	45	40	46	36	8

*—Less than 1 percent.

23(a) Now I want to read off to you a list of groups and people who have been prominent in the fight for Negro rights. For each I wish you would tell me how you would rate the job that person or group has done—excellent, pretty good, only fair, or poor.

	Total all inter-views		Total non-South		Non-South					
					Low income		Lower middle income		Middle and upper income	
	1966 %	1963 %	1966 %	1963 %	1966 %	1963 %	1966 %	1963 %	1966 %	1963 %
Urban League										
Excellent	25	27	31	31	25	13	26	31	32	37
Pretty good	25	27	32	33	21	25	32	32	34	42
Only fair	8	9	11	12	9	—	11	13	13	12
Poor	1	1	1	1	—	13	—	1	1	—
Not sure	41	36	25	23	45	49	31	23	20	9
SNCC (Student Non-Violent Coordinating Committee)										
Excellent	23	10	25	13	28	6	26	14	25	7
Pretty good	21	8	26	9	25	13	24	9	29	5
Only fair	10	3	9	2	9	—	7	2	9	2
Poor	4	1	6	1	—	—	3	1	6	2
Not sure	42	78	34	75	38	81	40	74	31	84
Southern Christian Leadership Conference										
Excellent	34	32	36	40	28	31	30	40	41	42
Pretty good	21	24	24	25	25	25	24	25	23	21
Only fair	5	9	7	6	9	6	7	5	7	9
Poor	1	2	2	2	3	—	—	2	3	2
Not sure	39	33	31	27	35	38	39	28	26	26

| | | South | | | | | | Age | | | Civil rights pace too slow | Negro community leaders |
| Total South | | Urban | | Non-urban | | Middle and upper income | | Under 35 | 35–49 | 50 and over | | |
1966 %	1963 %	1966 %	1963 %	1966 %	1963 %	1966 %	1963 %	1966 %	1966 %	1966 %	1966 %	1966 %
20	25	25	27	16	15	33	54	20	30	27	28	36
17	22	26	23	9	19	26	33	27	25	23	29	22
6	7	6	5	5	10	3	6	9	8	8	9	25
*	1	*	1	*	1	—	1	1	*	1	1	9
57	45	43	44	70	55	38	6	43	37	41	33	8
22	8	27	6	17	7	27	22	23	25	23	29	30
17	8	24	7	11	8	20	13	26	18	21	25	23
11	4	10	4	12	4	20	6	9	10	12	11	23
2	*	2	—	2	1	3	—	3	5	4	4	11
48	80	37	83	58	80	30	59	39	42	40	31	13
32	26	33	29	31	21	41	30	30	33	41	36	43
18	23	25	25	12	20	25	23	23	21	20	22	31
4	11	3	10	4	10	2	23	6	4	6	7	15
*	1	1	2	—	1	—	—	1	1	1	1	1
46	39	38	34	53	47	32	24	40	41	32	34	10

*—Less than 1 percent.

23(a) Now I want to read off to you a list of groups and people who have been prominent in the fight for Negro rights. For each I wish you would tell me how you would rate the job that person or group has done—excellent, pretty good, only fair, or poor.

	Total all interviews		Total non-South		Non-South					
					Low income		Lower middle income		Middle and upper income	
	1966 %	1963 %	1966 %	1963 %	1966 %	1963 %	1966 %	1963 %	1966 %	1963 %
Roy Wilkins										
Excellent	39	49	38	48	24	31	30	48	46	63
Pretty good	25	19	31	22	37	19	35	22	30	16
Only fair	6	6	8	9	14	—	10	9	8	9
Poor	*	1	1	1	—	—	—	1	1	*
Not sure	30	25	22	20	25	50	25	20	15	12
Ralph Bunche										
Excellent	33	42	35	41	31	38	29	25	37	38
Pretty good	20	20	25	20	23	22	27	38	27	21
Only fair	8	8	11	8	14	11	15	—	13	12
Poor	2	2	3	2	—	3	3	—	3	3
Not sure	37	28	26	29	32	26	26	37	20	26
Jackie Robinson										
Excellent	41	55	43	55	29	44	39	56	47	50
Pretty good	25	25	31	30	39	38	34	29	30	35
Only fair	10	7	12	8	20	6	9	8	13	9
Poor	1	1	2	1	3	—	3	1	2	2
Not sure	23	12	12	6	9	12	15	6	8	4
Bayard Rustin										
Excellent	10	X	13	X	12	X	8	X	10	X
Pretty good	12	X	15	X	9	X	17	X	17	X
Only fair	8	X	10	X	3	X	10	X	13	X
Poor	2	X	2	X	—	X	4	X	2	X
Not sure	68	X	60	X	76	X	61	X	58	X

*—Less than 1 percent.

| | | South | | | | | | Age | | | Civil rights pace too slow | Negro community leaders |
| Total South | | Urban | | Non-urban | | Middle and upper income | | Under 35 | 35–49 | 50 and over | | |
1966 %	1963 %	1966 %	1963 %	1966 %	1963 %	1966 %	1963 %	1966 %	1966 %	1966 %	1966 %	1966 %
40	49	46	54	36	38	59	68	35	39	45	42	44
19	17	22	17	16	17	17	19	28	26	21	26	18
4	4	5	3	3	6	4	4	7	4	7	8	20
*	—	*	—	—	—	—	2	1	—	1	1	9
37	30	27	26	45	39	20	7	29	31	26	23	9
30	47	32	42	29	45	45	32	27	34	39	36	27
15	26	20	19	11	20	17	18	21	20	19	21	22
5	9	8	5	3	4	8	7	11	6	7	11	17
1	2	1	1	1	—	—	1	2	2	1	3	15
49	16	39	33	56	31	30	42	39	38	34	29	19
39	55	40	59	40	46	56	68	37	41	46	45	22
21	21	26	24	16	18	21	21	28	28	22	28	36
7	7	7	5	7	8	6	6	11	8	10	10	22
1	—	1	—	*	—	—	—	3	1	1	3	6
32	17	26	12	37	28	17	5	21	22	21	14	14
8	X	11	X	6	X	13	X	6	13	12	12	22
9	X	12	X	6	X	9	X	13	12	11	14	31
6	X	8	X	5	X	8	X	6	10	8	10	24
1	X	1	X	1	X	2	X	1	2	2	2	7
76	X	68	X	82	X	68	X	72	63	67	62	16

23(a) Now I want to read off to you a list of groups and people who have been prominent in the fight for Negro rights. For each I wish you would tell me how you would rate the job that person or group has done—excellent, pretty good, only fair, or poor.

						Non-South				
	Total all inter-views		Total non-South		Low income		Lower middle income		Middle and upper income	
	1966	1963	1966	1963	1966	1963	1966	1963	1966	1963
	%	%	%	%	%	%	%	%	%	%
Thurgood Marshall										
Excellent	29	50	30	X	21	X	24	X	36	X
Pretty good	19	17	25	X	19	X	29	X	25	X
Only fair	5	4	7	X	3	X	6	X	8	X
Poor	1	*	1	X	—	X	2	X	1	X
Not sure	46	29	37	X	57	X	39	X	30	X
Charles Evers										
Excellent	31	X	34	X	42	X	23	X	35	X
Pretty good	23	X	29	X	24	X	35	X	30	X
Only fair	6	X	8	X	—	X	10	X	9	X
Poor	2	X	2	X	3	X	2	X	1	X
Not sure	38	X	27	X	31	X	30	X	25	X
Black Muslims										
Excellent	4	4	4	5	3	6	3	5	2	5
Pretty good	5	7	6	8	3	13	8	7	6	14
Only fair	6	6	7	8	3	6	11	7	6	14
Poor	43	38	52	43	57	25	47	43	60	49
Not sure	42	45	31	36	34	50	31	38	26	18

X—Not asked in 1963.

			South						Age			Civil rights pace too slow	Negro community leaders
Total South		Urban		Non-urban		Middle and upper income		Under 35	35–49	50 and over			
1966 %	1963 %	1966 %	1963 %	1966 %	1963 %	1966 %	1963 %	1966 %	1966 %	1966 %	1966 %	1966 %
29	X	30	X	28	X	40	X	20	33	36	31	66
14	X	18	X	11	X	17	X	19	21	19	19	15
3	X	3	X	2	X	2	X	4	3	6	6	7
1	X	1	X	*	X	–	X	1	*	2	1	11
53	X	48	X	59	X	41	X	56	43	37	43	1
29	X	33	X	26	X	39	X	29	33	33	38	32
18	X	21	X	15	X	27	X	26	23	22	25	36
5	X	5	X	4	X	2	X	5	6	8	6	16
2	X	3	X	2	X	1	X	3	2	2	2	1
46	X	38	X	53	X	31	X	37	36	35	29	15
5	3	6	2	3	2	5	6	4	5	4	6	4
4	5	4	5	3	5	3	2	8	3	2	5	17
4	4	5	3	3	3	5	13	8	6	4	7	16
34	30	43	29	26	27	49	49	44	45	41	49	48
53	58	42	61	65	63	38	30	36	41	49	33	15

23(a) Now I want to read off to you a list of groups and people who have been prominent in the fight for Negro rights. For each I wish you would tell me how you would rate the job that person or group has done—excellent, pretty good, only fair, or poor.

	Total all inter-views		Total non-South		Non-South					
					Low income		Lower middle income		Middle and upper income	
	1966 %	1963 %	1966 %	1963 %	1966 %	1963 %	1966 %	1963 %	1966 %	1963 %
Dick Gregory										
Excellent	33	38	37	X	27	X	39	X	39	X
Pretty good	23	24	30	X	33	X	30	X	28	X
Only fair	10	8	12	X	9	X	9	X	18	X
Poor	1	1	2	X	—	X	1	X	2	X
Not sure	33	29	19	X	31	X	21	X	13	X
Julian Bond										
Excellent	14	X	14	X	11	X	13	X	13	X
Pretty good	17	X	20	X	12	X	23	X	20	X
Only fair	10	X	13	X	12	X	12	X	15	X
Poor	2	X	3	X	—	X	2	X	2	X
Not sure	57	X	50	X	65	X	50	X	50	X
Whitney Young										
Excellent	16	X	17	X	6	X	16	X	16	X
Pretty good	17	X	21	X	22	X	20	X	23	X
Only fair	7	X	9	X	6	X	11	X	10	X
Poor	1	X	1	X	—	X	1	X	1	X
Not sure	59	X	52	X	66	X	52	X	50	X

X—*Question not asked in 1963.*

Total South		Urban		Non-urban		Middle and upper income		Under 35	35–49	50 and over	Civil rights pace too slow	Negro community leaders
1966 %	1963 %	1966 %	1963 %	1966 %	1963 %	1966 %	1963 %	1966 %	1966 %	1966 %	1966 %	1966 %
28	X	35	X	23	X	36	X	32	35	33	41	29
17	X	19	X	15	X	27	X	25	21	23	25	36
8	X	13	X	3	X	11	X	11	11	7	11	16
1	X	1	X	1	X	2	X	3	1	1	1	8
46	X	32	X	58	X	24	X	29	32	36	22	11
14	X	14	X	14	X	20	X	10	16	17	17	18
14	X	18	X	9	X	17	X	17	18	16	18	32
7	X	7	X	7	X	8	X	8	9	12	12	25
2	X	2	X	2	X	3	X	3	2	3	2	7
63	X	59	X	68	X	52	X	62	55	52	51	18
14	X	16	X	12	X	24	X	10	20	19	18	46
14	X	17	X	11	X	15	X	17	19	18	18	24
4	X	6	X	2	X	5	X	6	6	8	8	13
1	X	*	X	2	X	1	X	1	1	1	1	8
67	X	61	X	73	X	55	X	66	54	54	55	9

27(e) In the next five years, do you think the attitude of white people about Negro rights will get better, worse, or stay about the same?

	Total all inter-views		Total non-South		Non-South					
					Low income		Lower middle income		Middle and upper income	
	1966 %	1963 %	1966 %	1963 %	1966 %	1963 %	1966 %	1963 %	1966 %	1963 %
Better	69	73	69	71	67	44	75	72	73	70
Worse	2	2	3	1	8	13	2	1	2	—
Stay the same	13	11	15	11	10	13	12	12	16	9
Not sure	16	14	13	17	15	30	11	15	9	21

19(b) As far as all the things that have been going on lately with Negro rights, do you think things are moving about right these days, too fast, or too slow?

	Total all inter-views		Total non-South		Non-South					
					Low income		Lower middle income		Middle and upper income	
	1966 %	1963 %	1966 %	1963 %	1966 %	1963 %	1966 %	1963 %	1966 %	1963 %
About right	35	31	27	32	23	31	29	33	27	17
Too fast	4	3	2	2	3	—	3	2	1	7
Too slow	43	51	55	57	56	50	58	55	56	71
Not sure	18	15	16	9	18	19	10	10	16	5

Total South		Urban		Non-urban		Middle and upper income		Under 35	35–49	50 and over	Civil rights pace too slow	Negro community leaders
1966 %	1963 %	1966 %	1963 %	1966 %	1963 %	1966 %	1963 %	1966 %	1966 %	1966 %	1966 %	1966 %
69	74	70	81	68	61	72	98	70	70	70	72	59
1	2	2	1	1	3	–	–	3	*	3	3	5
12	10	11	7	12	15	15	2	13	17	10	13	8
18	14	17	11	19	21	13	–	14	13	17	12	28

Total South		Urban		Non-urban		Middle and upper income		Under 35	35–49	50 and over	Civil rights pace too slow	Negro community leaders
1966 %	1963 %	1966 %	1963 %	1966 %	1963 %	1966 %	1963 %	1966 %	1966 %	1966 %	1966 %	1966 %
43	32	42	32	44	35	46	17	30	37	39	–	9
6	3	3	3	9	4	4	–	3	5	5	–	–
31	46	41	48	22	38	39	70	54	41	35	100	82
20	19	14	17	25	23	11	13	13	17	21	–	9

18(a) Some Negro leaders have said that Negroes can only succeed in winning rights if they use nonviolent means to demonstrate. Others disagree. Do you personally feel Negroes today can win their rights without resorting to violence or do you think it will have to be an eye for an eye and a tooth for a tooth?

	Total all inter-views		Total non-South		Non-South					
					Low income		Lower middle income		Middle and upper income	
	1966 %	1963 %	1966 %	1963 %	1966 %	1963 %	1966 %	1963 %	1966 %	1963 %
Can win without violence	59	63	55	65	53	50	55	64	54	77
Will have to use violence	21	22	23	22	26	25	28	23	21	9
Not sure	20	15	22	13	21	25	17	13	25	14

15(b) On the whole, do you approve or disapprove of Black Nationalism?

	Total all inter-views		Total non-South		Non-South					
					Low income		Lower middle income		Middle and upper income	
	1966 %	1963 %	1966 %	1963 %	1966 %	1963 %	1966 %	1963 %	1966 %	1963 %
Approve	5	X	5	X	9	X	4	X	4	X
Disapprove	63	X	67	X	68	X	60	X	72	X
Not sure	32	X	28	X	23	X	36	X	24	X

X—*Question not asked in 1963.*

Total South		Urban		Non-urban		Middle and upper income		Under 35	35–49	50 and over	Civil rights pace too slow	Negro community leaders
1966 %	1963 %	1966 %	1963 %	1966 %	1963 %	1966 %	1963 %	1966 %	1966 %	1966 %	1966 %	1966 %
61	62	62	61	59	59	73	78	51	58	66	55	48
20	21	24	23	17	22	15	9	29	19	17	29	16
19	17	14	16	24	19	12	13	20	23	17	16	36

Total South		Urban		Non-urban		Middle and upper income		Under 35	35–49	50 and over	Civil rights pace too slow	Negro community leaders
1966 %	1963 %	1966 %	1963 %	1966 %	1963 %	1966 %	1963 %	1966 %	1966 %	1966 %	1966 %	1966 %
6	X	5	X	7	X	2	X	8	4	3	7	18
58	X	65	X	52	X	72	X	55	66	68	64	62
36	X	30	X	41	X	26	X	37	30	29	29	20

15(c) On the whole, do you approve or disapprove of the Black Muslim movement?

	Total all inter-views 1966 %	Total all inter-views 1963 %	Total non-South 1966 %	Total non-South 1963 %	Non-South Low income 1966 %	Non-South Low income 1963 %	Non-South Lower middle income 1966 %	Non-South Lower middle income 1963 %	Non-South Middle and upper income 1966 %	Non-South Middle and upper income 1963 %
Approve	4	6	5	9	9	13	4	9	4	14
Disapprove	66	53	72	59	71	57	64	31	78	56
Not sure	30	41	23	32	20	30	32	60	18	30

15(a) Some people are saying that Negroes have tried to work out their problems with white people and there's been a lot of talk but not much action. Now, they say, Negroes should give up working together with whites and just depend on their own people. Do you tend to agree or disagree with people who say this?

	Total all inter-views 1966 %	Total all inter-views 1963 %	Total non-South 1966 %	Total non-South 1963 %	Non-South Low income 1966 %	Non-South Low income 1963 %	Non-South Lower middle income 1966 %	Non-South Lower middle income 1963 %	Non-South Middle and upper income 1966 %	Non-South Middle and upper income 1963 %
Agree	11	X	8	X	7	X	10	X	9	X
Disagree	81	X	85	X	81	X	79	X	87	X
Not sure	8	X	7	X	12	X	11	X	4	X

X—*Question not asked in 1963.*

Total South								Age			Civil rights pace too slow	Negro community leaders
		Urban		Non-urban		Middle and upper income		Under 35	35–49	50 and over		
1966	1963	1966	1963	1966	1963	1966	1963	1966	1966	1966	1966	1966
%	%	%	%	%	%	%	%	%	%	%	%	%
2	3	3	3	1	2	1	4	6	2	3	6	15
61	48	68	50	54	39	77	75	63	68	67	69	62
37	49	29	47	45	59	22	21	31	30	30	25	23

Total South								Age			Civil rights pace too slow	Negro community leaders
		Urban		Non-urban		Middle and upper income		Under 35	35–49	50 and over		
1966	1963	1966	1963	1966	1963	1966	1963	1966	1966	1966	1966	1966
%	%	%	%	%	%	%	%	%	%	%	%	%
13	X	8	X	17	X	7	X	9	10	12	9	6
78	X	85	X	72	X	89	X	84	81	81	85	81
9	X	7	X	11	X	4	X	7	9	7	6	13

30(b) Do you favor or oppose the idea of "Black Power"?

| | Total all inter- views | Total non- South | Non-South | | | Total South |
			Low income	Lower middle income	Middle and upper income	
	1966	1966	1966	1966	1966	1966
	%	%	%	%	%	%
Favor	25	28	13	31	26	22
Oppose	37	40	40	31	45	32
Not sure	38	32	47	38	29	46

18(c) Some people have said that since there are 10 whites for every Negro in America, if it came to white against Negro, the Negroes would lose. Do you agree with this or disagree with it?

| | Total all inter- views | | Total non- South | | Non-South | | | | | |
					Low income		Lower middle income		Middle and upper income	
	1966	1963	1966	1963	1966	1963	1966	1963	1966	1963
	%	%	%	%	%	%	%	%	%	%
Agree	27	23	33	20	31	25	33	18	32	25
Disagree	49	50	46	53	54	52	49	55	48	50
Not sure	24	27	21	27	15	23	18	27	20	25

18(f) Do you think the riots that have taken place in Los Angeles and other cities have helped or hurt the cause of Negro rights or don't you think it makes much difference?

| | Total all inter- views | | Total non- South | | Non-South | | | | | |
					Low income		Lower middle income		Middle and upper income	
	1966	1963	1966	1963	1966	1963	1966	1963	1966	1963
	%	%	%	%	%	%	%	%	%	%
Helped	34	X	32	X	21	X	36	X	31	X
Hurt	20	X	26	X	15	X	25	X	28	X
Not much difference	17	X	19	X	30	X	20	X	19	X
Not sure	29	X	23	X	34	X	19	X	22	X

X—*Question not asked in 1963.*

	South			Age			Civil rights pace too slow	Negro community leaders
	Urban	Non-urban	Middle and upper income	Under 35	35–49	50 and over		
	1966	1966	1966	1966	1966	1966	1966	1966
	%	%	%	%	%	%	%	%
	20	24	19	31	25	22	30	51
	34	30	38	33	40	39	34	33
	46	46	43	36	35	39	36	16

Total South		South						Age			Civil rights pace too slow	Negro community leaders
		Urban		Non-urban		Middle and upper income		Under 35	35–49	50 and over		
1966	1963	1966	1963	1966	1963	1966	1963	1966	1966	1966	1966	1966
%	%	%	%	%	%	%	%	%	%	%	%	%
22	21	23	23	20	14	26	46	26	26	30	30	61
52	50	56	53	48	47	44	37	51	49	49	54	14
26	29	21	24	32	39	30	17	23	25	21	16	25

Total South		South						Age			Civil rights pace too slow	Negro community leaders
		Urban		Non-urban		Middle and upper income		Under 35	35–49	50 and over		
1966	1963	1966	1963	1966	1963	1966	1963	1966	1966	1966	1966	1966
%	%	%	%	%	%	%	%	%	%	%	%	%
35	X	42	X	30	X	33	X	38	37	31	41	38
15	X	15	X	15	X	20	X	21	19	20	19	23
16	X	12	X	19	X	14	X	15	19	16	18	16
34	X	31	X	36	X	33	X	26	25	33	22	23

18(h) Do you think there will be more riots in other cities in the months ahead or not?

	Total all inter-views		Total non-South		Non-South Low income		Non-South Lower middle income		Non-South Middle and upper income	
	1966 %	1963 %	1966 %	1963 %	1966 %	1963 %	1966 %	1963 %	1966 %	1963 %
Will be	61	X	62	X	75	X	65	X	64	X
Will not be	8	X	7	X	6	X	10	X	5	X
Not sure	31	X	31	X	19	X	25	X	31	X

X—*Question not asked in 1963.*

18(i) Would you join in something like that [riots] or not?

	Total all inter-views		Total non-South		Non-South Low income		Non-South Lower middle income		Non-South Middle and upper income	
	1966 %	1963 %	1966 %	1963 %	1966 %	1963 %	1966 %	1963 %	1966 %	1963 %
Would join	15	X	13	X	11	X	14	X	14	X
Would not join	61	X	62	X	71	X	61	X	61	X
Not sure	24	X	25	X	18	X	25	X	25	X

X—*Question not asked in 1963.*

Total South		South						Age			Civil rights pace too slow	Negro community leaders
		Urban		Non-urban		Middle and upper income		Under 35	35–49	50 and over		
1966	1963	1966	1963	1966	1963	1966	1963	1966	1966	1966	1966	1966
%	%	%	%	%	%	%	%	%	%	%	%	%
61	X	67	X	56	X	61	X	66	62	58	66	79
8	X	10	X	6	X	9	X	7	7	9	9	2
31	X	23	X	38	X	30	X	27	31	33	25	19

Total South		South						Age			Civil rights pace too slow	Negro community leaders
		Urban		Non-urban		Middle and upper income		Under 35	35–49	50 and over		
1966	1963	1966	1963	1966	1963	1966	1963	1966	1966	1966	1966	1966
%	%	%	%	%	%	%	%	%	%	%	%	%
18	X	21	X	14	X	15	X	19	15	13	19	1
59	X	60	X	59	X	64	X	57	60	66	56	75
23	X	19	X	27	X	21	X	24	25	21	25	24

CHAPTER VII

29(a) Now I want to ask you some questions about different types of people and situations. Do you know anyone who:

	Total all inter-views		Total non-South		Non-South					
					Low income		Lower middle income		Middle and upper income	
	1966 %	1963 %	1966 %	1963 %	1966 %	1963 %	1966 %	1963 %	1966 %	1963 %
Is an unwed mother	63	X	61	X	55	X	62	X	61	X
Is a teenager on dope	11	X	16	X	34	X	19	X	17	X
Is a high school drop-out	59	X	58	X	56	X	61	X	61	X
Has taken part in a riot	10	X	15	X	13	X	22	X	14	X
Has been sent to jail	36	X	41	X	40	X	35	X	46	X
Is a mother in a family where the father has left home	47	X	51	X	46	X	55	X	53	X

X—*Question not asked in 1963.*

29(d) In most Negro families, do you think the mother or the father is usually the one who teaches the children to behave right?

	Total all inter-views		Total non-South		Non-South					
					Low income		Lower middle income		Middle and upper income	
	1966 %	1963 %	1966 %	1963 %	1966 %	1963 %	1966 %	1963 %	1966 %	1963 %
Mother	51	X	51	X	58	X	59	X	48	X
Father	6	X	8	X	3	X	3	X	11	X
Both (volunteered)	33	X	32	X	26	X	30	X	37	X
Neither	1	X	1	X	—	X	1	X	—	X
Not sure	9	X	8	X	13	X	7	X	4	X

X—*Question not asked in 1963.*

		South						Age			Civil rights pace too slow	Negro community leaders
Total South		Urban		Non-urban		Middle and upper income		Under 35	35–49	50 and over		
1966 %	1963 %	1966 %	1963 %	1966 %	1963 %	1966 %	1963 %	1966 %	1966 %	1966 %	1966 %	1966 %
66	X	66	X	66	X	77	X	70	64	55	67	92
6	X	9	X	2	X	7	X	15	9	9	15	41
59	X	61	X	57	X	75	X	67	55	53	64	92
5	X	9	X	2	X	8	X	18	8	4	13	55
32	X	34	X	31	X	41	X	44	34	30	45	99
42	X	45	X	40	X	50	X	53	45	40	50	93

		South						Age			Civil rights pace too slow	Negro community leaders
Total South		Urban		Non-urban		Middle and upper income		Under 35	35–49	50 and over		
1966 %	1963 %	1966 %	1963 %	1966 %	1963 %	1966 %	1963 %	1966 %	1966 %	1966 %	1966 %	1966 %
49	X	45	X	52	X	57	X	52	52	51	52	60
5	X	9	X	2	X	6	X	7	5	7	8	3
34	X	35	X	33	X	28	X	35	35	30	32	17
1	X	1	X	—	X	—	X	*	—	1	*	—
11	X	10	X	13	X	9	X	6	8	11	8	20

*—Less than 1 percent.

6(d) Have any young boys or girls in your family dropped out of high school?

	Total all interviews		Total non-South		Non-South					
					Low income		Lower middle income		Middle and upper income	
	1966 %	1963 %	1966 %	1963 %	1966 %	1963 %	1966 %	1963 %	1966 %	1963 %
Yes	27	18	21	20	23	13	21	19	17	14
No	73	82	79	80	77	87	79	81	83	86

CHAPTER VIII

20(g) How would you rate the (Army, etc.) as a place for a young man to serve—excellent, pretty good, only fair, or poor?

	Total all interviews		Total non-South		Non-South					
					Low income		Lower middle income		Middle and upper income	
	1966 %	1963 %	1966 %	1963 %	1966 %	1963 %	1966 %	1963 %	1966 %	1963 %
Army										
Excellent	20	X	18	X	16	X	18	X	20	X
Pretty good	36	X	32	X	47	X	29	X	33	X
Only fair	15	X	17	X	6	X	20	X	19	X
Poor	5	X	7	X	6	X	9	X	7	X
Not sure	24	X	26	X	25	X	24	X	21	X
Navy										
Excellent	17	X	15	X	9	X	15	X	18	X
Pretty good	35	X	31	X	44	X	33	X	32	X
Only fair	14	X	16	X	3	X	17	X	18	X
Poor	6	X	9	X	13	X	11	X	7	X
Not sure	28	X	29	X	31	X	24	X	25	X

X—*Question not asked in 1963.*

		South						Age			Civil rights pace too slow	Negro community leaders
Total South		Urban		Non-urban		Middle and upper income		Under 35	35–49	50 and over		
1966 %	1963 %	1966 %	1963 %	1966 %	1963 %	1966 %	1963 %	1966 %	1966 %	1966 %	1966 %	1966 %
23	21	23	23	23	23	23	7	23	21	23	22	11
77	79	77	77	77	77	77	93	77	79	77	78	89

		South						Age			Civil rights pace too slow	Negro community leaders
Total South		Urban		Non-urban		Middle and upper income		Under 35	35–49	50 and over		
1966 %	1963 %	1966 %	1963 %	1966 %	1963 %	1966 %	1963 %	1966 %	1966 %	1966 %	1966 %	1966 %
21	X	21	X	21	X	21	X	16	23	22	19	13
40	X	41	X	39	X	42	X	36	33	38	32	30
13	X	14	X	13	X	17	X	19	14	13	18	11
4	X	4	X	4	X	2	X	9	4	4	9	18
22	X	20	X	23	X	18	X	20	26	23	22	28
19	X	22	X	17	X	18	X	16	17	20	15	9
38	X	36	X	41	X	43	X	33	32	40	31	18
13	X	14	X	11	X	14	X	18	15	12	18	21
3	X	3	X	3	X	1	X	9	5	3	10	20
27	X	25	X	28	X	24	X	24	31	25	26	32

20(g) How would you rate the (Army, etc.) as a place for a young man to serve—excellent, pretty good, only fair, or poor?

	Total all inter-views		Total non-South		Non-South					
					Low income		Lower middle income		Middle and upper income	
	1966 %	1963 %	1966 %	1963 %	1966 %	1963 %	1966 %	1963 %	1966 %	1963 %
Marine Corps										
Excellent	18	X	18	X	13	X	18	X	18	X
Pretty good	32	X	27	X	36	X	30	X	30	X
Only fair	14	X	17	X	14	X	17	X	19	X
Poor	7	X	9	X	9	X	9	X	9	X
Not sure	29	X	29	X	28	X	26	X	24	X
Air Force										
Excellent	24	X	25	X	28	X	21	X	29	X
Pretty good	35	X	30	X	35	X	30	X	34	X
Only fair	11	X	12	X	6	X	16	X	11	X
Poor	4	X	5	X	6	X	9	X	4	X
Not sure	26	X	28	X	25	X	24	X	22	X

X—*Question not asked in 1963.*

20(j) How would you rate the job President Johnson is doing in handling the war in Vietnam—excellent, pretty good, only fair, or poor?

	Total all inter-views		Total non-South		Non-South					
					Low income		Lower middle income		Middle and upper income	
	1966 %	1963 %	1966 %	1963 %	1966 %	1963 %	1966 %	1963 %	1966 %	1963 %
Excellent	18	X	14	X	13	X	9	X	13	X
Pretty good	36	X	32	X	32	X	28	X	40	X
Only fair	16	X	21	X	18	X	24	X	23	X
Poor	11	X	15	X	13	X	18	X	13	X
Not sure	19	X	18	X	24	X	21	X	11	X

X—*Question not asked in 1963.*

		South						Age			Civil rights pace too slow	Negro community leaders
Total South		Urban		Non-urban		Middle and upper income		Under 35	35–49	50 and over		
1966 %	1963 %	1966 %	1963 %	1966 %	1963 %	1966 %	1963 %	1966 %	1966 %	1966 %	1966 %	1966 %
18	X	24	X	12	X	17	X	18	16	20	16	11
37	X	35	X	38	X	38	X	32	30	37	30	19
11	X	9	X	14	X	15	X	17	16	9	18	19
5	X	5	X	5	X	4	X	10	6	4	10	18
29	X	27	X	31	X	26	X	23	32	30	26	33
24	X	27	X	20	X	28	X	24	23	28	25	17
38	X	38	X	38	X	37	X	35	32	36	31	25
10	X	8	X	12	X	13	X	13	12	8	13	13
3	X	4	X	3	X	2	X	7	4	2	7	13
25	X	23	X	27	X	20	X	21	29	26	24	32

		South						Age			Civil rights pace too slow	Negro community leaders
Total South		Urban		Non-urban		Middle and upper income		Under 35	35–49	50 and over		
1966 %	1963 %	1966 %	1963 %	1966 %	1963 %	1966 %	1963 %	1966 %	1966 %	1966 %	1966 %	1966 %
22	X	21	X	23	X	23	X	14	18	23	14	8
38	X	38	X	38	X	39	X	34	36	37	35	25
11	X	11	X	11	X	13	X	20	14	13	21	8
8	X	8	X	8	X	9	X	17	9	8	15	36
21	X	22	X	20	X	16	X	15	23	19	15	23

20(k) All in all, what do you think we should do about Vietnam? We can follow one of three courses: carry the ground fighting into North Vietnam at the risk of bringing Red China into the fighting; withdraw our support and troops from Vietnam, or continue to fight there until the Communists are defeated or sit down to negotiate?

	Total all interviews 1966 %	Total all interviews 1963 %	Total non-South 1966 %	Total non-South 1963 %	Non-South Low income 1966 %	Non-South Low income 1963 %	Non-South Lower middle income 1966 %	Non-South Lower middle income 1963 %	Non-South Middle and upper income 1966 %	Non-South Middle and upper income 1963 %
Carry ground fighting into North Vietnam	8	X	8	X	13	X	7	X	11	X
Withdraw	18	X	20	X	19	X	24	X	22	X
Continue to fight	37	X	40	X	24	X	36	X	40	X
Not sure	37	X	32	X	44	X	33	X	27	X

X—*Question not asked in 1963.*

20(c) If the United States got into a big world war today would you personally feel this country was worth fighting for or not?

	Total all interviews 1966 %	Total all interviews 1963 %	Total non-South 1966 %	Total non-South 1963 %	Non-South Low income 1966 %	Non-South Low income 1963 %	Non-South Lower middle income 1966 %	Non-South Lower middle income 1963 %	Non-South Middle and upper income 1966 %	Non-South Middle and upper income 1963 %
Worth fighting for	87	81	86	82	86	81	85	81	87	88
Not worth it	6	9	8	10	6	13	9	10	8	7
Not sure	7	10	6	8	8	6	6	9	5	5

| | | South | | | | | Age | | | Civil rights pace too slow | Negro community leaders |
| Total South | | Urban | | Non-urban | | Middle and upper income | | Under 35 | 35–49 | 50 and over | | |
1966 %	1963 %	1966 %	1963 %	1966 %	1963 %	1966 %	1963 %	1966 %	1966 %	1966 %	1966 %	1966 %
7	X	8	X	6	X	6	X	7	7	9	9	4
16	X	16	X	16	X	16	X	18	21	14	20	36
36	X	35	X	36	X	49	X	41	32	40	44	22
41	X	41	X	42	X	29	X	34	38	37	27	38

| | | South | | | | | Age | | | Civil rights pace too slow | Negro community leaders |
| Total South | | Urban | | Non-urban | | Middle and upper income | | Under 35 | 35–49 | 50 and over | | |
1966 %	1963 %	1966 %	1963 %	1966 %	1963 %	1966 %	1963 %	1966 %	1966 %	1966 %	1966 %	1966 %
88	80	90	78	87	79	90	88	85	88	90	87	73
4	8	5	11	2	5	5	6	10	4	3	8	9
8	12	5	11	11	16	5	6	5	8	7	5	18

20(e) Do you think the present draft laws are fair or unfair to Negroes?

	Total all interviews		Total non-South		Non-South					
					Low income		Lower middle income		Middle and upper income	
	1966	1963	1966	1963	1966	1963	1966	1963	1966	1963
	%	%	%	%	%	%	%	%	%	%
Fair	43	X	38	X	27	X	35	X	44	X
Unfair	25	X	30	X	32	X	36	X	28	X
Not sure	32	X	32	X	41	X	29	X	28	X

X—*Question not asked in 1963.*

43(a) Do you (and your family) own a car?

	Total all interviews	Total non-South	Non-South			Total South
			Low income	Lower middle income	Middle and upper income	
	1966	1966	1966	1966	1966	1966
	%	%	%	%	%	%
Yes	59	59	14	52	82	58
No	41	41	86	48	18	42

43(b) Do you (and your family) own a television set?

	Total all interviews	Total non-South	Non-South			Total South
			Low income	Lower middle income	Middle and upper income	
	1966	1966	1966	1966	1966	1966
	%	%	%	%	%	%
Yes	91	95	97	94	97	88
No	9	5	3	6	3	12

	South									Age			Civil rights pace too slow	Negro community leaders
Total South		Urban		Non-urban		Middle and upper income		Under 35	35–49	50 and over				
1966 %	1963 %	1966 %	1963 %	1966 %	1963 %	1966 %	1963 %	1966 %	1966 %	1966 %			1966 %	1966 %
47	X	44	X	50	X	57	X	44	39	47			38	21
20	X	21	X	20	X	20	X	27	29	21			33	58
33	X	35	X	30	X	23	X	29	32	32			29	21

South			Age			Civil rights pace too slow	Negro community leaders
Urban	Non-urban	Middle and upper income	Under 35	35–49	50 and over		
1966 %	1966 %	1966 %	1966 %	1966 %	1966 %	1966 %	1966 %
58	59	84	62	65	50	61	88
42	41	16	38	35	50	39	12

South			Age			Civil rights pace too slow	Negro community leaders
Urban	Non-urban	Middle and upper income	Under 35	35–49	50 and over		
1966 %	1966 %	1966 %	1966 %	1966 %	1966 %	1966 %	1966 %
91	85	97	92	95	87	93	99
9	15	3	8	5	13	7	1

Question from White Questionnaire

4(d) Some Negroes have suggested that since Negroes have been discriminated against for 100 years, they should be given special consideration in jobs, that they should actually be given a preference for a job opening, such as a veteran gets today in a government job. Do you agree or disagree with the idea of job preference for Negroes?

	Total 1966 %	Total 1963 %	East %	Midwest %	South %	West %
Agree	4	3	4	4	4	3
Disagree	90	93	89	90	91	94
Not sure	6	4	7	6	5	3

Index